AN INSIDER'S VIEW INTO ETHICAL
& SUCCESSFUL PREFORECLOSURE
SALES, AND PREFORECLOSURE

SHORT SALES

AN ETHICAL APPROACH

*"stiff legislation will help, not hinder,
the ethical, speculative investor"*

*"a must read for buyers **and sellers**
of foreclosed real estate"*

By **David M. Petrovich**
a/k/a TheShortSalePro™

AN INSIDER'S VIEW INTO ETHICAL
& SUCCESSFUL PREFORECLOSURE SALES, AND PREFORECLOSURE

SHORT SALES
AN ETHICAL APPROACH

Published in the United States of America
by:
CommonCentsFinancial
P.O. Box 142, Oakhurst, New Jersey 07755

ISBN 978-1-4116-9868-0

To the
bastards and charlatans
of real estate who have
tarnished
the real estate profession,
adversely impacted thousands
of American's households,
and made this book
a necessity.

Thanks To

*My wife, a very special person and
my best friend, for her interpretation
of the US Tax Code,*

*My immediate family
for all the obvious reasons,
including their unwavering support
of our family's moral compass,*

*Friends who have tried to understand
my continuing maturation and conviction,*

*Professional colleagues who
provide insight from every corner
of America, and*

*Those emotionally and financially
distraught homeowners whose candor
continues to provide
startling and upsetting views
into the dark side of
the mortgage foreclosure industry.*

CONTENTS

DISCLAIMER

BAD FAITH, in a realty transaction, is, in my opinion, the absence of honesty. Bad faith can be intentional, or, a result of ignorance. I'm neither an attorney, nor accountant, and while nothing I've written should be construed as legal, or tax advice, I've had enough experience to be able to recognize 'red flag' warnings that indicate an unconscionable, or predatory, real estate transaction In my opinion, if a proposed foreclosure real estate deal lacks full disclosure (honesty), it should proceed if and only if all parties are fully informed. There is an **abundance** of intentional, and unwitting bad faith in the foreclosure real estate industry

I am an advocate for the distressed homeowner, but I am not against real estate speculators. I am, however, against those who rely upon deceptive practices and become unjustly enriched at the expense of their prey, the financially unsophisticated. This book is a collection of my interpretations, my opinions, and my conclusions which, hopefully, will help you spot "red flags" in your transactions. There are people who will disagree with my interpretations, my opinions, and my conclusions. They'll say I have distorted the facts by telling only one side of the story. They'll point to thousands of distressed homeowners who benefit from 'foreclosure rescue' practitioners, and entrepreneurs who devise 'outside the box' realty transactions. They'll call what I have to say "typical, left leaning, chicken little, knee jerk reaction type garbage." Who are these critics? These are the folks whose desire to make money becomes the most important thing in their lives. Making money and doing whatever it takes to make more money governs their decisions, actions, and moral compass. They believe it's OK to make misleading statements or lie to homeowners, or falsify applications or other documents. Mostly, my critics are the ones who think it's perfectly OK to cross the line and cut corners. If people get harmed, so what? They justify their actions by saying, "Hardly ever does anyone get caught…" In my opinion, not getting caught doesn't make anything OK.

ABOUT THE AUTHOR

The Author, recently celebrating his fiftieth birthday, has been actively involved in the business of real estate for more than 25 years, at times working as a contractor, Realtor®, a construction project manager, a landlord, an independent fee consultant, an appraiser, a mortgage loan officer, a consulting partner for a quarter billion dollar waterfront redevelopment project, a non-performing asset manager for a national mortgage loan servicer, and for the last 8 years, as Executive Director of a non profit, housing counseling organization whose services include, but are not limited to, post purchase/pre default/and pre-bankruptcy counseling. His 501(c)(3) Corporation has been an outsource resource to the Mortgage Bankers Association of America, investigating allegations of mortgage loan servicing error, predatory lending, and real estate transaction fraud. He has served as expert (mortgage loan servicing) witness in several Federal Bankruptcy Courts (New York, New Jersey, and Pennsylvania). In those capacities, he has been involved, directly or indirectly, with thousands of preforeclosure, preforeclosure short sale, Sheriff's Sale, and REO sale transactions.

He has appeared as a guest on television news segments, drive time NY area radio talk shows, and has been featured in the real estate section of the Sunday New York Times. Representing his non-profit organization (www.SPOCH.org), his interview will appear in the upcoming credit industry film documentary's DVD version of <u>Maxed Out!</u>

INTRODUCTION

This book isn't as much about assigning blame, or faulting, specific acquisition techniques (although I do!) as much as it is about faulting the individuals who don't anticipate, or respect, the consequences of their actions. In some instances, this book will take the reader for a literary walk in the shoes of the homeowner, the principled investor, and the evil, predatorial, speculators.

While there is no justification for shortsightedness, it seems foresight is in short supply and more attention is paid to the end result (making money) than the path chosen. Little attention is afforded to the casualties. Few 'goal oriented' foreclosure acquisition practitioners think much about the consequences! It seems everybody wants to get rich quick, and only the shortest path to the anticipated riches will do. (read: short cut) Some other words to describe a short cut include dodge (as in tax dodge), evade (as in tax evasion), avoid (as in shirk responsibility), circumvent, etc. Well, not only are short cuts not free, but they come at a price someone has to be willing to pay. Oftentimes the cost of a short cut is a failed transaction that results in the avoidable loss of homeownership, or unconscionable enrichment of one party at the expense of the other. More often than not, it's the deals that die on the vine that go unnoticed, and under reported. In my opinion, deals that don't close do the most damage to the parties.

I want your deals to close. But I want your deals to be mutually and financially beneficial to all parties. I want you to be able to sleep well at night knowing you've approached a potential deal ethically, and at all times sought (win/win) solutions which are just, and favorable to all concerned. If you come away with nothing else from this book, please understand the need to know what's around the corner instead of blindly forging ahead in callous disregard, and or ignorance. If just one family in foreclosure can avoid the involuntary loss of their home, or stripped of their equity, as a result of your reading of this book, please let me know.

Incidentally, all proceeds from the sale of this book have been dedicated to the charitable pursuits of The Society for the Preservation of Continued Homeownership, a NJ, non profit, 501c3, tax exempt corporation. (www.SPOCH.org)

The material herein, and other information available on my website(s) was originally intended to help distressed homeowners and speculative investors, understand the acquisition technique known as a mortgagee approved, preforeclosure short sale, and, to be able to recognize and avoid potential problems that often arise sometime between the identification and prequalification of the short sale candidate, and the anxiously awaited response from the mortgagee(s) to your formal proposal. It also is an excellent primer for foreclosed homeowners who need to quickly educate themselves about those wanting to "help" them.

While many things you learn here will help you, much of your success will depend upon your own imagination and ability to blend gathered market data, physical field data, negotiation skills, and presentation skills. The skill set needed to prepare a compelling preforeclosure short sale proposal is transferable in your quest for FSBOs, preforeclosures, and REOs.

Since failed transactions are of benefit to no one, and quite detrimental to the distressed homeowners who have placed their trust in you, (the speculative investor), I wrote this manual in the hope speculative investors will recognize poorly qualified short sale candidates, and attempt fewer short sales on those transactions destined to fail. Consequently, the speculative investor will able to complete more transactions by utilizing other, more conventional, acquisition techniques.

Not every preforeclosure situation indicates short sale. If the only tool in your toolbox is a hammer, you'll look at every deal as if it were a nail.

In most major TV markets, late night viewers are invited to "get rich quick" with little or no effort while working part-time from the convenience of their own homes. They're asked to plunk down their hard earned bucks for the latest entry into the foray of real estate investment courses, books, tapes, or seminars. They're told that they'll learn the 'secrets' of buying discounted real estate including land trusts, sub2's, lease options, municipal tax liens, or any number of techniques heralded as, "the best method of real estate investment' as pitched by the TV infomercial gurus.

Is any one method of real estate investment superior to all others? Should one technique be used above all others?

Will the mastering of any single technique, including "short sales" make one rich? No. But I do think each investment technique or "tool" that's learned will better enable a speculative real estate investor to identify and capitalize on more opportunities. The more tools you know how to use, the better prepared you are when faced with opportunity.

Let me repeat: Not every preforeclosure situation indicates short sale. If the only tool in your toolbox is a hammer, you'll look at every deal as if it were a nail.

A successful *short sale* can create equity and opportunity where none previously existed. But, you must be both clever, and professional in your approach. Most casual speculators overlook property(s) that appear to have little or zero equity.

Let's pretend for a moment that real estate investment is in many ways like the game of golf. An "investor" is a golfer about to play a round of 18 holes. For those of you unfamiliar with golf, it is a game of skill played (mostly) by white men wearing brightly colored, expensive clothing over a (battle) field more than four miles long. Many boast how great their business is doing while trying to move a small, round ball into a distant, slightly larger, round hole by striking the ball with crooked sticks using as few strokes as possible. These crooked sticks are called clubs and include metals, woods, irons, wedges, or putters and are the 'tools' of the game. If that isn't challenging enough, the golfers must negotiate all types of weather conditions, stands of trees, great ponds of water, or white beaches of sand. They must also endure distractions some intentional, some not, including but not limited to buzzing wasps, swarming mosquitoes (New Jersey), alligators (Florida) or other loud, obnoxious players (New York).

Each crooked stick or tool is designed in such a way as to propel the struck ball with a certain trajectory and distance in anticipation of a desired result. For example, a "wood" will send a properly struck ball about 284 yards toward the green (or closing table). From there, a wedge will more accurately carry the ball closer to the green.

A sand wedge will blast the ball from the green side bunker onto the putting surface. An experienced golfer, requiring a club designed for a short and accurate shot, would properly select and use his putter to send the tiny, round ball into the only slightly larger hole.

The game of golf, not unlike the real estate business, is as much about knowing the right club or tool to use in a given situation as executing the technique required by each club or tool.

What does this mean? A golfer, challenged by dynamic course conditions, must know which clubs he owns, and which to use to overcome a particular set of obstacles.

If the golfer finds himself in a sand trap, he would know to use a with the desired result. Similarly, a real estate professional must know what technique or 'tool" to use to identify and exploit an opportunity. This introduction to unique, complex, but potentially rewarding realty transactions commonly known as a ***short sale,*** is intended for real estate brokers, brokers' agents, mortgage brokers, real estate investors, or potential speculators who want to learn about the discounted, pre foreclosure acquisition of distressed real estate. If you don't have a basic understanding of real estate terms, transactions or finance, you should keep handy a real estate and business terms dictionary. I've included a glossary of terms at the end of this book. Will an understanding of ***short sales*** make you rich? No. But once the process is demystified, you will be able to close deals that others are afraid to touch, or don't even realize are there.

This manual will address the technique known as **The** (mortgagee approved, preforeclosure) **Short Sale**, some frequently asked questions, and several short sale scenarios.

This is not a step by step cookie cutter approach to the art of short sales, but will help you to understand what is needed and why. Foreclosure laws, practices and customs vary from State to State, and in some places, from County to County. This manual will not differentiate security instruments including mortgages, deeds of trust, or security deeds, nor will it specifically address strict foreclosure, judicial foreclosure, or non judicial foreclosure procedures. I apologize in advance for any spelling errors, and for any number of my many, uncorrected (bad) grammatical habits.

Separation, divorce, unexpected medical expenses, and un(der)employment are some of the most common causes for financial hardship and resultant mortgage foreclosure. To better understand the Homeowner's situation, it might be helpful to read Bob's Story. Bob, a typical homeowner who has experienced a loss of income, is fighting to save his home. If you don't want a sanitized glimpse of what it might like to be the homeowner in a preforeclosure scenario please skip Bob's Story.

SURVIVING MORTGAGE FORECLOSURE: BOB'S STORY

Unless you've been in Bob's shoes, you can't imagine what it's like to be on the other side of preforeclosure, or have a sheriff knocking on your door. Imagine if you were in Bob's shoes. After a year of heavy borrowing on plastic for necessary home improvements, you consolidated a handful of those high balance, credit cards by refinancing your mortgage loan. Because you had a few late pays, your credit hadn't been perfect, so the interest rate and monthly payments on the new mortgage loan were a bit higher than you had hoped. Still, you were saving about $150 every month.

Three months ago your regular hours at work were cut back but you considered yourself lucky because most of your department was laid off. Even though your regular paycheck has been less, the bills have stayed the same, and it's been impossible to pay all the bills on time. You've had to choose which bills to pay, and which ones to delay, or not pay at all. You hope that work picks up, and you can get back to working more hours. Just as you were about to leave work for the day, you are called into the personnel office and told you have worked your last day. Ouch!

Five months later, you still haven't been able to find a new job commensurate with your experience. The unemployment benefits barely cover food and utilities. You learn about COBRA. Your wife took a part-time job outside the home just so the kids could keep up with their after school activities.

You hadn't been able to pay the mortgage for the last 3 months, ABC Mortgage Company is pressuring you for payment, so you took the last available cash advance from 3 credit cards to catch up. On the day that you are sending in your payment, the mortgage company is sending you a demand letter. You sent the mortgage company a triple payment and thought things were okay. A couple days later, you receive a certified letter from the lender advising that they will foreclose unless payment is received. You call the mortgage company wanting to tell them you had sent in payment, but were unable to get through to their customer service department. Either the line was busy, or you were directed to an overflowing voice mail box The next week you open a letter from the lender and learn to find out that the check you had sent was returned because it 1) wasn't in certified funds, 2) didn't include late fees and returned check charges, and 3) your loan is now in default. They were demanding an extra $1,750 just to bring the loan current. So you tear up the check and, instead of paying the mortgage, you pay down the cable TV bill, the AOL account, the car insurance, the orthodontic bill, go on a long overdue grocery shopping trip, and must choose between COBRA, and replacing some badly worn tires on the family car.

You are almost afraid to answer the telephone because you just know it's one of those collection calls. The calls are from any one of about 4 credit card companies, or the mortgage company. The credit cards have exceeded their limit, payments are past due, and their collection reps have been calling and calling, and calling. Their line of questions imply that you are *choosing* not to pay. "You aren't a deadbeat, are you Bob? Why aren't you paying us? Out of work? Why are you home answering the phone, Bob, you should be out looking for work!?"

ABC Mortgage Company calls every other day around dinner-time. "Hi, Bob, this is Mr. Self-Important at ABC Mortgage Company. Say, when are you going to send in that payment? If you don't send it in soon, you might as well start packing because we're going to take your house! Ha Ha Ha. When can I expect your check, Bob?"

Sometimes, in an effort to get you to make promises to send payments, the more aggressive mortgage loan collectors will ask for your boss's telephone number at work, or ask you to confirm your friend's and neighbor's telephone numbers implying that they would be placing calls to your workplace, friends and neighbors. They'll tell you that you can be tossed out into the street if you don't make the payments or that they would be sending someone by to appraise your home.

By this time you now know that even if you could manage to send in a payment of anything less than the full amount due, it'll be returned to you, uncashed, attached to a note advising that your loan has been sent to their foreclosure department. Unless you bring the account current, or make acceptable payment arrangements, your loan will be foreclosed. Like most people, you really aren't sure what that means. The next day you get two letters in the mail from your lender; one certified, receipt requested, and one sent regular mail. They both say the same thing. It's a formal, "Notice of Intent to Foreclose."

The first step [in the foreclosure process] is to send to you an official Notice of Intent to Foreclose. This starts the foreclosure clock ticking. Up until this point, your inability to send the mortgage payments has been a financial problem. Now, it's been compounded into a legal & financial problem. If you don't bring the loan current within 30 days, the loan will be foreclosed. The letter says that to reinstate your loan you would need about $6,000 which would cover back payments, penalties, and other fees. It also invites you to call them and ask about 'non-foreclosure' options and alternatives.

"Where did they come up with that figure?" you wonder. Then you decide to call the telephone number for their loss mitigation department. You tell the voice on the other end that you want to save the home, and they agree to send you an application for a 'loan workout.'

Foreclosure and a foreclosure timetable means different things in different parts of the country.

In New Jersey, a "judicial foreclosure" state, the process can take as long as a year or more.

The 5 Phases Of NJ Judicial Mortgage Foreclosure:

1. Collection (up to 60 days from date of 1st missed payment)
2. Preforeclosure (from 60 to 90 days from 1st missed payment)
3. Foreclosure (from 90 to 180 days from the 1st missed payment)
4. Sheriff's Sale (12 months from the 1st missed payment)
5. Right of Redemption (10 days following a NJ Sheriff's Sale)

Most mortgage companies don't even pretend to be interested in your problems. They don't care that you're out of work. They don't care your job interview next Tuesday has been cancelled, or there is a serious illness in your family. All they care about is getting their money. Their objective is in getting you to promise that you'll send in their money. They employ professional collectors trained in the art of wheedling blood from stones.

If you can demonstrate your temporary financial hardship has now been resolved, you are now working and able to begin making payments again, they may offer a forbearance and reinstatement plan. But if you can't, and their threats aren't working on you they'll ship your loan to their foreclosure attorney who will initiate foreclosure proceedings.

Around day 50, following the Notice of Intent, you begin to receive letters from bankruptcy lawyers, real estate brokers, mortgage brokers, private investors, and 'foreclosure rescue' companies offering to help you to save your home from foreclosure.

"How do they know what we are going through?" you ask your wife.

You choose from one of about three dozen letters from mortgage brokers who advertise that they offer foreclosure bailout loans but learn that you must have about 30% equity before you would be considered for a loan. Even if you had the equity, the loan's interest rate, terms, and fees would make it quite unaffordable.

Sometime after the 60th day following your receipt of the Notice of Intent, in the evening around 9 PM, there is a loud and startling knock/pounding on your door. You wonder why whoever it is didn't use the doorbell.

Standing on your doorstep is an impatient, burly guy with a clipboard. His car is left running in the driveway. Your heart begins to pound when he announces himself to be a Sheriff's Deputy dutifully serving a Summons. He asks for you and your wife by name.

Your hands begin to tremble as he opens the screen door and pushes himself into the doorway. He confirms your identity, hands you the clipboard, and instructs you where to sign your name. As he looks around, you notice his badge and holster. Your wide-eyed kids are peering from behind a chair, wondering what this man is doing talking to their Mommy and Daddy. The Sheriff's Deputy, satisfied that you've signed where he has indicated for you to sign, hands you and your wife some papers, and steps outside.... The "service" lasted all of 90 seconds. Within the first 10 minutes, your hands shaking and feeling as if you were punched in the stomach, you'll reread the papers three times.

You don't know exactly what the papers say. Most of it's redundant and in legalese, but you know it can't be good. You can't sleep that night, and you really don't know what you will do tomorrow. As you toss and turn, you decide that tomorrow you would call a lawyer.

The next day you sift through the growing pile of letters from lawyers, real estate brokers, mortgage brokers, 'foreclosure consultants' and speculative investors. You call a bankruptcy attorney for the free consultation and are told that to save the house, bankruptcy may be your only solution. No surprise. You call the real estate broker who advises that you sell your home. No surprise. If you called a car dealer, he would advise that you buy a car. No surprise.

Just about everyone you call will have some service to sell. How do you choose what's right for YOU? You really don't want to file a petition for bankruptcy and even if you do, there's no guarantee that you'll be able to keep your home. The bankruptcy laws have changed, making bankruptcy more expensive. An attorney will charge about $3,000 just to prepare and file a Chapter 13 plan. If accepted, a Chapter 13 plan requires that you resume making your regularly scheduled payments and make an extra payment each month for a portion of the payments that you've missed. Many people facing foreclosure find this to be an unaffordable option, especially if the underlying problem (not enough income) hasn't been fully resolved.

Your long awaited job interview was going well until you were told about the salary. The job offers much less than what you had been making, and some quick math suggests that the estimated take home will only be a little more than unemployment (which runs out next week). Without a job, you don't qualify for a new mortgage loan. Without a job, you can't qualify for bankruptcy. You need this job, so you take it, and agree to start work in one week. You tell yourself that it's a start on the road to recovery.

You call your lawyer who says that even with the new job, you still don't qualify for a Chapter 13 Bankruptcy Plan, and advises that you liquidate, and let the house go. He gives you the name and number of his friend, a real estate broker. Even though you really don't want to sell, you may be forced to sell or lose it at Sheriff's Sale.

You've got a letter in the mail waiting from you from a company whose claims sound pretty good. They say that they can help even if your home is in foreclosure and even if you owe more than your home is worth. So you call.

A soothing voice assures you, "Don't worry, Bob, we can stop the foreclosure and make the home payments more affordable for you." You say that you want to learn more about their special program, and set up an appointment. The soothing voice says, "Don't forget to bring the deed, Bob, and your checkbook."

If Bob kept the appointment, he would be asked to sign over his house to the company, and it would collect rent, and lease it back to him. The company, while collecting Bob's rent would (in theory) try to acquire Bob's mortgage loan (at a steep discount) from the foreclosing mortgagee.

You get another job interview. Though you've already accepted a new job, and you're not too optimistic about finding another one, you decide to go on the interview with another company, anyway. After all, what did you have to lose? So you went on the interview, and (knowing that you already had a job) you were relaxed and conversational.

"They offered me a better job! I start next week!" you excitedly tell your wife. "Let's call ABC Mortgage Company and see what we can do to save the house."

You're finally able to get through to someone in their loss mitigation department who advises that since the loan has been sent to foreclosure, it's too late to do anything. But you persist. You tell them that although your financial hardship has been ongoing, it was a temporary situation. You tell them that you've been out of work for awhile, but now you have found a great job. You want to know what you can do to get the loan out of foreclosure, and reinstated so that you can begin making payments again.

"Well, let me see what I can do for you," says the ABC's loss mitigation specialist, "How much of a payment can you send in now?" You are thinking to yourself that you can barely scratch up the next payment, let alone an extra amount.

"To bring the loan current you'll need about $8,000 plus attorney's costs of about $2,000. Can you send in $10,000?" she asks.

"No, I'm just going back to work. I don't have that kind of money. If I did, I wouldn't be in this mess."

"Can you send in $5,000? I'm going to need something to show as your good faith payment towards a reinstatement. I could probably make this work if you could send in $5,000."

"No, I can't pay $5,000, but if I had to I could sell the car, or maybe withdraw $2,500 from a 401K retirement plan. I can do that. I can do $2,500," you tell her.

"Okay, I'll send you a workout package." she said, "There are some financial forms for you to complete. Provide your income tax returns from the past two years, your pay stubs (Mr.'s and Mrs.'s), your bank account statements, and a letter describing why you couldn't pay the mortgage, and what has changed so that you can begin paying again. And include your check for $2,500."

"It'll take some time to sell the car or borrow against the 401K. What if I sent in the paperwork right away, and then sent the check to you in 2 weeks?" you asked.

"Well, you haven't been scheduled for a Sheriff's Sale yet. If you have to wait two weeks I suppose it'll be all right, but the foreclosure costs will keep increasing until you send in the check," she advised. "I'll overnight you the workout application. No guarantees, but I think my boss'll approve it."

You promised to complete the paperwork right away. You were able to make an application for a hardship withdrawal from your 401K (subject to income tax, and penalty) to pay the $2,500 good faith deposit. They said that you would have the check in about 10 days. You completed and returned the financial forms and kept a careful eye on the calendar.

Your workout application was approved. After paying the $2500 (approximate costs for attorney's fees) there was a delinquency balance that could be repaid over a period of 18 months. That meant that you will now have to make the regularly scheduled payments, plus an extra 1/2 payment each month for the next 18 months. The payments will have to be in certified funds, and received on-time. If any payment is late, or not sent in certified funds, the foreclosure picks up right where it left off. Once you've made the 18th consecutive payment, the foreclosure will be canceled. You breathe a sigh of relief 6 months coming. You know that as long as you keep your job, you're home free. Your wife will have keep her part time job to help offset the higher payments, and it'll be tough. But you consider yourself lucky.

Bob *was* lucky. He didn't lose the house to foreclosure, or to an investor. Many people aren't so lucky, aren't able to find work, or able to draw on a 401K plan. Many people do lose their homes to Sheriff's Sale, or are forced to sell as their only viable alternative to mortgage foreclosure. Even folks who owe more than their homes are worth.

In cases when the financially distressed homeowner decides to sell, but there is little, or no equity, and the home is in need of cosmetic or more comprehensive repairs you may have a good, short sale candidate.

Since short sale approvals can take anywhere from 45 to 90 days or more, it's best to know how a short sale candidate is pre qualified for feasibility, and how it's structured, negotiated, and completed.

WHAT IS A SHORT SALE?

Short Sale A type of preforeclosure sale in which the mortgagee agrees to let you sell the property for less than the full amount due, and accept the proceeds as payment in full. The sale of property at a fair market price that's lower than the loan balance(s). A *mortgagee approved, preforeclosure short sale* is a realty transaction which occurs when anticipated proceeds from a sale are insufficient to payoff all lien holders (usually the mortgagee) in full. In advance, the lien holders agree in writing to facilitate the sale by accepting less than it is contractually due, though it is under no (legal) obligation to do so.

Before clear title to real estate can pass from seller to purchaser, all liens and encumbrances including mortgage(s), property taxes, judgments, costs of sale, etc., against the property must be paid. Typically, that payment is made at the time of passing of title using disbursements from proceeds of sale. Sometimes, when anticipated proceeds from the sale are insufficient to payoff all liens against the property, the seller, alerted by the closing agent, must be prepared to make up the difference in cash between proceeds from the sale and what is owed to the lien holders. But what happens if the seller ar-

9

rives at closing without cash, and can't convey clear title because the proceeds from sale aren't enough?

The buyer won't want to pay more than the contract price, so unless the shortage could be negotiated, the closing would be postponed, and the transaction would probably die. Could the deal be saved if the mortgagee(s) had agreed in advance to accept less than they were due? Absolutely.

In fact, many mortgage lenders do agree to let a financially troubled homeowner sell in an attempt to recover as much of the mortgage balance as possible, rather than foreclose, even if the sale proceeds won't satisfy the total amount due on the mortgage. For example, let's consider a financially distressed homeowner whose mortgage loan is delinquent, in default, or in foreclosure.

No longer able to afford the cost of keeping the home, he considers selling, but knows that he owes more than the property is worth. He doesn't have the cash to pay the difference between what is owed, and what would have to be paid to the mortgagee(s) at closing. If it could be demonstrated to the mortgagee(s) that it would be in their best, financial interest, to permit a passing of title, the mortgagee(s) would have the option of mitigating potential future losses by accepting less than they are due. An effective short sale proposal will motivate the mortgagee(s) to accept and approve as payoff in full anticipated proceeds to complete the short sale transaction.

To obtain mortgagee(s)' short sale approval, a **Short Sale Proposal** must be prepared, presented, and negotiated. A comprehensive, factual, compelling, and forward thinking short sale proposal is designed to convince the foreclosing mortgagee to agree to accept less than it is due as an alternative to taking back another, perhaps under marketable REO and all costs associated with that foreclosure. What costs? Foreclosure Sale fees, additional legal fees, eviction costs including damage to property, property insurance, property taxes, property preservation fees, and ultimately, REO liquidation sales commissions, and more legal fees.

According to a recent study published by FHLMC (Freddie Mac), a sample of loans that went through the full formal foreclosure process, the total cost including lost interest during delinquency, foreclosure costs, and disposition of the foreclosed property exceeded $58,750 and the process took an average of 18 months to resolve. By accepting a short payoff, the mortgagee would save both time, and money. How much would the lender save in time and money by accepting your proposal? That's something for you to consider and include in your proposal.

Irrespective of who seeks to benefit from a mortgagee approved short sale, it is the financially distressed homeowner who must be qualified to seek relief in the form of short sale approval from the foreclosing mortgagee(s). It is the homeowner who requests the application for short sale consideration from the mortgagee's collection, loss mitigation, or foreclosure department. It is the homeowner who, with assistance from a short sale facilitator, completes the application to be used in conjunction with a short sale proposal.

The short sale facilitator can be the seller, purchaser, real estate broker, or a private consultant hired to structure and facilitate the proposed transaction.

The Six Basic Steps To Short Sale Success

1) Preliminary prequalification of the seller, the mortgagee, and the real estate that indicates financial sense for the mortgagor and mortgagee to agree that a short sale is in their best interest;

2) Information gathering (field & empirical) for analysis and its manufacture into supportive data;

3) Preparation of a compelling, benefits driven proposal;

4) Presentation of that proposal to the appropriate body and/or individuals;

5) Negotiate terms for mortgagee(s) approval;

6) Anticipate all obstacles, then close the deal.

FHA/VA VS. CONVENTIONAL CRITERIA

All Mortgage Loans And Their Servicers Are NOT The Same

Mortgages, and mortgage loan servicing rights are bought and sold everyday. Institutional and portfolio investors buy, sell, or hold their collateralized investments and oftentimes hire a mortgage loan servicing company to accept and record payments, negotiate workouts, and supervise the foreclosure process in the event of a default.

Most mortgage loans are VA, FHA, or conventional (not insured by HUD or guaranteed by the VA). Each type of mortgage loan has its own origination and servicing criteria imposed by the entity that owns &/or insures the mortgagee against loss due to borrower default.

When considering short sale applications, conventional loan servicers, in addition to the investors' criteria, may also be governed by private mortgage insurors' criteria. Typically, conventional short sales are less bureaucratic than loans that are government backed.

FHA insured loan servicers can offer defaulted borrowers the option of selling their property via a preforeclosure sale (PFS), even if anticipated proceeds aren't enough to satisfy both the mortgage, and costs of sale.

Preforeclosure short sale consideration is predicated upon the severity of borrowers' demonstrated hardship, and their inability to otherwise cure the default using other loss mitigation techniques. Short sale approval is conditioned upon the transactions' financial parameters such that net proceeds from an arm's length sale must be at least 82% of the property's as-is, fair market value, **and** the ratio of the appraised value to outstanding mortgage indebtedness must be at least 63%.

FHA Preforeclosure/Short Sale

Eligibility will be determined using the NET PROCEEDS, which must be 82% of the "as-is" appraised value.

The ratio of the appraised value to outstanding mortgage indebtedness must be equal to or greater than 63%.

A Second Mortgagee is permitted a maximum of $1,000

To qualify:
NET ≥ 82% of FMV
FMV ÷ MTGE ≥ 63%

Example:
FMV = $150,000
mtge = $175,000
NET = $125,000

82% of $150,000 = $123,000 → NET ≥ 82% OK
& $150,000 ÷ $175,000 = 85% → 85% > 63% OK

From HUD's Mortgagee Letter 00-05
(preforeclosure short sale criteria)

The 10% Threshold

"Properties which have sustained serious damage (flood, fire, earthquake, tornado) are NOT eligible for PFS if the cost of repair exceeds 10% of the AS-REPAIRED value. Lenders may exercise their discretion to accept or reject damaged properties when repairs costs are less than the 10% threshold, but should document their decision in the claim review file."

In my experience, most needed repairs result from deferred maintenance, NOT a catastrophic event. I placed a call to HUD's National Servicing Center in Oklahoma for an interpretation of the Rule, and to ascertain if the costs to cure deferred maintenance could be an exception to the Rule. I was advised that under no conditions would the 10% threshold be waived. This rigidity is due to the mortgagee's FHA claims for reimbursement procedure.

The FHA servicer may also require that the subject property be listed for sale with a licensed real estate broker, and require that restrictive language be included in both the listing agreement, and any contract of sale. This language may differ slightly from lender to lender, but essentially the documents must state that the sale is subject to written, mortgagee PFS approval, that the property is to be sold in its as-is condition, and that the seller is to receive zero proceeds from the sale.

A VA Compromise Sale, equally difficult, generally accepts net proceeds of not less than 88% of the property's confirmed, as-is, fair market value.

One of the first steps in the preforeclosure short sale process, is to first pre qualify the circumstances for having short sale feasibility since not all (or even most) preforeclosure situations are short sale candidates.

ESTABLISH SHORT SALE FEASIBILITY

The seller must be qualified to receive relief from the mortgagee. The seller must have experienced an involuntary, financial hardship, not have the financial capacity to repay the loan in it's entirety, tried (unsuccessfully) to market the property at a higher than market price needed to break even, and agrees to fully cooperate with both the mortgagee and the purchaser during the short sale process.

The mortgage loan servicer must be *authorized* to participate in a short sale. All liens that attach to the property should be identified, the total lien amount should be equal to or greater than the mortgagee's perception of the real estate's as-is, fair market value.

Anticipated loan payoff(s) and negotiated terms of short sale approval must meet with both the seller's need, and your own business requirements.

Before even suggesting that the mortgagee consider accepting a short sale, learn as much as you can about the mortgage loan(s) in question. Who owns the mortgage loan? Is the loan servicer authorized to accept a short payoff? Is it a senior or junior lien? What type of loan is it? Conventional? FHA insured? VA insured? Is there PMI? Was the loan subsidized in any way? Is the mortgage loan part of a servicing pool? When was the loan originated? What is the remaining principal balance?

If you feel that a short sale is the indicated acquisition technique, you would begin the process by having the mortgagee furnish an application for short sale consideration. Once the homeowner provides the lender their written permission to communicate with you about the mortgage loan account you can speak to the account rep about the process, and formally request the application. (It's best to keep a log of your phone calls.)

Identify potential problems early on in the process. If, after speaking with the account rep, you conclude that a short sale might not be the indicated acquisition technique, consider other methods.

SHORT SALES AND BANKRUPTCY

"I'm not an attorney, nor should anything I say or do be construed as legal advice."

You should get used to this phrase, especially when dealing with the less financially sophisticated. Everyone you speak with in your capacity as a real estate entrepreneur is a potential lawsuit waiting to happen. Especially if your negligence results in the homeowner's additional hardship (a deal gone bad). The homeowner will perceive you to be a professional. So will the homeowner's attorney, the prosecuting attorney, and the Judge. Bankruptcy is a legal process, and the decision to enter into a bankruptcy or discuss the various benefits or disadvantages of individual chapters can constitute providing legal advice. You don't want to be accused of providing legal advice, especially inaccurate legal advice (without a license). For that matter, you don't want to be accused of engaging in the practice of real estate that would otherwise require a NJ sales or brokers license. Ditto CPA.

Bankruptcy Should Send Up A Red Flag Saying, "Proceed With Caution!"

The two common types of Bankruptcy for consumers are Chapters 7 and 13. Any realty transaction that involves a consumer in bankruptcy will require the express approval of the Bankruptcy Trustee and the Bankruptcy Court. Before the homeowner-in-bankruptcy can enter into a contract, even a listing agreement, the Bankruptcy Trustee and the Bankruptcy Court should give their consent.

Additionally, since the negotiation of a short sale is technically a collection activity the foreclosing mortgagee will probably defer negotiations until the lifting of the stay, or the dismissal of the bankruptcy.

Since it's the Bankruptcy Trustee's mission to maximize the recovery for unsecured creditors, he/she won't be too quick to approve a transaction that results in the loss (transfer from the bankruptcy estate to you) of equity that would otherwise be distributed to the unsecured creditors. You can either gain their approval, or, you can wait, and wriggle into place if and when the foreclosing mortgagee seeks and is granted a lifting of the automatic stay removing the property from under the protection of bankruptcy and opening the window of opportunity.

SHORT SALE PROPOSAL CONSTRUCT

Simply completing and returning an application for short sale consideration that had been provided by a mortgagee is not, in itself, a proposal. An application only tells one side of the story. The proposal is your chance to plead your case. The completed application is but one part of *The Short Sale Proposal*. The proposal should include all the information necessary for the mortgagee to make its decision on whether or not to accept a short payoff. That information should include, but not be limited to a statement of the problem, a realistic solution to the stated problem, and all physical and financial data that supports a favorable decision and encourages willingness to proceed.

Though a pretty cover alone won't get an approval for an ill-conceived proposal, I believe that a professional presentation is important. I utilize Avery Direct Print Custom Labels which can be purchased in single or four packs of 5 or 8 tabs. Typically, the sections of the proposal include a cover w/title, an executive summary; the mortgagor's hardship & financial update; the real estate section;

the proposal & contact names, addresses, and numbers; and the appendix. Make sure that all information is easily accessible to the reader.

I have at least 8 sets of the proposal professionally wire coil bound (not plastic comb that can come apart), with three copies designated for the mortgagee, one copy for the client, one copy for my reference, and the remaining sets available to be redelivered if needed. To improve the chances for an approval, your proposal must be compelling, *forward thinking*, and both anticipate and address mortgagee's questions, whatever those questions may be.

In addition to the boilerplate application forms that most mortgagees require, your accompanying proposal should quickly identify its **potential benefits** inured to the reader, and ask them to accept your proposal. Place a reasonable time limit for their response.

If the reviewing mortgagee has any doubts, and/or unanswered questions following their review of the application & proposal, it may:

1. request additional information
2. conditionally accept the offer
3. make a counteroffer
4. reject, or ignore the proposal
5. or worse, package and sell the mortgage &/or servicing rights forcing you to resubmit to a new mortgage loan servicer.

Assume that the mortgagee will misplace, lose, or deny ever having received your short sale application at least once. When the homeowner assembles the required financial information (bank statements, pay stubs, tax returns, etc.) he/she should make at least three sets of all worksheets or *proofs* that are created for each mortgagee that will receive a short sale proposal. Never send in original documents, and always send correspondence via a national carrier that can trace their packages.

Your proposal must QUICKLY speak to the need/benefit of the mortgagee. Your proposal should include all the information necessary for the mortgagee to make its decision on whether or not to accept a short payoff.

Suggested components of the proposal and organized with Custom Divider Tabs:

- cover with title
- executive summary
- table of contents
- authorization from seller to mortgagee(s)
- lender specific short sale application
- listing agreement w/restrictive language
- contract of sale w/restrictive language
- purchaser's qualifications (good to go!)
- estimated HUD 1
- borrower's chronology of hardship
- borrower's updated financials
- comparable market analysis, appraisal,
- review appraisal, or BPO w/color photographs and w/supportive data
- big ticket repairs estimates
- preliminary title report
- the Ask
- cost benefit analysis
- provided "Letter of Short Sale Approval"
- contact telephone numbers

THE HUD 1

an estimated settlement statement explained by a mortgage broker

(this section is used with permission)

The HUD-1 is a form used to itemize all charges imposed upon a borrower and seller for a real estate transaction. Be careful when estimating costs to include costs that will continue to accru until closing.

When Is The HUD-1 Used?

The statutes of the Real Estate Settlement Procedures Act (RESPA) require the form be used as the standard real estate settlement form in all transactions in the United States, which involve federally related mortgage loans.

When Is The HUD-1 Distributed?

RESPA states you should be given a copy of the HUD-1 at least one day prior to settlement. In real life, entries may still be coming in a few hours before closing. Most buyers and sellers study the statement on their own, with their real estate agent, and with the set-tlement agent. The more people who review it, the more likely that errors will be detected. Ask as many questions as necessary to help you understand all charges.

Line	Heading	Description Of Amounts Put On The Line
100	Gross Amount Due From Borrower	This section groups items that detail the amounts due and to whom they are due
101	Contract Sales Price	Filled in only for purchases
102	Personal Property	If non-real property is involved in the transaction. A manufactured home is personal property
104	Payoff to xxx lender	The amount paid to satisfy an existing loan. This line is used for refinances only.
106	Taxes	Taxes being paid
200	Amount Paid By Borrower	This section lists the money being brought to the table (or already held in escrow) by the borrower/buyer
201	Earnest Money Deposit	This is the amount already paid by the borrower/buyer
202	Principal amount of new loan	This is the borrowed amount
300	Cash at Settlement To/From Buyer	These totals summarize sections 100 & 200
400	Gross Amount Due to Seller	This section sums up the transaction similar to section 100, only from the seller's perspective
500	Reductions in Amount Due to Sellers	With a purchase, if the seller had an existing mortgage loans, they would be listed here
600	Cash To/From Seller	These totals summarize sections 400 & 500
700	Realtor Fees	These amounts split the real estate commissions paid by the buyer and/or seller

800	Items Paid in Connection with Loan	This section describes all one-time fees that are part of the process of approving and make the loan at the interest rate you have requested.
801	Lender's Loan Origination Fee	The fee charged to the borrower by the lender for making a mortgage loan. It is usually computed as a percentage of the loan amount.
802	Lender's Loan Discount Fee	Points charged by the lender to offer the interest rate you are receiving. Each point is equal to 1% of the mortgage amount. This is tax deductible (entire amount in first year on purchase, spread over life of loan on refinance).
803	Appraisal Fee	Payment to an independent and licensed appraiser to research and assess the market value of the property. The appraisal is required in order to determine the security of the loan and the borrower's loan to value (LTV) ratio.
804	Credit Report	This fee is charged by a credit service agency to provide the lender and us with a report detailing a borrower's credit history. We require an independent credit report.
808	Tax Service Fee	Each property is reviewed to confirm that the taxes are paid in full and up to date. Any unpaid property taxes are a liability to the lender and must be paid at closing.
809	Underwriting Review	This is what the mortgage company is charged for the review of your application by the lender's underwriter.
814	Yield Spread Premium	This amount is paid by lenders to our company for closing your loan. This amount is not paid by you, nor does it increase your closing costs.
816	Origination Due Broker	This is a fee. It is a tax deductible amount, either 100% during first year of a purchase, or spread over life of loan for a refinance.

818	Processing Fee	The mortgage company's fee for handling your paperwork.
819	Escrow Waiver Fee	If you choose to pay your taxes and insurance separately from your regular monthly mortgage payment you may pay this one time fee to the lender. The fee is usually 25% of the loan amount.
900	Items Required by Lender to be Paid in Advance	This section lists that a borrower may be required to prepay at the time of settlement, such as accrued interest, mortgage and hazard insurance premiums.
901	Interest for XX days at $XX per day	Prepaid interest due on the new loan from the date of funding to the end of the month If you close early in the month you will owe more interest, if you close later you will owe less.
902	Mortgage Insurance Premium	Private Mortgage Insurance (PMI) may be required on certain loans (usually above 80% loan to value). It is paid by the borrower and insures the lender against certain losses in the event of a foreclosure.
903	Hazard Insurance Premiums	The lender will require you to insure the property you are buying, since the property is the collateral for the loan
904	Flood Insurance Premiums	If your property is in a flood zone Flood insurance may be required. It is paid by the borrower and insures the borrower and lender against certain losses in the event of a flood.
1000	Reserves Deposited with Lender	Reserves held by the lender in an escrow account to pay for the borrower's future insurance premiums and taxes are detailed in this section.
1001	Hazard Insurance: months at $xx/mo.	Impounds may be required on loans with Loan to Value (LTV) ratios over 80%.
1002	Mortgage Insurance: months at $xx/mo.	Impounds may be required on loans with Loan to Value (LTV) ratios over 80%.

1004	Property Taxes: months at $xx/mo.	Estimated amount necessary to set up your escrow account. Your property taxes are being estimated at this point, and may be high or low in this assumption. .
1006	Flood Insurance Im- pounds	Impounds may be required on loans with Loan to Value (LTV) ratios over 80%.
1100	Title Charges	In this section the costs of a variety of ser- vices performed by the title company and others are specified.
1101	Settlement of Clos- ing/Escrow Fee	The fee paid to the escrow company for han- dling all the financial transfers and payments associated with the transaction. GFE pro- vider will estimate the fee, but is set by the closing firm you select.
1105	Document Preparation Fee	Pays for the service of creating your loan documents.
1106	Notary Fee	Several documents you sign during the loan must be notarized.
1107	Attorney Fee	Closing fee individually negotiated.
1108	Title Insurance	Guarantees that your home has no other liens on the property and guarantees your undis- puted ownership. All lenders require that you have title insurance on the home.
1112	Title Search	Most closing firms will require the title his- tory on your loan to be reviewed before they can issue a new title policy.
1200	Government Recording Transfer Fees	In this section, details about charges for the fees paid by either the buyer or seller at the time the purchase agreement is executed are found.
1201	Recording Fees	The recording fee, which varies by state, is paid to the county.
1202	City/County Tax/Stamps	Stamps, affixed to the deed, showing the amount of transfer tax paid.

1203	State Tax/Stamps	Stamps, affixed to the deed, showing the amount of transfer tax paid.
1300	Additional Settlement Charges	The final section describe other miscellaneous fees and credits.
1301	Survey	Some states require a survey before the loan can be fully approved and cleared for closing.
1305	Flood Certification	Cost of the flood zone determination to confirm if the property is /is not in a flood zone.
1307	Funding Fee	The cost of the wire transfer to deliver funds to the closing.

More On The HUD-1
(this section used with permission, too)

Section L, Settlement Charges

Section 700, Agency Commissions

This section deals with the commission paid to real estate agencies. Lines 701 and 702 show how commissions are split between two participating agencies. Commissions are usually paid from the seller's funds. However, a buyer's agent who sells a for-sale-by-owner home may be paid by his or her client, not the seller.

Section 800, Items Payable in Connection with Loan

The entries on these lines are most often paid from the buyer's funds, although in some cases sellers agree to pay specified amounts to help the buyer close.

Line 801 shows the fee the lender charged for processing or originating the loan. If the fee is a percentage of the loan amount, the percentage will be stated. Line 802 is used to record the "points" charged by the lender. Each point is 1% of the loan amount. Line 803 is used to record appraisal fees. You may have paid the fee when you applied for the loan. If so, it should be marked "POC," for paid outside of closing. The amount would be shown, but would not be included in the total fees you bring to settlement. Line 804 is used to record the cost of the credit report if it is not included in the Origination Fee. Line 805 includes charges for inspections done at the request of the lender. Other pest and structural inspections are recorded in another area.

Line 806 is for an application fee that might be required by a Private Mortgage Insurance (PMI) company. Line 807 is only used for loan assumption transactions, where the buyer takes over the seller's existing mortgage. Lines 808 to 811 are used for miscellaneous items connected with the loan, such as fees paid to a mortgage broker.

Section 900, Items Required by Lender to be Paid in Advance

These charges are typically paid by the buyer. They are all items which the lender requires, but which are not always paid to the lender.

Line 901 is used to record interest that is collected at settlement for the time period between closing and the first monthly payment. Line 902 shows mortgage insurance premiums that are due at settlement. Escrow reserves for mortgage insurance are recorded later. If your mortgage insurance is a lump sum payment good for the life of the loan it should be noted. Line 903 is used to record hazard insurance premiums that must be paid at settlement in order to have immediate insurance on the property. It is not used for insurance reserves that will go into escrow. Lines 904 and 905 are for miscellaneous items, such as flood insurance, mortgage life insurance, credit life insurance and disability insurance premiums.

Section 1000, Reserves Deposited with Lender

This section is used to itemize escrow funds collected by the lender from the borrower for such things as hazard insurance and property taxes. The number of months charged varies, but there are limits as to how much the lender can collect. The borrower paid current charges for the expenses in Section 900.

The entries on lines 1001-1007 are for funds used to start the borrower's escrow account, from which the lender will pay next year's premiums. Each mortgage payment includes an amount that covers a portion of these recurring expenses. Line 1008 is an escrow adjustment calculated by the settlement agent by comparing different escrow formulas. This step is to make sure the lender is not collecting more escrow funds than are allowed. The figure is always zero or a negative number.

Section 1100, Title Charges

Title charges include fees directly related to the transfer of title, such as the title examination, title search, document preparation, and fees for the title insurance policy. They are normally charged to the buyer. Legal fees include fees for both the borrower's and seller's attorneys, and sometimes an attorney for the lender. Other items covered in this section are fees for closing agents and notaries. When one person performs many tasks fees may be lumped together. Line 1101 is used to record the settlement agent's fee. The fees for the abstract or title search and examination are entered in lines 1102 and 1103. If the same person performs both duties, a lump sum will be entered in line 1103. If the person doing the work is a title company or attorney, charges are entered later, in lines 1107 or 1108. Line 1104 shows charges for the title insurance binder (also called a commitment to insure). Payment for title insurance policies is entered later.

Line 1105 records charges for deed preparations, and such bills as work on mortgages and notes. The fee charged by a notary public for authenticating the execution of the settlement documents is entered on line 1106. Line 1107 discloses an attorney's fees. Line 1108 is the cost of title insurance (except the cost of the binder). Lines 1109 and 1110 are informational lines that disclose the costs for the separate title insurance policies for borrower and lender. (Only line 1108 is carried forward.) Lines 1111 to 1113 are used to enter other title-related charges which vary by location. Entries might include a fee to a county tax collector for a tax certificate or a fee to a private tax service.

Section 1200, Government Recording and Transfer Charges

This section is used to itemize charges such as costs for recording deeds and mortgages and fees for tax stamps.

Sections 1300 & 1400, Additional Settlement Charges and Totals

Section 1300 is used to record survey fees and inspections for such things as pests, lead-based paint and radon. Structural inspections and inspections for heating, plumbing, or electrical equipment might also be included. If either party is buying a home warranty, the charge will be entered in this section. Line 1400 is for the total settlement charges paid from borrower's and seller's funds. They are also entered in Sections J and K, lines 103 and 502.

Section J, Summary of Borrower's Transaction

Section 100, Gross Amount Due from Borrower

Line 101 states the gross sales price of the property. Charges for personal property (such items as draperies, washer, dryer, outdoor furniture, and decorative items being purchased from the seller) are listed on 102. Line 103 shows the total settlement charges to the borrower that are brought forward from Line 1400. Lines 104 and 105 are for amounts owed by the borrower or previously paid by the seller.

- Entries charged to the borrower include a balance in the seller's escrow account if the borrower is assuming the loan.

- The borrower may owe the seller a portion of uncollected rents.

Lines 106 through 112 are for items which the Seller has paid in advance. For instance, the buyer must reimburse the seller for his prorated portion of county taxes if the seller paid an annual bill. Each person pays charges for the time they owned the property. Line 120 is the gross amount due from borrower. It is the total of Lines 101 through 112.

Section 200, Amounts Paid By or In Behalf of Borrower. These are all entries for funds the borrower will receive at closing.

Line 201 gives the buyer credit for the amount of earnest money paid when the offer was accepted. Line 202 is the amount of the new loan, which is being paid to the borrower by the lender. Line 203 is used when the borrower is assuming a loan or taking title subject to an existing loan or lien on the property. Lines 204 through 209 are used to list miscellaneous items paid by or on behalf of the buyer. They may include such items as an allowance the seller is making for repairs or replacement of items. This area is also used when the seller accepts a note from the borrower for part of the purchase price. Lines 210 through 219 are for bills which the seller has not yet paid, but owes all or a portion of Taxes and assessments are listed, but the area might also include rent collected in advance by the seller for a period extending beyond the settlement date. Line 220 is the total for all items in Section 200. The total is added to the borrower's proceeds.

Section 300, Cash at Settlement From/To Borrower

Line 301 is a summary of the total amount due from the borrower. Line 302 is a summery of all items already paid by or for the borrower. Line 303 is the difference between lines 301 and 302. It most often shows how much money the borrower must bring to closing. It could be a negative number, indicating that the borrower will receive funds back at closing.

Section K, Summary of Seller's Transaction

Section 400, Gross Amount Due to Seller

The amounts in this section are added to the seller's funds. Line 401 states the gross sales price of the property. Entries for personal property (such items as draperies, washer, dryer, outdoor furniture and decorative items that the seller may be selling to the buyer) are listed on 402.

Lines 404 and 405 are for other amounts owed by the borrower or previously paid by the seller, such as:

- If the borrower is assuming the seller's loan, he/she must reimburse the seller for the balance in the seller's escrow account.

- The buyer may owe the seller a portion of uncollected rents.

Lines 406 through 412 are for items which the Seller has paid in advance. For instance, the buyer may need to reimburse the seller for a prorated portion of county taxes if the seller paid an annual bill but will not own the property during that entire year.

Line 420 is the gross amount due to the seller. It is the total of Lines 401 through 412.

Section 500, Reductions in Amount Due to Seller

The amounts in this section are subtracted from the seller's funds.

Line 501 is used when the seller's real estate broker or another party holds the borrower's earnest money deposit, and will pay it directly to the seller. Line 502 contains the figure from Line 1400, the seller's total charges as computed in Section L. Line 503 is used if the borrower is assuming or taking title subject to existing liens which are deducted from the sales price. Lines 504 and 505 are for any first and/or second loans which will be paid-off as part of settlement (including accrued interest). Lines 506 through 509 are shown as blank lines for miscellaneous entries. Line 506 is used to record deposits paid by the borrower to the seller or another party who is not the settlement agent.

This is slightly different than the entry in 501. In this case the party holding the funds transfers it to the settlement agent to be disbursed at closing. These lines may also be used to list additional liens which much be paid at settlement to clear title to the property. Lines 510 through 519 are for bills which the seller has not yet paid, but owes all or a portion of. Taxes and assessments are listed, but the area might also include rent collected in advance by the seller for a period extending beyond the settlement date. Line 520 is the total for all items in Section 500. The total is deducted from the seller's proceeds.

Section 600, Cash at Settlement To/From Seller

Lines 601 is the gross amount due to the seller, from line 420. Line 602 contains the total of reductions in seller's proceeds, from line 520. Line 603 is the difference between lines 601 and 602. It usually indicates a cash amount paid to seller, but it's possible for the seller to owe money at closing. For instance, the seller might owe more on first and second mortgages than is recovered in the contract.

You can prepare the estimated HUD1 without assistance, or you can commission your title insurance company or closing attorney prepare it for you.

Make certain that your cost projections are as accurate as possible.

Anticipate costs, including the accrual of property taxes, and the mortgage payoff amount through the anticipated closing date.

PRESENTING THE PROPOSAL

Early on, you should try learn who will be making the decision to accept, counter offer, or reject your proposal. Your first line of contact will be the *foreclosure account manager,* or *loss mitigation specialist,* who will pre qualify the possibility for short sale consideration as an alternative to foreclosure. If the loss mit rep determines that a short sale is feasible, he/she is responsible for requesting and collecting the basic information needed for short sale consideration. Lenders will have their own *checklist* but it's reasonable to assume that the Homeowner will be asked to produce the last few month's bank statements, pay stubs, a financial worksheet, credit card account statements, a property tax bill, a home owner's insurance policy, etc. Once all items on the loss mit rep's checklist are assembled, a preliminary determination will be made, and that information is submitted to his/her superiors for their consideration, and approval.

While maintaining a professional and respectful demeanor, you'll want to try to learn who the superiors are, and the location of their offices. They might be in the same building, across the street, or in another part of the country.

Send your proposal to the highest ranking members of the loss mitigation department, but don't forget to send a courtesy copy of your proposal to the loan workout rep who sent you the application for short sale consideration in the first place. In addition to an internally prepared application for short sale consideration, you will send your own, comprehensive and compelling, short sale proposal to the appropriate body or individual(s). Why? Since you can't be in the same room with them as they review the application for short sale consideration, your proposal will have to speak for you.

Your proposal should be factual and compelling, and address any objections or questions that may be raised. I always send my short sale proposals via US Priority Mail, Certified, with Return Receipt Requested. Even if and especially if request the application be FAXed. In my opinion, the proposal loses its impact when FAXed.

I think presentation is critical, and an original sets the proposal apart from others spat out from the FAX.

Assume That The Mortgagee Will Misplace, Lose, And/Or Deny Ever Having Received Your Short Sale Application At Least Once, Maybe Twice. So Make A Few Copies.

WHAT IF THE PROPOSAL IS REJECTED?

Initially, many short sale proposals are rejected, however, an initial rejection isn't necessarily the end of the negotiation. Many times, the loss mitigation specialist is waiting for an interpretation or an update to servicer's policy, and isn't in a position to process your application. Or, he/she is too busy working on other applications to respond. Or, the file hasn't been tagged "urgent," and the lender isn't too concerned about the pending foreclosure. So, you wait until their perception changes to one of concern.

If your proposal has been rejected, ask for a specific reason, in writing, why the request for short sale consideration was denied. More often than not the reason is that the anticipated net proceeds do not meet minimal short sale criteria for that particular loan type. Sometimes a proposal is rejected due to a basic flaw, omission, misstated information in the presentation, a missed deadline, stale information, or it hasn't been presented to the appropriate body or individual(s). Sometimes, the *appropriate* body or individual changes after the short sale proposal has been submitted.

With increasing frequency, *troubled* mortgage loan servicing rights are transferred from one mortgage loan servicer to another servicer, perhaps with more experience in foreclosure, and liquidation.

If this happens, and the foreclosure time line permits, the request for short sale consideration must be repackaged and resubmitted to the new mortgage loan servicer whose criteria for short sale consideration may be similar, dissimilar, or nonexistent. It's important to be diplomatic with and respectful to everyone that you contact during the process.

The last thing that you would want to do would be to make an unappreciated remark, or express your impatience or dissatisfaction with any loan servicing representative who has anything to do with your short sale proposal. You'll need their continued cooperation to advance to the next level. If you lose their cooperation your short sale application might stall, without good cause.

SAMPLE SHORT SALE APPROVAL LETTER

You will always need a written agreement with the lender if the property can be sold via short sale. The lender will want to make sure that the property is being sold at its best, possible price because the higher the price, the greater their net recovery. At the time of agreement for short sale, make sure that it states that the lender WILL NOT SEEK payment on the balance of the debt

date

RE: mortgagor(s)
property address

mortgage loan account # _____

To whom it may concern:

Mortgagee issues its approval to sell the subject property which will result in a short payoff of the mortgage, and mortgagor(s) acknowledge they waive any and all rights to any escrow balance, insurance proceeds, or refunds from prepaid expenses.

As agreed, when mortgagee is in receipt of the proceeds of sale and all required documentation, we will amend reporting to the credit bureau to reflect 'agreed settlement short of full payment" which should be reflected within 60 to 90 days from date of modification and waive any deficiency rights, if any.

This approval is predicated upon   the purchase contract dated _____ between Mortgagor(s), the Seller(s), and _____, the Buyer(s),   for a purchase price of $_____ .

The terms of our approval and instruction to the settlement agent are as follows:

This Approval is contingent upon 1) the property is to be sold in an as-is, condition, there are to be ZERO allowances for repairs, 2) the Seller is to receive ZERO proceeds from the sale, and 3) The Seller must provide an executed, non transferable sales contract with a sales price of $_____ .

Payment must be in the form of CERTIFIED FUNDS ONLY, and must be accompanied by a copy of the final, net settlement statement (HUD1). Any surplus funds shall be paid directly to Mortgagee.

Our Customer must acknowledge their agreement to the terms outlined herein this letter by their signature at the bottom of this letter. This Offer shall be valid through ___ / ___ / 2006.

 Failure to comply with any of the above may result in a delay of any release of lien, and the voiding of this Offer.

In accordance with the above conditions, and upon receipt of an executed contract, a final net settlement statement, and payment in certified funds, Mortgagee agrees to cancel any deficiency.

Sincerely

_____

Mortgagee, Title / date

FINANCING THE SHORT SALE ACQUISITION

Congratulations, now that your proposed transaction has been approved, you've got to prepare for closing, and quickly, too. Once the contract of sale has been approved by the foreclosing lender, the purchaser will have a short window of time to complete the transaction. Typically they'll be asked to close within 30 to 45 days before incurring a penalty, or the recession of the short sale approval. As is often the case, preparations for closings, especially when the purchaser needs an acquisition mortgage loan, can take more than the window allows. The purchaser's lender's closing requirements may include the need for an appraisal, property survey, and in some cases, repairs. Sometimes, the foreclosing lender will agree to a postponement, and it's not uncommon for them to ask that additional monies be paid (nonrefundable, in advance) to offset their additional costs.

It's best to identify both your acquisition and exit strategy well in advance. **Cash is King!** Plan to use cash, an acquisition mortgage loan, assign the contract, or schedule simultaneous or a double closing.

Assigning a mortgagee approved short sale contract is becoming more and more complicated as lenders seek to restrict the practice of 'flipping' that results in a less than maximum recovery. A post closing review that indicates a change from the original contract can send up a red flag, jeopardizing the deal. One way to avoid this problem is to cause the named purchaser to be a limited liability company (LLC). Even though the named purchaser on the contract won't change, the members that comprise the LLC can be added, or removed.

Instead of assigning the contract, and causing someone other than the named purchaser to close (may be in violation of the terms and conditions of short sale approval) simply add the purchaser to the LLC as a member and when it comes time to close, the new member can identify himself as a member of the LLC, and bring funding to the table. If that funding is in the name of the purchaser, he can explain prior to closing that his mortgage lender requires that he take title in his own name a very plausible explanation.

The closing attorney would have no reason to suspect that the contract was assigned, placing the closing in jeopardy of violating (foreclosing mortgagee's) closing instructions.

A simultaneous closing occurs on the same day: either back-to-back, or within a few hours of each other. All of the ownership paperwork, titling, and monies are finalized, and transfers effected basically at the same time at the same title company - hence the name *simultaneous* close.

Not all title companies who perform closing services, or closing attorneys, are professionally comfortable with conducting simultaneous closings. It's best to interview several before you actually need their services. You should specifically ask if their services can include a simultaneous or double closing.

Another factor to consider would be to identify *seasoning* requirements imposed by your buyer's mortgage lender. If there are no seasoning requirement, or if your buyer is paying cash… you'll be on your way to a smooth closing.

FOUR SHORT SALE SCENARIOS

Short Sale Scenario #1
Assignment Of Contract

I was contacted by a homeowner who faced the loss of her home. Efforts to effectuate a workout with her mortgagee had failed, and she was also found to be ineligible for a bankruptcy Chapter 13 re-payment plan. She wanted very much to bring the loan current and stop the foreclosure, but was not able to access the resources to do so. I agreed to consider her problem.

The home was an older, legal two family dwelling in distressed condition. The top floor apartment had a terrific view (from New Jersey) of the New York skyline. It had been her dream plan to pur-chase the home, spruce it up, and, while living on the top floor apartment, rent the ground floor apartment. Shortly following the purchase two years earlier, she learned that the condition of the dwelling was much worse than she had anticipated. Needing sub-stantial repairs at considerable expense, the lower unit would not be issued a certificate of occupancy. She knew that without the rental income, the mortgage payment would be unmanageable.

To further compound the problem, the dwelling's roof needed a total replacement, as did the old wooden doors and window sashes. What had been a dream-come-true for the homeowner, quickly became an all-too-real nightmare. Desperate, the homeowner (illegally) leased the bottom floor apartment to an acquaintance who promised to make some repairs in exchange for some rent. Within a couple of months, that situation turned ugly. The homeowner was cited for leasing the premises without having a certificate of occupancy, and making repairs without a building permit. The local fire marshal and building inspector red tagged the unit, rendering the entire structure uninhabitable. The homeowner made some emergency repairs that conditionally enabled her to resume her top floor occupancy.

Despite the pending foreclosure, and the physical condition, she wanted to stay in her home. She purchased the home for $178,000 financed by a $160,000 conventional mortgage loan. Due to multiple missed payments, penalties, and foreclosure related costs, she now owed about $180,000. The property needed between $25,000 and $40,000 in repairs. In it's as-is condition, I estimated it's value to be about $130,000. After repairs, the dwelling could have had a value of about $250,000 or more.

Generally, it isn't advisable to keep the former homeowner as a tenant **unless** the new owner is family, or a friend who specifically devised a sale and leaseback for the former homeowner's benefit. In this case, since it was a legal two family dwelling, an occupied conveyance might be of interest to an Investor, while meeting the desire of the seller. I again met with the homeowner, outlining the possibility of a transaction known as a (short) sale and leaseback. The property could be sold to an investor who would have to agree to lease the premises to her as he "worked around her" making essential repairs to dwelling. The Investor would first complete repairs to the exterior, then renovate the ground floor apartment. Upon completion of the ground floor unit, she would then have to relocate to the ground floor to accommodate the top floor unit's construction schedule. Once the property was renovated, and provided that she remained current with her lease payments, she would have an opportunity to purchase the property from the new owner at its then, market value in a fully repaired condition as established by a

43

certified appraisal. She agreed with the plan and agreed to meet me again in a few days.

I crunched the numbers and knew that to be attractive to an investor, this would have to be a short sale. I prepared three documents: 1) a ShortSalePro services agreement & applicable authorizations, 2) a contract for sale at a price of $125,000, w/ an assignment clause, and 3) a separate lease agreement. The homeowner signed a Short-SalePro services agreement and paid the initial installment of my fee. She also signed the contract for sale, and agreed to provide other information and documents necessary for the short sale proposal, including pay stubs, W-2s, tax returns, financial worksheets, a letter of hardship, a contract for sale, and a net sheet (estimated HUD 1) etc.

Multiple objectives were as follows: 1) to keep the present owner in the house as a tenant, 2) to identify and secure a qualified investor who would purchase the property, make necessary repairs, and offer the tenant a opportunity to purchase the property pursuant to a conditional right of first refusal, and 3) realize a profit for me, the facilitator.

To assemble the standard documentation that most *short sale applications* require was a matter of routine. I had the cooperation of the homeowner. The manufacture and justification of an as-is, fair market value to make the deal work would be relatively easy. Based upon the physical conditions I had observed, supported by municipal inspection reports and summaries of violation, I felt confident that the numbers would work. The tough part would be to find an investor who would agree to the conditions of the sale and leaseback.

There are about a zillion potential investors or wannabe investors for every qualified real estate opportunity. A simple classified advertisement in the local newspaper a year earlier had resulted in a list of pre qualified, real estate *speculators* who were desperate to throw money into real estate, eager to try what the infomercial gurus promised to be the source of great riches. Of the scores that called, those who seemed *real* were added to my dynamic list of potential investor/speculators.

Over the next couple of weeks, as I worked to prepare the short sale proposal, I dropped a few hints to the folks on my list that there might be an opportunity available in a month or so, requiring about $50,000 cash plus some short term mortgage finance. My thinking was that if an investor were to purchase the property for $125,000 plus closing costs, then spend another $40,000 in repairs, carrying the property for at least a year (offset by 12 month's rental income from the former homeowner) there was a potential pretax profit of about $75,000. What would the investor need? A down payment, a purchase money mortgage loan, plus rehab and carrying costs. I had to describe the deal a few times before I narrowed the list to three candidates who would be given an opportunity to inspect the property, and review the contracts.

In addition to completing the mortgagee's boilerplate *application for short sale consideration* checklist, I developed other components of the proposal. The two most important elements of a short sale proposal are (1) the mortgagees' perception of the subject property's as-is, fair market value, and (2) anticipated net payoff to the mortgagee(s).

Since a proposal should be based on as much data accepted as true by the mortgagee, I decided that I would begin with the mortgagee's origination appraisal of $178,000, and from that manufacture a credible, as-is, fair market value. In anticipation of the mortgagee's objection that the then FMV had increased due to appreciation, I multiplied $178,000 by the area's documented rate of appreciation for the 18 months of ownership, and estimated a range of value from $195,000 to $205,000. From that I deducted repairs costs that were line itemized and supported by photographs from the extensive list of required structural and cosmetic repairs. I deducted lender's estimated foreclosure (pre REO) costs. From that subtotal, I deducted lender's estimated REO costs: eviction proceedings, property preservation, property taxes, insurance, lost opportunity costs, and liquidation expenses. The grand total, rounded off, came to be the basis for an as-is, fair market value to the mortgagee of $125,000.

Once the short sale proposal had been completed and presented to the foreclosing mortgagee, I knew I had a few weeks to secure an investor who would purchase my contract via an assignment, and complete the transaction. I found such an investor. Good credit, access to cash. He was a builder in need of a project. He liked the numbers, though he thought that my estimates for repair were too high. "$40,000? I can get that done for less than $30,000." he said. Which is exactly what I wanted to hear because it made the deal that much more valuable to him. And to me. He hadn't seen the contracts, and we still hadn't discussed my assignment fee. I wanted him to get excited about the project before an assignment fee was discussed. I'm sure that he didn't know that he was buying the 'deal' from me. All he knew was that he was buying a house that needed repairs, and he could make a handsome profit in a short time.

Long story short, the short sale was approved by the mortgagee, in writing, for $125,000. I agreed to assign the contract to the investor for $7,500. He was hesitant to pay the assignment fee before he had acquired the property, but did agree, however, to place the sum in trust with an attorney who was instructed to release the $7,500 to me upon presentation of closing documents. As closing approached, and the documents were reviewed, the mortgagee balked when it learned that the contract had been assigned to another buyer and threatened to rescind their short sale approval. What triggered their reaction was the purchaser's mortgage loan commitment for $165,000.

I wasn't aware that the buyer had applied for and was approved for an FHA 203K mortgage loan in the amount of $165,000. An FHA 203 loan finances both the purchase price, PLUS the estimated costs to repair the dwelling. It took a few days to resolve the glitch, but ultimately the transaction closed. The FHA appraisal confirmed a FMV of $125,000, and called for $40,000 in repairs. The ARV was estimated at $265,000, and more than justified the loan.

The former homeowner remained as a tenant. Following the completion of renovations, the property was placed on the market for sale. The former homeowner, now tenant, was offered first right of refusal to purchase the property, but elected, instead, to agree to a lease cancellation for cash.

The Only Numbers That Really Matter Are The Mortgagee's Perception Of The As-Is, Fair Market Value, And Their Net Proceeds From The Sale

Short Sale Scenario #2
Choose Your Battles

An investor/speculator presented his "at risk" deal to me and asked if there was anything I could do to get the deal closed. He had attempted to work out a short sale on his own with the foreclosed homeowner, but the mortgagee had rejected the application due to the amount of the offer ($100,000) and their anticipated net recovery on a loan with a balance of $180,000.

The short sale application itself was adequately prepared, meeting the criteria set forth by the mortgagee for short sale consideration. The distressed homeowner had a bona fide hardship, and was unable to bring the loan current. The fair market value was less than the mortgage loan balance. There was an offer to purchase the property in its as-is condition, with closing to be scheduled within 30 days.

The subject property was an older home in disrepair with a mortgage balance of about $180,000 in an area of newer, $350,000 to $450,000 homes. The short sale had been conditionally approved, subject to the results of an appraisal performed by a bank approved, certified appraiser. The bank ordered an appraisal, but to the dismay of the buyer, the appraised value came back at $150,000.

Consequently, the mortgagee rescinded its approval, and suggested that unless the buyer submitted another offer, one with a sales price of $150,000, the mortgagee's attorney would move to reinstate the Sheriff's Sale. Had the buyer met with the appraiser on site before the appraisal was performed, he might have been able to influence the appraiser's opinion of value. But, he didn't. He left the single most important element of the short sale application process to chance.

Let me repeat that. **He left the single most important element of the short sale application process to chance.**

Once the opinion of value was 'certified' in the form of an appraisal, and presented to the mortgagee (appraiser's client), it would be difficult to have that perception of value reversed.

Before I could consider accepting the challenge of resurrecting this short sale, I needed to see a copy of the bank's appraisal, and needed to review the appraisal by physically inspecting the property.

The buyer agreed to produce a copy of the appraisal and meet me at the property the next morning.

After introducing me to the homeowner, he handed me the appraisal and drove away. I scanned to the boilerplate appraisal's indicated value of $150,000 in its as-is, condition. I gave it a cursory read, but knew that in order to get the mortgagee to reconsider, I'd have to invalidate the appraisal's conclusion. The homeowner offered to walk me through the house.

I grabbed my field pack (umbrella and boots, flashlight, pocketknife, small binoculars, camera, extra film, extra batteries, a 25 foot tape measure, torpedo level, small plastic sandwich bags, some wooden popsicle sticks, a roll of double stick tape, a lead paint swipe test, and a one dollar bill, and a twenty five cent piece, and took the tour. The home, in its day, would have been majestic in its authentic, colonial beauty.

A true colonial farmhouse set on about an acre of what had been a 100 acre farm. With the bank's appraisal in hand, I walked through the aged house making notes and taking photographs. I photographed everything that seemed in need of repair. Cracks in plaster walls, peeling or blistering paint, water-stained ceilings, out of level floors, out of plumb walls, asbestos insulation and pipe wrap, the old oil furnace, water heaters, electrical service panel, clusters of electrical wire, damaged floors, broken windows, anything and everything. For reference to size, I place a dollar bill, a quarter, or my tape measure next to the defect, and took a snapshot. Sometimes, I held my flashlight in such a way as to highlight cracks or depressions (that would otherwise be indiscernible). If walls were out of plumb, I placed a level on it and photographed the bubble. In older homes, I always conduct a lead paint swipe test (I ask the homeowner to take a photo of my hand as it presses the test swipe to the painted surface) I always try to schedule the inspection on trash collection day. A home always looks worse with several overflowing garbage cans in front. As I took snapshot after snapshot, I listened as the Homeowner described the various problems and repairs made over the years. After about 45 minutes of locating most of the obvious defects (major and minor) and making the homeowner's wife quite embarrassed in the process, I thought that I had enough information to refute the appraisal.

I then accepted the invitation to walk the property with the owner. I listened as he described both the farm's and family's history. As the homeowner told me about his large back yard and what it once was, he pointed to a garden's rock walls, and said that was where the well had been. As he talked I listened and learned that the farmhouse wasn't connected to the city sewers, but had instead (illegally) tapped into the new sewer line belonging to the house of his next door neighbor.

"I saved $2,000 by tapping into her line," he said. With that, I said good-bye to the homeowner and knew that I would have little trouble refuting the appraiser's opinion of value. Why? Because I took the little extra time to listen.

I called the buyer from the road and told him that I thought I could salvage his short sale, and we negotiated the terms of our agreement. I took the film to be processed and within a few hours had drafted the basis for requesting that the appraisal's value be revised. I contacted the appraiser, and said that I had some additional information regarding one of his appraisals, and asked if I could drop off my 'notes' for his review. He didn't seem too receptive, but agreed that he would take a look at it.

The presentation format to the appraiser included the most supportive photographs to illustrate my motion for reconsideration, a scope of repairs schedule, estimated costs for labor and materials, and, using the appraiser's own comparable market data, recalculated the subject's as-is, fair market value from $150,000 to $100,000. On a separate letter to the appraiser, I asked that he reconsider his appraisal's conclusion, revise, and resubmit a revised appraisal report to reflect the additional information. Within a day of receiving my report, he acquiesced. The revised appraisal was submitted to the mortgagee and referenced my report, a copy of which was attached.

The mortgagee, upon receipt of the revised appraisal, issued a short sale approval letter to the homeowner at $100,000, and the buyer (my Client) was able to complete the short sale purchase.

SHORT SALES – AN ETHICAL APPROACH

Short Sale Scenario #3
The One That Got Away

A foreclosure investor/speculator called about his 'at risk' deal that was about to implode and asked that I look over his file. The subject property had a fair market range of value from $750,000 to $850,000 with two, foreclosed mortgage loans that totaled $1.1 million.

The investor had obtained a quit claim deed to the property from the mortgagor (subject to the mortgages, and delinquent property taxes), then entered into a contract to sell the property for $825,000 to a cash buyer. His $550,000 cash offer to the mortgagee(s) to purchase the mortgages at a discount was rejected. He couldn't get the mortgagee(s) to budge on their demand for payment in full, $1,100,000. He was frustrated and anxious to salvage this deal. He had spent thousands of dollars in landscape upkeep, pool maintenance, and utilities while the property was marketed by a local real estate broker. Once the property was under contract, though, the gardeners weren't called back. Nor was the pool guy.

I declined his offer of a $25,000 success fee to save his deal. I knew that this would be an extraordinarily tough assignment, so I countered, and he agreed that he would pay me $1,000 to prepare a short sale proposal, and another $4,000 to present and negotiate the proposal. In advance. Additionally, if the proposal were accepted with terms favorable to complete his transaction, he would pay me an additional 5% of his net profit.

I set about preparing the short sale proposal by getting access to the property in its million dollar neighborhood. I knew the house right away. The grass was about two feet tall! Seeing the real estate broker parked in front, I grabbed my field pack (umbrella and boots, flashlight, pocketknife, small binoculars, camera, extra film, extra batteries, a 25 foot tape measure, torpedo level, small plastic sandwich bags, some wooden popsicle sticks, a roll of double stick tape, a lead paint swipe test, and $1.25) and went to meet her at the door. I should mention that when I have to travel any distance, I sometimes invite my Dad for the ride. He is a retired science teacher, and I value his company, and astute observations. On this day, I asked my father to keep the real estate broker busy in another part of the house as I prepared the scene. Calling this a single family residence a simple "house" did it a disservice.

It was more like a single family resort. There was an indoor pool in a room with a retractable roof. More bathrooms than I could count. But, there were problems, and my immediate task was to identify and document the problems in hope of convincing the mortgagees that their collateral wasn't worth $1.1 million dollars, and that it was in their best financial interest to accept less. Much, much less. My photographs concentrated on the indoor pool area. There were some mold/mildew problems due to a lack of ventilation in the once steamy room. Some ceramic floor tiles were coming up, and the sound system had been removed leaving obvious voids in the woodwork where speakers had been. While I was carrying an overflowing trash can from the garage into the kitchen, it 'accidentally' tipped, spilling its contents across the ceramic tiled floor. I noticed, and adjusted a few loose floor tiles, snapped a picture or two, then carefully replaced the tiles into their original position, and returned the scattered trash into the trash can. I used whatever was available to me to make the condition appear in need of repairs, and in an under marketable condition. After about an hour (inside and out) I reunited with the real estate broker, thanked her as she locked up, and watched her drive off.

My Dad had gleaned some valuable information from her. This dwelling had been the 'model' home in that development, the builder's own residence. Rumor was that the builder refinanced, then skipped town. Another suburban scandal! My Dad also pointed out a few things that I had overlooked. I amended my notes, took a few more exterior photographs, then took my "helper" to lunch. As was usually the case, he bought lunch for me.

Since I would be facilitating the discounted purchase of a mortgage(s), there was no need to have written authorization from the mortgagor. This would be a straightforward business proposal made to an asset manager of non performing loans.

Every proposal for short sale consideration should include both a physical evaluation of the property, and a financial analysis. To determine the as-is, fair market value of the subject, I started by using an insurance adjuster's cost repair guide to methodically prepare a 'scope of repairs' and its likely cost. I also considered the 'stigma' factor. The house was robbed of its equity, then abandoned by the builder, eventually becoming an eyesore in the upscale community.

While selecting photographs to incorporate into the proposal, I noticed a series of high tension towers and wires in the background, so I included a generic paragraph on the adverse impact power lines exact upon marketability.

It took about a week, but I finally was comfortable with the proposal. The data justified an offer of $625,000 for the two mortgages (held by the same mortgagee). The proposal included a signed "offer to purchase mortgage via an assignment" contract. I attached my client's good faith check for $6,250. I sent three copies of the completed proposal via US Priority Mail, Certified, with Return Receipt Requested to the appropriate individual with whom I had several, material conversations.

I called the next day to make sure that the proposal had been received. He said that it was, he reviewed it, was impressed, and it would go to committee the next morning after which, he would call me. He didn't foresee any problems with them accepting the offer. I called my client and told him that the proposal had been received, and we should have a favorable decision by the next afternoon. But, by the next afternoon, there had been no call back as promised.

I called my contact the next morning only to be told that no decision had been made. The proposal was still in committee. The next day I was told that the proposal had been accepted, and the appropriate paperwork was being prepared by their attorney. I asked that their approval be reduced to writing and FAXed to me. But the promised FAX didn't come as promised. A few more days passed, and my calls were no longer being accepted, and my messages were not being returned. This went on for a few more days. I was getting anxious. My client was beside himself as the foreclosure sale date rapidly approached, his end-buyer was screaming, and his/our profit at risk!

My last call to the mortgagee proved damaging, but informative. I was informed that the mortgages had been packaged with other mortgages, and sold to a Dallas, Texas mortgage servicing company! Instead of taking the hit, they sold the loans to an institutional loan servicer. It could take weeks for the files to be shipped, inventoried and assigned a new mortgage loan number, its status reviewed, and assigned to a foreclosure, or an REO management team.

I didn't have that kind of time. I would have to present the proposal to the new mortgagee within a matter of days since a sheriff's sale had been scheduled within a week. I placed a call to the attorney of record who filed the foreclosure lawsuit. He indicated that his client had not advised him to postpone the sale, and the sale would proceed as scheduled.

I called the new mortgagee's foreclosure department. They had no record of the mortgage, and suggested that I call back in a couple of weeks. I moved my way up the chain of command and soon spoke to the new product administrator whose job it was to process new portfolios for servicing. I was able to identify the incoming portfolio of which "my" mortgage was included. There were about 100 new files, all had been scheduled for a foreclosure sale. It would take a few weeks for her to sort through them.

I explained that I had presented an offer to purchase the mortgage, and had a verbal approval from the former mortgagee. "Then it'll be in the file. When I find it, I'll let you know," she said, adding, "I've got about 100 new files and I can't make any promises."

My client was in panic mode. He agreed that the only way to get some action on this was for me to meet the processor face to face and physically place the file in front of her. He agreed to pay for my flight from NJ to Texas, overnight accommodations, car rental, and my per diem for 2 days. Within a few hours, armed with three copies of my proposal, I was on my way to try to salvage the deal for my client. I called the processor, and advised that I would be in town the next day, and wanted to drop off a copy of the time sensitive proposal. She agreed to see me.

Upon my arrival, I immediately called her to confirm the appointment to meet with her the next day. She said she hadn't even located the file, but to come by the following morning. I used that afternoon and evening to learn as much as I could about the new mortgagee as possible. Who were they, what was their specialty?

The next morning I took a cab from the hotel to the mortgagee's headquarters for my 10 AM appointment. Making my way from one security conscious level to the next, I was finally was able to announce myself to the casually dressed receptionist (it was Casual Friday), and waited in the outer office. And waited. It was close to noon when I was told that the woman with whom I was to meet was too busy to see me. In fact, they were all so busy that they wouldn't even be able to break for lunch. This was something for which I hadn't prepared. I thought that I'd be able to at least meet with her, if only for a few minutes.

I walked away, dejected, thinking that I had wasted my time. I looked for a public telephone with a phone book to call a cab, when I noticed a restaurant's advertisement for "free delivery" in the pay phone's stall. An idea came to me! I ordered platters of sandwiches, salads, bottles of soda, and bags of chips to be delivered to the 4th floor processing department.

I placed the charge on my credit card, but insisted that the order must be acknowledged as received by guess who? The woman that was too busy to meet with me!

I waited until I saw the restaurant's free delivery van park outside the building. I accompanied the delivery guy, helping him carry what didn't exactly fit on his wheeled cart. We went right up to the 4th floor's receptionist who seemed delighted that somebody had ordered lunch for the entire department. When told who had to sign for the assortment of food, she made a call and within about 30 seconds, we were taken back to a small office located in the rear of a cavernous, new product processing center. Long story short, I introduced myself and said that though I appreciated that she had been too busy to meet with me, as promised, I wanted to take just a few, short minutes with her during lunch.

She grabbed a plate and sandwich. Sitting at her computer, she located the file and within a few minutes it was delivered to her desk. Expecting to see a copy of my proposal, I was surprised that there was no mention of the proposal, or the former mortgagee's acceptance. "I'm not at all surprised it's not in here," she remarked as I handed her a copy of the proposal. "I'll put it in the file, and pass this along to the asset manager. We might have to send this mortgage back. But don't expect anything to happen quickly. Nothing ever does " she said.

I arrived back at my office Monday morning, preparing to call my client with an update when he called to tell me, "The buyer backed out the deal is dead. Thanks for trying."

About a week later, I got a call from the mortgagee's asset manager who had reviewed my proposal, and expressed an interest in accepting the offer. He asked for access to order a new appraisal. I thanked him, then told him that the decision had been too long in coming, and the investor went with another deal. He said he understood, then asked if I had any other clients who would be interested in purchasing non performing mortgage loans at a discount. We spoke further, and to this day he FAXes to my office his listings of REO, and prelisted REO properties.

Short Sale Scenario #4
Exception To The Rule

Often, financially distressed homeowners, in an effort to avoid foreclosure, list their homes for sale at an asking price of just enough to payoff the mortgage(s), and real estate commission irrespective of the property's market value. Sometimes, the asking price exceeds the property's as-is, fair market value, and the listing remains unsold.

Unable to convince the sellers to reduce their asking price, many real estate brokers have overpriced, stagnant listings in their inventory of unsold homes.

Invitations are sometimes extended from local real estate brokers asking me to speak to their agents about accepting listings with 'upside down' mortgage loans, or properties that faced mortgage foreclosure. In exchange for a percentage of the transaction fee, I would make myself available to those agents who had questions, or needed help in working a short sale listing.

A broker called with a problem listing, "It's about $20,000 overpriced and the Sellers are driving me nuts with phone calls. I sold them the house two years ago, and, instead of it's appreciating in value, it's value has decreased. They say that they can't reduce the price because they owe more on their mortgage that the home is worth. They don't have the cash to make up the difference and they just want out. Can you work a short sale?"

I met with the sellers at their home the next afternoon, explaining that if I did agree to negotiate a short sale in their behalf, there would be some paperwork involved, and I discussed my fee schedule. The young family had purchased the single family home about 2 years earlier, and it appeared that there was new vinyl siding, windows, and appliances.

The primary mortgagor was fully employed as a telecom engineer, his wife a stay-at-home Mom who took care of their two preschool aged children. Their reason for selling, I was told, was they no longer liked the neighborhood.

After a walk through their home, and cursory review of their finances, I quickly decided that they probably wouldn't qualify for a negotiated short sale. There was no unemployment, no illness, and I saw no financial hardship. The mortgage loan payments and property taxes were current. I told them that I would speak with their real estate broker who would call them later on in the week.

I told the broker that I didn't think that I could build much of an argument for a short sale, and I explained my reasoning. He wasn't very happy, he wanted to get the house sold, and asked me to reconsider. I told him I'd think about it though I had no intention of accepting the assignment.

The next morning I got a call from Mrs. Homeowner who implored me to accept their case. I told her that I didn't think that there was much of a chance that I would be successful, and I didn't want to waste my time, or take their money. She was insistent that I try and said that she understood that I do not guarantee results. I relented, and agreed to meet with them again. "When do they pick up your trash?" I asked, and explained that I would agree to meet them on the next trash pick up day.

I prepared for the meeting by setting up a short sale file folder, assembling the application checklist, and other documents that I would need to prepare the short sale proposal.

I stopped by to see the broker and asked for a copy of the listing agreement, and a *conservative* comparable market analysis. As he thought about what comparables to use for the CMA, we spoke about the property. It was listed for sale at $115,000, but in the five months it had been exposed to the market, there were no offers, and had become stale with little or no market interest. It was his opinion that at an asking price of $115,000, the listing would sit. He indicated that it could probably sell for $95,000. With a mortgage loan balance of about $105,000, plus costs of sale, the home would have to sell for just about $112,000. He handed me a CMA with an indicated range of value from $90,000 to $110,000. We drew up a transaction brokers' shared fee agreement, and I was off to meet the sellers.

There wasn't too much wrong with the subject's interior or mechanical systems, in fact, they had been both upgraded, and well maintained. I arrived at the property about 30 minutes before the scheduled appointment, read over the CMA, then walked the exterior, taking about two dozen photographs of the subject, and its neighboring homes, some of which were in disrepair. I made certain that I saw all the homes that were used for comparables, and photographed them, too, carefully recording their addresses.

I met with the homeowners, and had them sign the applicable documents, including a ShortSalePro services agreement which contained an authorization for the mortgagee to release information. I also left a generic financial disclosure form to be completed, and asked them to make three sets of copies of all documents, including their income tax returns, W-2s, monthly bank statements (checking/saving), and a letter describing their hardship. On the way back to the office, I stopped to photograph some homes that were for sale in a nearby "neighborhood in decline" as well as the local elementary school, and dropped off several rolls of film to be processed.

While researching for the proposal, I visited a web site for a local newspaper, reading a few unflattering articles about the rising crime, increased property taxes, and anything that suggested that the area was *stigmatized*. A few hours later, my data suggested and supported an as-is, fair market value of $90,000.

Within a day, the homeowners had furnished all the requested financial documents, and authorized the price reduction from $115,000 to $90,000. Of course, the restrictive, short sale contingency was included with the price reduction.

As I reviewed the seller's financial disclosures, I noticed that there was about $30,000 in unsecured credit card debt that had been consolidated by a credit repair agency into a single, monthly payment plan. The sellers hadn't mentioned that they had had ongoing credit problems so I called and asked them to provide a current credit report, which they did. I called the mortgagee and explained that I wasn't going to ask any specific information about the account at that time, but for me to send a letter of authorization I'd need the name of the account manager, the specific mailing address, and phone and FAX numbers, which they gladly provided. Now that I had a contact, I sent the mortgagee a written authorization (their permission to speak with me) from their borrower, and my initial letter which alerted them to the possibility of a problem, and requested that a loan workout application be sent to the borrower ASAP.

Within a few days, the broker called and advised that there was an offer on the property for $85,000. He also told me that the seller had received additional financial forms from the mortgagee that needed to be completed and returned. I called the seller and recommended they accept the offer, and asked that they go to the broker's office to sign the contract, and leave a copy of their completed workout forms where I would get them.

A few days later, the short sale proposal in the hands of the mortgagee, I get a call from the mortgagee's account manager who said that he needed an appraisal of the property pursuant to their review process. He asked if I could call his local appraiser and facilitate access to the premises. I agreed, and met the appraiser at the property with the supportive comparables provided by the listing broker. I also handed the appraiser copies of the selected newspaper articles, and my photographs of the houses from the neighborhood-in-decline.

I was very surprised when I got **the call from the seller advising that their short sale had been approved. In my opinion, the seller simply didn't qualify for short sale relief. I speculated that the mortgagee was acutely 'loss averse' to approve an $85,000 offer. When it comes to short sales, I'll never say never again.**

QUESTIONS FROM THE E-MAILBAG

Here are dozens of randomly selected questions and brief, consistent responses. If you still have answered questions, or disagree with a given response, please feel free to email me directly at: ShortSaleBlue@aol.com

Q. Who are the Players in a Short Sale?

The homeowner/seller, the purchaser, the broker or short sale facilitator, and the foreclosing lender. The lender &/or mortgage investor is the holder of a note secured by a mortgage or deed of trust. The lender &/or mortgage investor could be privately owned and managed portfolio investment groups including insurance companies, banks, REIT's, pension funds, or semipublic agencies including, but not limited to FNMA, FHLMC, or HUD. The lender &/or mortgage investor sets loan servicing criteria which must be observed by the mortgage loan servicer. The mortgage loan servicer is paid by the lender &/or mortgage investor to administer the loan, including collecting monthly payments and penalties on late payments, keeping track of the amount of principal and interest paid at any particular time, acting as an escrow agent for funds to cover property taxes and insurance, and, if necessary, curing defaults and foreclosing when a mortgagor is seriously delinquent in repayment.

Q. Under what conditions is a short sale be considered by a mortgagee?   (mortgagee = lender)

The mortgagee may (or may not) be authorized to accept a short payoff under certain conditions. Factors include both internal company policy, and mortgage loan servicing criteria. If accepting less than due is in the mortgagee's best financial interest, they'll consider it. Some material indicators include a high LTV mortgage loan that's delinquent, in default, or in foreclosure. The property would be in less than perfect condition, having depreciated in value, and its owner, having a demonstrated financial hardship, cannot bring the loan current, nor can afford the cost to keep the home. If the mortgagee's exposure to financial liability is estimated to be less by participating in a preforeclosure short sale than by pursuing lengthy and expensive foreclosure proceedings, including post sale holding and liquidation costs, they'll be more inclined to consider a preforeclosure sale option.

Q. Why would a seller agree to a short sale to receive zero proceeds from sale?

Financially troubled homeowners who participate in short sales find adverse credit report information resulting from a short sale is *less damaging* than bankruptcy, or a full term foreclosure. A credit report might reflect a bankruptcy or foreclosure from 7 to 10 years. Additional motivation might be to avoid the stigma of losing the home at a forced, public sale; to prevent additional damage to future credit worthiness; and to preserve dignity by having some degree of control of the sale/moving process.

Q. What will the seller's credit report say if a mortgagee accepts the short sale?

The credit report will not erase past late payments, or hide the mortgagee's efforts to foreclose. An updated credit report should indicate that the foreclosure lawsuit was dismissed, and the account marked paid as agreed. How a foreclosing lender reports the short sale transaction can and should be negotiated. It's difficult to predict how a future creditor will interpret the seller's current situation, but will no doubt be influenced by the type and severity of the hardship, and how the seller faced, and overcame the hardship. The former homeowner can prepare and submit to the credit reporting agency a consumer statement that explains the derogatory credit information, and what steps were taken to resolve the problem.

Q. Is the seller responsible for the deficiency?

Lender's policy on pursuit of deficiency should be determined early on. Depending on the sellers' financial health, the lender may forgive the entire remaining balance, require a *cash at closing contribution*, or may require that the seller agree to an unsecured loan for the balance. If the seller is capable of repaying the debt, the lender may agree to release its security interest (mortgage) but require that the seller honor the note (promise to pay) until the debt is repaid in its entirety. Sometimes, the deficiency is incorporated into a newly established credit card account subject to monthly payments.

Q. What are the tax consequences for the seller who sells short?

The cancellation of debt can result in an exposure to income tax liability. The IRS treats a loan as income which is offset by the obligation to repay the loan. If the debt is forgiven and the promise to repay is removed the IRS may treat the amount of the forgiven debt as taxable income, and subject to tax. However, the IRS imposes specific criteria or a *test* to determine the extent of tax liability. If a seller can demonstrate *insolvency* then the forgiven debt would probably be exempt from taxation. To establish insolvency the former mortgagor (or tax professional) would provide to the IRS a letter of explanation concerning the discharged debt as indicated on form 1099C, and a schedule that demonstrates that at the time the debt was forgiven the seller had more debt than assets. Visit www.IRS.gov and search for IRS form 982. It's best to recommend that the seller consult a tax professional.

Q. What's the difference between discounting the mortgage and a short sale?

When buying a mortgage at a discount you would seek to purchase a piece of paper that evidences debt, and contains a promise to repay that debt. If successful, you would not own the real estate that secures the mortgage loan. The buyer of the mortgage purchases the instrument at discount, and pays in funds acceptable to the seller of the mortgage. The mortgage is then assigned to the new mortgagee who would record the assignment in the appropriate county office. If the former mortgagee had initiated foreclosure proceedings, your purchase via an assignment would place you *in the shoes* of the former mortgagee. The new mortgagee could continue the foreclosure and force payment, and/or force the property to Sheriff's or Trustee's Sale. It's also possible for the mortgagor to convey his ownership interest to the mortgagee via a contract for sale, or quit claim deed. A *negotiated short sale* involves the purchase of real property.

Q. What would be an average discount (%) on a 1st or 2nd mortgage loan?

Except in the cases of government insured mortgage loans, the 1st mortgage loan balance or amount in arrears is immaterial. The only numbers that really matter are the mortgagee's perception of the as-is, fair market value, and their anticipated, net proceeds from the sale. Usually, a first mortgagee will agree to accept net proceeds of about 85% of their perception of the subject's as-is, fair market value. An *at risk* 2nd mortgagee may agree to accept pennies on the dollar rather than risk being extinguished at foreclosure sale.

Q. What about VA and FHA insured mortgage loans?

In a *VA compromised* sale, the VA seeks at least 88 - 91% of appraised as-is, FMV. An *FHA pre foreclosure sale* must be sold for at least 64% of principal balance, and from 82% to 87% of the appraised as-is, fair market value. It's important to remember that the only relevant numbers are the mortgagee's perception of the market value of the home, and their net recovery. They'll also want to confirm that the home is owner occupied, and that the mortgagor seeking relief has not transferred title to a third party.

Q. When submitting a short sale offer on an FHA insured loan (which usually will settle at 82%), do you make your first offer to the bank at a 40% discount?

I've found that FHA short sale criteria is pretty much set in stone. They simply won't consider a net amount of anything less than 82% of the property's fair market value. Those are the rules, and they're telling you that if you want to proceed, this point is NOT open for debate. OK, so you can't overcome the 82% threshold. If you've done your homework, your Proposal should be able to influence their perception of the as-is, fair market value. However, if your Proposal can't support an as-is, fair market value at a number that is conducive to your business requirements, then you didn't pre qualify this opportunity as having short sale potential. In my opinion, submitting a ridiculous or *low ball offer* would be a waste of everyone's time. If the transaction doesn't pre qualify for a short sale, try another technique.

Q. I am working a short sale on an FHA loan. Is there any special paperwork involved?

Yes. Plenty! FHA preforeclosure short sales (PFS) require, among other things, the Seller to submit a HUD-90036, and, if qualified, will receive a HUD-90045. Get ready to jump through hoops providing information as requested. Give them what they want when they want it. Failure to comply with minutia can result in the application's grinding to a stop.

Q. How can I profit on Short Sales?

How you choose to profit on a short sale transaction is preordained in your business plan, if you have a business plan. As with other acquisition strategies, you can keep the property as a primary residence, rehab and flip, or lease it out for an income. Prior to seeking mortgagee short sale approval, you may also be able to assign the rights to purchase the property to an investor for cash, or for a promise to share in anticipated profits. Most potential transactions that appear to offer little or no profit are passed over in favor of more lucrative, and highly sought deals. By creating equity where there was none, you manufacture profit potential, and have very little competition in the process. If there are great deals everywhere, should you pass over a more lucrative opportunity in favor of a short sale? Probably not, but it's worth a cursory look. If deals are scarce, and a potential short sale opportunity drops into your lap, should you ignore the opportunity? No. Take a good look. If it makes sense and there is a profit to be earned via a rehab and flip, then do it. You can either keep it, or sell the deal to another investor/speculator for cash.

Q. Do banks require CASH from a short sale buyer?

That depends. The foreclosing lender will want to close within 30 days from their approval which means you would either have to have cash, or some financing prearranged. Be careful. You don't want to be in a position of holding contradictory appraisals. After submitting market data designed to denigrate the real estate's as-is, fair market value, can you imagine being asked by the foreclosing mortgagee that the Purchaser provide a copy of his acquisition and mortgage origination appraisal?

Q. Do I need to grab the deed?

In traditional transactions, a buyer and seller attend the *closing* at which time the buyer pays the seller for the property and receives from the seller a deed of ownership. The taking of a deed before traditional payment and satisfaction of liens is in direct conflict with the majority of conditional short sale approvals, especially in an FHA approved short or a VA compromised sale. Perhaps this is a generalization, but simply because some infomercial gurus advocate *grabbing the deed* to control the property, it doesn't legitimize the taking, and should not be attempted while seeking a mortgagee approved short sale. In the majority of legitimate real estate transactions, contractual agreements can effectuate an appropriate level of control. The one way to gain the trust of a distressed seller is to treat him/her fairly, with honesty and respect. *Grabbing the Deed* in my opinion, is tantamount to *pulling a fast one* on somebody. Occasionally, I am asked to investigate allegations of predatory lending and *untoward* real estate practices for the Mortgage Bankers Association of USA. The majority of real estate related complaints by Homeowners result from practices known as **Deed Stealing** and **Equity Theft**. Almost all complaints came from homeowners who participated in ill-fated transactions that resulted in (unconscionable) loss of equity or loss of home ownership. In my opinion? Have an honest and mutually respectful relationship with the seller. Enter into a contractual agreement and effectuate the deal. No need to take the deed. But, that's just my opinion, and based upon my experience. I've heard some good arguments in support of taking the deed, but I, personally, don't embrace the concept. If a seller gets 'cold feet' or decides to implement another strategy to save the home…and renegs on our contractual agreement, so be it. Chances are that sooner or later they'll realize that I have their best interest at heart and ask me to reconsider helping them on my terms. Or they'll determine that someone else was able to offer better results. Again, either way I'm OK with their decision.

Q. How would the seller's bankruptcy impact a short sale?

When a mortgagor files for protection from creditors via a petition for bankruptcy, the action of filing provides an 'automatic stay' which temporarily halts all creditors' collection activities If a mortgagor is in bankruptcy, just about any proposed contractual transaction must be pre-approved by the bankruptcy court via the bankruptcy trustee. Even a listing agreement must be approved for it to be valid. Most mortgagees won't consider accepting a short sale proposal unless/until the mortgagor's bankruptcy is discharged, dismissed, or the bankruptcy trustee formally abandons its interest in the property. Why?. Because, technically, a lender's consideration of a preforeclosure short sale is a collection activity. Though some lenders disregard the Federal Bankruptcy laws, and risk severe penalties... that doesn't make it right.

Q. Who does what to prepare the proposal?

It's a team effort, and every team should have a (team) manager or short sale facilitator. The facilitator will assemble all components, and be responsible for every facet of the short sale proposal, including its preparation, presentation, negotiation, and completion. The facilitator will authorize the real estate broker to valuate, list, market, and produce a ready, willing, able, and informed purchaser. Oftentimes, the purchaser *is* the short sale facilitator. The real estate broker will assist the facilitator in the manufacture of an essential element of a successful short sale proposal by identifying and supporting the as-is, fair market value of the property. The mortgagee's perception of the as-is, fair market value, and their exposure to loss is crucial. The homeowner must seek and complete the initial application for short sale consideration from the mortgagee. The homeowner must provide current financial data, and should prepare a (draft) *Letter of Hardship* that includes a chronology of events and the specific hardship(s) leading to the default, and specific steps taken by the homeowner to extricate himself/herself from the dilemma. Legitimate hardships may include the death of a family member and any resultant expenses, involuntary unemployment, an involuntary reduction in income, disability or prolonged illness, divorce, financial reversals, incarceration, or any catastrophic event. Exacerbating circumstances could include an inability to sell the house for what is owed due to its condition, market downturn, or both. The real estate broker can provide specific and supportive market data. With draft Letter of Hardship in hand, the facilitator should help prepare an easy to read, *concise* (one or two pages) Letter of Hardship that demonstrates that the seller cannot possibly bring the loan current, has no other assets, and the only way to mitigate potential loss would be for the mortgagee to accept less than they are contractually due. Any evidence that supports the hardship should be referenced (death certificate, medical bills, divorce decree, letter of termination of employment, etc.) and included in the short sale proposal.

Q. Can you explain a cost benefit analysis w/ time value of money scenario?

This section addresses the financial interest of the mortgagee. The cost benefit analysis w/ time value of money scenario, a forward thinking hybrid, indicates and itemizes potential benefits resulting from a decision to accept the short sale proposal, calculating the cost of the decision, then demonstrates that the benefits outweigh the cost. Incorporated into this hybrid is a concept that money available now is worth more than the same amount or a lesser amount in the future. An understanding of the specific foreclosure laws and customs of the applicable jurisdiction is crucial in demonstrating the foreclosure time line. Our time line originates from the point of mortgage default, and projects the date and costs associated with an executed foreclosure through an REO liquidation.

Q. Do you need to use a broker, and can any broker handle a short sale?

A growing trend is for mortgagees to require a licensed, real estate broker's participation in the short sale process. Many brokers, however, won't want to touch a listing in foreclosure in fear that the property will be sold at foreclosure sale before they can produce a buyer, or that their commission will be reduced or eliminated. It's true that most often the short sale real estate commissions are reduced which makes no sense to me whatsoever. Sometimes a buyer cannot be secured before the property is sold at a forced, public sale. Unless properly pre-qualified, structured, and administered, *listings in foreclosure* & especially *listings requiring short sales* can be problematic. But foreclosures are a fact of real estate life. In New Jersey, there are more than 16,000 foreclosures every year, and three times as many bankruptcies that involve real estate. It makes sense that brokers and their agents would know how to manage this specialty listing, but most don't, and don't want to learn. That lack of proficiency and willingness to service foreclosure listings has resulted in a largely under served market.

Q. What exactly is a net sheet?

A *net sheet* could be any disbursement schedule of proceeds from sale, or an estimated HUD 1 Settlement Statement. A preliminary net sheet is most always required by a mortgagee considering an application for short sale consideration. The net sheet provides an estimate to the lender as to what will be their net recovery from proceeds of sale.

Q. What is the restrictive language that is used in listing agreements, and contracts for sale?

I've had short sale proposals rejected because they didn't contain some specifically required, restrictive language in the listing agreement, and sale agreement. Since then, I always cause the insertion of the following clauses in the listing agreement, and in the contract for sale.

It is in the contract for sale where I would assert my right to assign the approved contract w/mortgagee preforeclosure short sale approval. Despite the insertion, most lenders' approvals contain boilerplate language, irrespective of what might be in the contract between the buyer and seller.

1. The sale of this property is subject to mortgagee(s)' written, short payoff approval at terms favorable and acceptable to the seller.
2. This property is to be sold in an as-is condition. The seller will make no repairs, nor financial concessions to the purchaser.
3. sellers are to receive ZERO proceeds from the sale.
4. Mortgagee(s)'s written approval or rejection may take from 45 days to 90 days, or more.
5. The purchaser reserves the right to assign this con tract to a qualified third party who will abide by the terms and conditions of mortgagee's short sale approval.

Q. When it's done, to whom do you present the Short Sale Proposal?

The Facilitator tries to place the Short Sale Proposal into the hands of the person or persons who are empowered to make the decision to accept the Proposal. The Proposal simply isn't Faxed to the loan officer or loss mitigation rep, unless, of course, that loan officer is empowered and part of the decision making team. Usually, a *collection clerk* gathers the essential information before it's placed in front of his/her superior for consideration. I'll make sure that I learn the name, address, and telephone number of the VP for Loss Mitigation (if one exists) or another, equally empowered representative. Three or more sets are sent into the hands of the authorized/empowered representatives their delivery scheduled to coincide with their weekly staff meeting.

Q. How long is the foreclosure process?

Foreclosure laws, practices and customs vary from State to State, and County to County. In some states an uncontested foreclosure can take a matter of weeks. In some states, a contested foreclosure can take years.

Q. How long does a Short Sale usually take?

From the moment the mortgagee has been alerted to a possible short sale application, to the execution of a contract for sale, is an unknown variable. However, once a completed short sale proposal has been submitted to the appropriate and empowered body, that body's acceptance or rejection of the short sale proposal could take from 45 to 60 days, or more. Generally, proposals to second mortgagees are reviewed and responded to more quickly than those submitted to senior mortgagees.

Q. Why was my Proposal rejected? I've sent them everything they've asked for, when they've ask for it. Why

would a mortgagee reject a short sale proposal? What should I do now?

Some reasons that your proposal was rejected might include that the homeowner doesn't qualify for the relief requested, that the net proceeds are insufficient to satisfy their dynamic, internal criteria, the mortgagee is unwilling to postpone a scheduled foreclosure sale, there isn't enough time available to permit the mortgagee its due diligence, the mortgagee is not authorized to participate in a short sale, or any combination of these. Your proposal should start with a solid foundation. Spelling, neatness, and accuracy counts. If you want an "A" on a research paper, would you hand your professor a disorganized pile of papers, some handwritten, some typed, some missing? No. A short sale proposal should be prepared and presented in much the same way as you would a comprehensive research paper. I don't bang out 100 short sale proposals (cookie cutter style) per year. However many I prepare stand out and apart from the boilerplate applications that sit in piles upon the asset managers' desks.

Q. What can I do to make sure that my proposal is considered favorably?

It's got to make sense, and quickly identify the benefit to the reader. The proposal both identifies a problem, and proposes a solution to that problem. You've got to make sure that the information contained in the proposal is as accurate and credible as possible, and supportive of your proposal. A cost benefit analysis is, in my opinion, the essence of a successful short sale proposal. A CBA is a way to measure the anticipated benefits of an expected decision. Your proposal must include all the information needed to make a favorable decision. That decision being that it would be in their best financial interest to accept your proposal. In my opinion, simply completing an application is not, in itself, a compelling proposal. They won't be making a financial decision predicated on a few snapshots. While important, they simply support your stated opinion of value which is included in the financial presentation. Though the infomercial gurus might think that this is overkill, that banks will casually and heavily discount a loan in default that's not been my experience. It takes some insight, some work, some professionalism, and some luck. Why leave anything to chance? You've got a narrow window of opportunity to effectuate a short sale. Make the proposal all it can be.

Q. I receive a list of approx. 50 notice of defaults per day. I also noticed that 95% are not listed or for sale. Why don't they?

That's about 1,000 per month, or a little less than we see here in New Jersey. Some of the NOD's (Notice of Defaults) or NOI's (Notice of Intent to Foreclose) are filed by junior lien holders and represent two separate foreclosures on the same property, some are filed prematurely &/or in error, and are rescinded by the mortgagee. Some mortgagors have moved and don't even know about the NOD or NOI. Some of those that face default have already placed their property on the market for sale, either FSBO, a discount broker, or a Realtor. Others have the means to cure the default and do so immediately while others must wait and try to refinance their mortgage loan. Some seek a bankruptcy repayment plan. Still others have participated in creative means to circumvent the foreclosure process. Some don't care, or feel their situation is hopeless, especially if they owe more than their homes are worth. Potential short sales could be a great way to acquire distressed real estate at a discount. Some brokers don't want to be involved in distressed real estate.

If a broker were to list a property in foreclosure, &/or to list a property that requires a short sale he/she must have at least a basic understanding of the short sale process, be able to anticipate potential roadblocks, and a have willingness to overcome those obstacles. Generally speaking, most brokers and their agents don't want to list properties in bankruptcy or foreclosure because they fear that their commissions will be slashed or eliminated, or that the property will be sold at a forced, public foreclosure sale before they can introduce a ready, willing, and able purchaser. A little bit of knowledge can foster an understanding that is crucial to working in a niche market.

Q. I am interested in purchasing an empty home in my neighborhood scheduled for Sheriff's Sale. What do I need from the owners to be able to talk to the mortgagee about shorting the loan, and where can I find the forms that I need?

You'll need a *Letter of Authorization*. Ask the owners to show you the last letter(s) they received from their mortgagee, and the *Notice of Intent to Foreclose*. You can learn a lot about the mortgage loan and who to contact from those documents. Help compose a letter from the owners to their mortgagee(s) that gives the mortgagee(s) written permission and authorization to discuss their mortgage loan account, and possible non foreclosure alternatives with you. Once the owners sign the *Letter of Authorization*. FAX it to the individual &/or the specific department named in the last letter the owners received from their mortgagee. Be sure the *Letter of Authorization* includes the mortgage loan account number, the property address, and your name, address, and contact numbers.

Q, Some people contacted me after their sheriff's sale (about 40 days after and have a 6 month redemption period) wanting me to help them. They owe 110k on their mortgage plus about 9k in charges. The house is worth around 130k. They claim the house needs few, if any, repairs. I'm going to see the house today. They have a real hardship - medical problems ending in loss of jobs (she has to take care of him at home) and want out before their credit is ruined. They want to down size and have some cash for the move, but not enough to save the present home. Is there a chance the bank will short sale?

There might be a chance, but it depends upon the former mortgagee's short sale criteria. You've got to interview them, and learn as much as you can about the former mortgage loan. Also, when you visit the house, bring a camera and photograph each and every defect or area in need of repairs, especially in the basement. Document any adverse conditions. As with any short sale opportunity, it's important to increase the (former) mortgagee's perception of an exposure to risk, and simultaneously denigrate their perception of the subject's value.

Q. I am working on an FHA short sale application. The owner of the property tried, but couldn't sell his house. He rented it to Tenants who stopped paying rent. The application for short sale consideration was rejected because the property had been used as a "rental", and therefore disqualified for an FHA pre foreclosure short sale.

It's important for those who attempt to utilize a short sale technique to pre qualify the candidate before devoting energy &/or resources. In this case, as in just about all FHA pre foreclosure short sale applications, a basic requirement is owner-occupancy. Try to learn, in advance, the specific short sale criteria for individual mortgagees, and loans insured by the VA, USDA, pooled loans, and subsidized loans. This criteria can change from month to month, and lender to lender.

Q. In your experience, what's the average time one has available from the time a lis pendens (or NOD) is filed to auction? I know this can very from bank to bank, area to area, but I just want to get some educated guesses. 4 weeks? 4 months?

The answer depends primarily upon the mortgagee, and the foreclosure laws and customs particular to that state and county. The answer also depends upon the actions of the mortgagor. If the mortgagor wants to contest the foreclosure and confound the mortgagee every step of the way, it's possible that an auction might not be scheduled for years. I had first hand knowledge of a mortgagor who dragged out the process for 11 years.

Q. I have a home owner in foreclosure who owes 103k on the first, 17k on the second, and needed repairs that will cost 7,500. Owes another 2k between property taxes and other liens. Does the owner make the offer or do I? The comps come in at 140k. The only way I can see doing this is if the bank accepts 67k with the second being wiped out.

You have to manufacture the comparable data into a reasonably accurate FMV. If the estimated, as-is, fair market value is $132,500 ($140,000 less costs of repairs), forget about a short sale with the first mortgagee. There is sufficient equity to make the first mortgagee whole, and there is no incentive for it to accept less than it is due. The second, however, might be more receptive to releasing their security interest for less than they are due. But you would have to present a compelling Proposal. In my opinion, this is not a worthwhile candidate for short sale.

Q. The owner of a vacant house in my neighborhood is three payments behind (bank has not started foreclosure) and is interested in selling his house. He owes more ($143,000) than the house is worth ($135,000 ARV) and knows it. I suggested we try a short sale and he's ready and willing. I'd like to flip it.

This might be a good candidate for a *short sale*, however, you must do some homework, more than simply running the numbers. You must learn about type of mortgage loan, and the Investor's criteria for *short sale* consideration. If it's an FHA insured mortgage loan, the fact that the home has been vacated could be problematic.

Q. If you can get the bank to agree to a short sale are there any positive or negative consequences for the seller other than getting out from under a problem?

The short answer: tax liability, and a blemish on their credit. The blemish on their credit for a short sale isn't as harmful as would be a completed foreclosure sale, and how it's reported to the credit agencies is negotiable. There is some 'after the sale' follow up that can soften the adverse impact, too. When a mortgagee forgives all or a portion of a debt, the mortgagee will report the forgiven debt (their loss) to the IRS. The IRS, in turn, will treat that forgiven debt as income to the homeowner. As you know, some income is taxable. In the majority of short sale scenarios, the Homeowner receiving debt forgiveness will receive a 1099 reflecting the forgiven debt as income. They may or may not have a liability to pay tax on that income. In most cases, they have no liability, but must demonstrate to the IRS why that income should be exempt from taxation.

Q. How do I assign a short sale contract?

If you are not the primary purchaser to a short sale transaction, closing won't be easy. In most cases, if the approving mortgagee thinks that there is a profit to be made via an assignment, they'll reconsider and probably revise or rescind their approval. If the purchaser to the initial PSA is an entity such as an LLC (limited liability company) with members and/or partners, you could sell, assign, or modify your interest in the LLC and be replaced in the LLC by the end-buyer for a fee. The LLC completes the purchase. To obtain the approval, the LLC would have to demonstrate the financial capacity to complete the purchase. It's very difficult to obtain an approval without demonstrating the ability to close within 30 days from the approval. You would have to have a Buyer ready to commit to the purchase and have already extended their financial resources to the LLC. In some states it's fairly simple and inexpensive to set up an LLC. It would be prudent to seek the advice of an attorney to set up a boilerplate process.

Q. It seems that you need a broker / Realtor to be involved in the short sale. However as I understand they are only needed to make appraisal and comps, etc, Would it then make sense to take a Realtor which takes the least commission, or a flat fee?

The role of the broker is that as an informed member of your team. It is the seller who must engage the services of a real estate broker to list the property at it's as-is, fair market value, subject to the restrictive, short sale contingency provision. You may recommend to the seller a real estate broker to list the home, write up the offer, and help facilitate the short sale proposal, but remember that the broker works for the seller.

If you do not have a cooperative real estate broker, I can recommend a (local to you) broker to list the property, and write up your short sale offer. The broker would provide comparables that suggest and confirm the as-is, fair market value. The mortgagee anticipates the payment of brokers' fee, and usually mandates a reduction from the custom and usual commission.

Q. I am not clear about the appraised value and comps the Realtor is supposed to come up with? Is it supposed to be a true and fair one like anyone not doing a short sale would get. Or is supposed to be made as low as can be? (it seemed from one of your scenarios (#1) in the book, that the fair market value you submitted in the short sale proposal was not lower, you just deducted the repairs, and losses the bank would incur as result of foreclosure, etc.

Whatever information you present to the mortgagee as part of your short sale proposal will be subject to confirmation by the mortgagee. The broker providing the comparables should be instructed to provide reliable data that accurately reflects the as-is, fair market value. This is the same information that will be available to the mortgagee's appraiser. It is that 'raw data' that you will manufacture to coincide with your short sale offer.

Q. What are the initial steps of pre-qualifying a short sale?

The pre qualification process begins with a telephonic interview with the homeowner. You want to ask specific questions whose answers would either support, or eliminate the possibility a short sale. For example, if the home is in excellent condition, and there appears to be ample equity, the probability of a mortgagee approved short sale is all but eliminated. You should learn why the loan is in default, and if the homeowners have considered bankruptcy, or the sale of their home. You should find out the loan types and balances on the mortgage(s), and the approximate market value. If it seems that a short sale might make sense, then you can make an initial appointment to meet with the Homeowners. At that meeting, they can sign their Letter of Authorization in your favor. Ask for an initial walk through, record the number of rooms, condition, etc. Make no formal proposal to them at that meeting, but promise to meet with them again within a few days. Then, with LOA, contact the mortgagee(s) and learn what you can about the loan, and their hierarchy.

Q. Regarding repair estimates and evaluations, I see you are really a pro in this! Do I need to do this myself or hire someone?

The mortgagee will have a pretty good idea as to what services cost. It's a good idea to have a few estimates (at least 2), and offer those in support of your summary.

Q Can I give the seller cash, say, for moving expenses? What is the maximum you can give the seller? Can this be considered a kick back and illegal?

Most short sale approvals require that the Seller receive zero proceeds from the sale. You may be able to pay the Seller (by separate agreement) for personal goods or services. For example, you could agree to pay the Seller for 'trash removal' services, or for the appliances or window treatments.

Q. If I get the bank to accept the offer, and agree not pursue a judgment against the seller for the difference will this show up on the seller credit report as "settled" or "paid in full"?

How the mortgagee reports the settlement is a matter of their own internal policy, and may be negotiable.

Q. What is an assignment fee?

An **assignment fee** would be what you could charge to assign your interest in a contract to another Buyer/Investor. If you didn't have the funds to acquire the property, or you are simply in the business of structuring transactions, then transferring or assigning the approved contracts to another Buyer/Investor for a fee then you would be paid via an *assignment fee*, usually through a pre devised entity such as an LLC (limited liability company)

Q. Is there an online list service for up to date pre foreclosures and REO's?

I don't think that 'up to date' lists are that critical. IMHO it's not who speaks to the distressed homeowner first it's who makes the most sense to the homeowner, who follows up with the Homeowner, and who last speaks with the Homeowner that makes the deal. I don't believe that having the 'freshest' pre foreclosure information is necessarily critical to the process. Why compete with 60 to 100 others whose boilerplate solicitations fill the distressed homeowners' mailboxes? The overwhelmed Homeowner will first seek conventional, non-foreclosure alternatives. Then, after he/she realizes that they aren't qualified for a refi, mortgagee approved workout, or bankruptcy repayment plan, they'll be more receptive to unconventional and/or creative strategies. If you are first in line, you'll meet a homeowner in denial. Wait awhile, and he'll have already gone a few rounds. It's he who speaks to the Homeowner last that makes the deal. As far as REO? Get connected with a broker who specializes in REO. Not generic FHA/VA stuff. But a well established broker who handles regional REO portfolios for mortgage loan servicers. You'll be expected to take the broker to lunch, dinner, or treat him to a round of golf as his best customers do. You'll have to promote yourself as a 'player' and try out for his team. When a deal comes in, you'll be on his short list of investors he'll call. You'll also be expected to act quickly, and be ready to purchase the property in an as-is condition. And be able to close when you say you will.

Q. Anyone ever deal with XYZ Company with a short sale?. If so, are they difficult to deal with. Also does any one have the Loss Mitigation number?

XYZ Company (or any lender) may be the holder of the mortgage, or acting as a mortgage loan servicing agent for an Investor. It's good to know a bit about the mortgage so that you are better able to 'frame' your inquiry. The degree of 'difficulty' you face is predicated upon the mortgagee's criteria, and the strength of your proposal. Typically, an under supported or poorly presented proposal will result in difficulty. However, even a well prepared, comprehensive, and logical Proposal is often met with resistance. Usually, the Homeowner will receive a few letters from the loss mit department's assigned rep. The letter should include the rep's name, department, and location. That's a good starting point. If the letter is stale, the file will likely be reassigned to another rep in another location depending upon the type of mortgage, and that particular mortgagee's workout criteria. If you don't have a letter handy, just call XYZ Company's toll free customer service #. They'll ask for the mortgage loan # and you'll be on your way. Be certain to preface your inquiry by stating that you are not seeking specific information about the account, but merely need to know to which representative your formal LOA should be presented. Ask for the rep's name, department, department's manager, mailing address, and direct telephone and telefax numbers.

Q. Does anyone have an XYZ Company short sale package they could send me?

I'm certain that XYZ Company services many different types of loans owned by an assortment of investors so knowing who owns the loan, or what type it is could point to a specific application. The ss criteria and application for a Gov't backed or insured loan is a bit more involved than for a conventional loan workout but your question doesn't indicate whether it's a conventional, gov't insured, or if it's even a first mortgage loan. A FHLMC loan will have different criteria for ss consideration that a FNMA loan. A loan insured with PMI will have different ss criteria than a loan without PMI. XYZ Company might use as many as a dozen or more different ss applications but, a generic app would be a good start. A generic application could include the mortgagor's updated application for credit, copies of bank statements, tax returns, a property tax statement, evidence of a paid up homeowners insurance policy, any junior mortgage loan statements, plus a letter of hardship, and a letter requesting relief. Also, a CMA, a listing agreement, and an executory contract for sale. A basic application should be incorporated into a Short Sale Proposal.

Q. How many Homeowners actually receive a 1099 or get a deficiency judgment?

It's important for you to know that the lender doesn't pursue a deficiency judgment <u>and</u> issue a 1099 simultaneously. If the deficiency is waived as a condition to the short sale, the homeowners should and probably will receive an IRS 1099. But, the fact is that many mortgagees that waive the pursuit of a deficiency will neglect to issue a 1099 due to inadequate internal controls. That doesn't relieve the Seller from the responsibility to pay tax, much like if your employer 'forgot' to issue a 1040. The earner is still required to include/report the income on the return. To my knowledge, there is no statute of limitation on when the mortgagee can issue the 1099 could be next month, next year, or a few years down the line. A late issuance would require the payment of a fine by the mortgagee to the IRS. The Seller would likely be audited and required to pay the tax, plus penalty and interest. Most folks who participate as Seller in a PFSS have no real liability to pay tax on the forgiven debt, but must demonstrate proofs to the IRS that the income should be exempt from tax. In my opinion, it's best to be proactive and face the matter before it escalates instead of waiting to be caught.

Q. I have found an owner with a 1st and a 2nd thinking of doing a Deed in Lieu of Foreclosure. Would this affect the 2nd? 1st=83k, 2nd=25k FMV = $120k.

The first will likely **not** accept/consider a DIL. The second might consider accepting a bit less than it's owed. Though mortgagees' boilerplate workout literature includes a DIL option, they rarely consider that option, and almost never when there are junior liens. They also want to avoid holding costs insurance, taxes, security, etc. It's much easier to simply foreclose and extinguish the juniors. No fuss. No muss. The reasoning for them accepting a DIL must be soooo compelling that the act of interrupting the foreclosure process, and taking title (with all its ramifications) outweigh the risks. Lenders prefer a Sheriff's Deed or Trustee's Deed to a DIL. Usually, the mortgagee will first attempt to cure the default via forbearance, then recommend preforeclosure sale, and, if necessary, preforeclosure short sale.

Q. I know some people charge fees to help people work out a repayment plan with their bank. I am doing this to help two people currently, and was wondering how other people do it.

Yes, in some cases I do impose a fee to the homeowners to facilitate a workout usually, it's predicated upon the number of mortgages, and the amount of their regular monthly payment. If it's their primary residence, or if they really can't afford to pay a fee for the service I waive the fee. I do charge speculative investors to structure, prepare, present, and negotiate preforeclosure short sales.

Q. One of the forms required on this FHA short sale I'm negotiating is the "homeownership counseling certification." Do you actually have the homeowners talk to a counseling agency, or what?

With more and more frequency, a distressed borrower seeking to participate in an FHA approved, PFS needs to 1) be counseled, and 2) obtain a certificate sealed by an approved HUD counseling agency. The counselor will review generally acceptable options and alternatives (approved by HUD) to foreclosure and issue a cert to the borrower. If your deal is straightforward and you are honest with the distressed borrower you have nothing to fear from the counseling. If you are trying to screw over the homeowner then counseling may expose the proposed transaction as predatory.

Q. I had a SS approved for $80K, the FMV is $116K. The Seller said he owed some taxes, but the title search showed that the seller owed $11K in Child Support and $10K with NJ DMV. Child Support and DMV will not negotiate their liens. What would you recommend?

Consider it tuition and write a check. This problem was avoidable. Part of the speculator's job is to anticipate problems when the Seller indicated he owed a few grand in taxes that's a RED FLAG. The presence of a variable has been disclosed. It's the speculator's job to define that variable. Now. Today. Not wait until closing that smacks of ill preparedness. Nothing personal, just an observation based upon a forensic review of hundreds of cases. In this case, presenting the short sale proposal before all facts were in evidence was premature and it blew up in your face. The speculator can walk away and move on to the next deal and leave the Seller in worse shape. Most of the Johnny come lately speculators profess that they "want to help people" but then blame others when their deals fall apart (Joe wasn't doing that, but many people do). It boils down to properly pre qualifying the short sale candidate. Before you go into contract. Before you spend time. Before you raise everyone's hopes. In this case, Joe (and many, many others) relied upon a function of closing instead of being proactive. I work with folks across the USA who face the loss of their home due to foreclosure. Increasingly, following a bungled attempt by 'speculators' to creatively avoid foreclosure. Most of the transactions were bungled due to faulty preliminary work. Avoidable. The better and more comprehensive your preliminary work the greater your chance for transactional success.

Q. I am contemplating a short sale on one of my rental properties. Will I be able to walk away?

A prime criteria for short sale consideration is owner occupancy. If the subject property is non owner occupied it will impact how they'll structure their approval. Once the lender learns that you have other property, and/or other assets they'll likely approach your short sale request a bit differently. While they may agree to release their lien, accepting proceeds from the sale allowing you to sell, they may not agree to forgive the remaining debt. They'll ask to place a mortgage against your other property provided the property has equity. You may be rid of the property but you still may have the debt. and monthly repayment responsibility.

Q. I have been an REI for a couple years. I have bought REO and I am about to try to put together my first short sale. Problem is I don't have a good enough idea of what is customary from particularly a "what to offer" standpoint. Anyone who can give me a bit of guidance. Thanks. Here it goes: Worth Repaired- approx. $290,000 1st mort bal.- $210,000..2nd- $45,000 (both 4 months behind).

Any short sale is predicated on the as-is fair market value not what it might be worth someday in an improved condition. That number is only important to you. Loan types are important, too. If the first is an FHA insured loan, with a hefty second... the second would have to agree to accept $1,000 as payment in full before the first could consider accepting a nickel less. In most scenarios, it's the second who takes the biggest hit and it should be the second that gets your attention. You'll have to guestimate what the second would get if the foreclosure went full term. Your proposal will have to convince them that it's in their best financial interest to accept less, now, then to continue a costly, and lengthy foreclosure. Sometimes, they aren't motivated to accept less, now. They'll push foreclosure in an attempt to be made whole. It's when they aren't convinced that they will be made whole that you'll have a shot at short sale.

Q. Currently working with a homeowner that has a 1st & 2nd with the same lender. The first is foreclosing. How will the lender handle this with them holding both mortgages in regards to a discount. 1st balance is 75K & 2nd is 35K. FMV 105-110K home is in good condition. I recently contacted the lender and have spoken to them about the 1st mortgage they said they are willing to do a S.S. but didn't discuss the 2nd. Any input on what I can expect. Thanks in advance..

"How will the lender handle this with them holding both mortgages in regards to a discount?" A couple of things.. just because both loans happen to be serviced by the same company don't assume that both loans are held by the same investor. Different owners, different default resolution criteria. A voice on the phone saying that they (the first mortgagee) are willing to do a short is different than them saying they would *approve* a short sale perhaps that class of loan includes a ss as a loss mit option but from your numbers it doesn't make sense that the first would eagerly entertain a short My guess is that once they crunch the numbers they'll change their tune.

It will be the second that takes the serious hit, and on the second that you should concentrate your efforts. If its an FHA first the second would have to agree to accept $1,000 (?) before the first would budge a nickel.

Q. After about 2 weeks of calling and leaving messages, I finally got the rep. at Countrywide call me back. She ordered an appraisal and then countered my offer of 35k with the original loan amount of 57K . The homeowner is still living in the property and he's prepared to move to an apartment. How should I approach her on this deal?

Countrywide's job is to maximize the recovery for their client, whoever the owner of the mortgage might be. It's important to find out the type of mortgage loan, who owns it (if you can), identify PMI if applicable, and get a handle on the marketability of the property. You must denigrate the lender's perception of value, and convince them that accepting your offer is in their best financial interest. Not all preforeclosure situations indicate the need for a short sale. It's all about value. You'll need to know with a degree of certainty what its worth. I try to establish a rapport with each loss mit rep early on in the fact-finding. After all, "negotiation" includes the sharing of information. Your tidbit of info is that the property will soon be vacated. Give some info, get some info. I try to arm myself with as much info as possible before I start speaking about numbers or making an offer. The more bullets in your gun, the longer you'll last. Shoot your only shot too early and it's time to pack up and go home. Negotiation is a process.

Q. Have you ever done a shortsale on a condo? How do you discount since there is no roof, fence, and etc. The only thing I can think of is a interior discount.

Check to see if it's a subsidized unit restricting it's resale value; check to see if the Association has raised its fees impacting affordability, or will have to raise its fees for common expenses (roof, fence, pool, parking, insurance, etc.) Check to see the number of owner occupied units, vs. the number of non owner occupied units, the number of units in foreclosure, and determine the rate of collection for HOA fees. Check to see if the Association is defendant to a lawsuit. Check to see the average DOM for comparable units which would impact the lender's holding costs.

Q. What is a reasonable fee to pay a company to negotiate a Short Sale on a $40,000 property? And should that fee be paid after closing of the Short Sale?

The amount of work to choreograph a preforeclosure short sale on a $40K property is probably the same as it would be for a $400,000 property. I determine the fee on a case by case basis subject to the anticipated difficulties, number of mortgagees, etc. Whatever the agreed upon fee, I take a non refundable retainer, and either split the balance over three installments, or have the fee held in escrow by a third party (bank/lawyer) to be released upon proof of mortgagees approval of terms for short sale. Sometimes, I don't charge a fee for putting together a successful preforeclosure short sale, especially when the Buyer is a concerned friend or family member of the Seller who wants to help but aren't sure how to go about it. Not all short sale sellers are in acute financial distress. Some are Investors who have overpaid and/or over leveraged, who want to liquidate and quite willing to pay a fee in exchange for eliminating a problem.

Q. I have a motivated homeowner under contract for a property that has no equity in it. I intend to do a double closing on this deal.

a. Does the lender require me to be qualified to buy the property from the homeowner. Like will they want to check my credit, require personal financial statement or request Bank records? Obviously, I am not buying the property so do not know how to approach this.

b. The escrow amount I heard is usually $ 500. Is there a way to make it lower or eliminate that completely?

c. The property is in great condition. I am at my wits end, cause I don't know what to tell the lender as the BPO will probably come in high. I need to convince the lender to let go of the property. Any Ideas?

a) the foreclosing lender might and will probably ask to see the Buyer's mortgage loan prequalfication, preapproval, commitment, or proof of cash as part of the Short Sale Proposal/Application, or they might just say, "you've got 30 days to close good luck!"

b) Fully negotiable

c) Not every situation is a candidate for short sale

Q. Some lenders will only accept my SS packets via fax. I would rather send it FedEx, or even snail mail, so I can include a more comprehensive packet including pictures, comps, etc. Some of these faxes are over 30 pages. Any suggestions?

I think that presentation is key to convey professionalism. It's OK to FAX any supplemental info that might be requested, but (with first mortgagee submissions) I always send several copies of the bound Proposal via FedEx or similar. Not only does it present well, but it makes the f/c clerk feel important.

Q. Does it look like I have any chance here? Background: Six months ago, Owner paid $541,0000 with a 1st mortgage of $432,800 and a 2nd mortgage of $54,100. The seller lost her job soon after the house was purchased, has not made a payment since, and has abandoned the house. It looks like the owner overpaid. Comparable houses in the neighborhood are listed at $450K-$480K and aren't selling. I estimate the FMV is around $400K . I would like to purchase it for around $320K. I figure I will try to short the second mortgage first, and get it down as low as possible, since it looks like they will not get anything if it goes to foreclosure.

If I were the lender with a second or third month default, I wouldn't act quickly to accept a short sale, I would investigate the transaction for fraud. My first call would be to the underwriter. I would check all the documents including a sales contract to learn about the original Seller, the mortgage origination application to learn about the Buyer, and, of course, the appraiser's status. I would immediately order another appraisal from a different appraiser. Then, I would look at whoever was making a pitch to purchase via short sale to see if they were somehow connected with the Seller, but I wouldn't make a move unless I was confident that things were as they appeared.

Q. I have the list of foreclosures, and I'm looking for a short sale deal. I have a situation. The first isn't fore-closing, but the second mortgage is. There is no equity. I understand if the 1st were foreclosing that the 2nd would not get anything. So, I'm a bit confused.

I don't recommend that you go out in search of "short sale" deals just be prepared to do one when their ugly head pops out because in reality, they are twice the work for half the profit but knowing how to do one will allow you to complete deals that others pass by. And in times when deals are in short supply, you'll be ready. Oftentimes, when the first mortgagee forecloses, the second mortgagee either joins the lawsuit as Plaintiff, attends the foreclosure auction (as jurisdiction indicates) and bids up to its limit of exposure or acceptable upset price, or otherwise redeems and continues the foreclosure. In some situations, junior lienhoders are extinguished but to say that the second would get nothing is an oversimplification, and not quite correct. Typically, a foreclosing junior lien would foreclose the rights of the mortgagor to the property, and take ownership subject to the senior mortgagee.

Q. I recently heard someone speak on doing pre-foreclosure Short Sales who brought up the subject of "negotiating away the deficiency". They said that in some cases that the lender would get a Deficiency Judgement in the courts or use a 1099. Could you elaborate on this?

A foreclosing lienholder may either 1) accept proceeds from sale as payment in full and "write off" the deficiency and in doing so trigger a 1099 event. This means that the lender will report the forgiven debt to the IRS via a form 1099. The IRS views forgiven debt as taxable income. BUT in most cases the income is exempt from tax due to the borrowers' insolvency; or 2) the lender will agree to accept proceeds from sale and release its security interest AND address the deficiency via an unsecured Note. Just to be clear the "payment in full" option will allow the preforeclosure short sale with no pursuit of a deficiency, and no requirement for an unsecured note but it does trigger the 1099 event (even if the lender doesn't issue a 1099, the borrower is responsible for reporting the forgiven debt income) The IRS has several tests to determine insolvency and borrowers' insolvency can be used to render the "forgiven debt income" exempt from taxation. An accountant whose clientele include the financially distressed (not their favorite class of client) can help with the preparation of the next year's income tax preparation and filing.

Q. I am a homeowner facing foreclosure and have found an investor that is interested in buying my property via a short sale. The investor wants me to complete the following documents: quit claim deed, and power of attorney. He stated that the lender would not talk to him about the property without having these documents. Is this true?

No, not true. And it seems that the Investor found you, not the other way around. All that the mortgagee requires is a simple letter of authorization giving them permission to speak with the named third party. If you signed the power of attorney, you would give the buyer permission to do everything and anything with the property. By signing a quit claim deed you transfer your rights of ownership but still obligated on the mortgage.

Q. Does listing the property with an agent delay the foreclosure?

Generally, the mere act of listing the property with a real estate broker will not delay the foreclosure process. The foreclosing lender may, upon notification that the mortgagor is taking steps to mitigate the problem (listing the property for sale to avoid a forced, public sale), may not pursue the foreclosure as aggressively.

Q. I thought I understood what a short sale involved, but today someone told me that you cannot do a short sale if

the value of the home is equal to the mortgage balance. I thought a short sale could be done if (1) the homeowner was behind 60-90 days on their mortgage; (2) the home has not gone into foreclosure; (3) there is evidence that the homeowever will probably not make any more payments; and with those items present, the mortgage company may negotiate a lower mortgage balance to at least recover some of their money.

A negotiated preforeclosure short sale is a realty transaction where the mortgagee(s) allow the mortgagor to sell the property for less than the full amount due, and agree to accept proceeds in exchange for the release of their security interest (mortgage). Typically, short sales are considered if the mortgage loan(s) are in default, or in foreclosure, and the borrower cannot bring the loan(s) current, and cannot sell the property at a sales price that would generate sufficient proceeds to payoff all liens including mortgages, taxes, judgment liens, and costs of sale. Any mortgagee asked to consider accepting less than the full amount due will use different criteria when evaluating the request. Generally, they'll look to the confirmed, as-is value of the subject property as a basis and 'guestimate' their anticipated net recovery from foreclosure sale vs. accepting less earlier on in the process. The mortgagee's job is to maximize the net recovery. Sometimes it makes sense to accept less via a preforeclosure short sale. Sometimes, the proposal doesn't make financial sense to the mortgagee. And sometimes, due to their internal policies, they simply cannot accept less even if it makes financial sense to do so. Short Sales are both time consuming and complicated. But they are a vehicle to create equity where little or none previously existed, and work especially well in down markets.

Q. What's a NET SHEET?

A "net" sheet is a basic outline a condensed and preliminary HUD1 with broad line items that highlights the anticipated disbursement of proceeds, and indicates the dollar amount of the check that the mortgagee(s) would receive if the Proposal were accepted in other words, what the mortgagee will 'net' from the closing. Be sure to state that the 'net' sheet is an estimate, a projection but make certain it is subject to adjustment due to a current title search. (I usually request a copy of their own title search which is typically ordered by their foreclosure attorney)

Q. I hope you can help me. There is a house that is listed with a broker and has a foreclosure sale date for a month from now. How would I be able to do a short sale with it being listed already?

Before you know that it's a feasible short sale candidate, for starters you'll have to know what's owed against it, and what it is worth. The fact that the property is listed is a good thing because the broker can help you confirm the as-is, fair market value, and document marketing activities (DOM) which can be useful if making a short sale proprosal.

Q. What lenders are open to selling the mortgage note if the short sale isn't successful?

That depends entirely upon who owns the mortgage and note, and their criteria. Most "lenders" are really servicers they service the mortgage loan for the investor (entity) that actually owns the mortgage. Many "lenders" service loans for dozens of investors.

Q. If I were able to successfully negotiate a short sale deal with the lender/loss mitigation, would it be legal for me to sell my position to another real estate investor since I don't have the funds/credit to purchase & rehab the house.

Legal? Probably. But an assignment would likely be in contradiction to mortgagee(s)' terms of short sale approval and closing instructions. Most, but not all mortgagees require that the named Seller complete the purchase. There are techniques that can circumvent that problem. But generally, I discourage the assignment of a negotiated short sale. They represent a lot of work and to increase profitability, I suggest that the named Buyer buys, makes value added repairs, then sells retail, or slightly less than retail.

Q. Do I need something unique to offer lenders to approve my short sale request?

Try to always be respectful to the loss mit reps they'll remember that. They have no real power other than to champion your proposal to their superiors or to discard it as being meritless. Your offer makes financial sense to the loan servicing rep, or it does not.

Q. I called about a preforeclosure home I saw online and was told it was a divorce case. I searched court records and learned that the home was owned by single man, and this was NOT a divorce matter. So, the agent lied. The asking price of $400,000 was right for the area. I learned that he owes $300,000. Is this a short sale candidate?

On its face it doesn't appear that a preforeclosure short sale is indicated. Simply because a property faces foreclosure doesn't necessarily mean it becomes a terrific acquisition opportunity for a speculator/investor a well managed foreclosure can and often does result in a retail sale by the seller. There seems to be plenty of equity. It's simply a question of time constraints. If you have a cash offer make that offer known and let it stand against retail buyers but put a time limit on the offer.

Q. My short sale proposal was approved. I've been told by the lender that the seller will receive a 1099 for the difference between the note and the payoff amount, which, in this case, is about $60k. The Loan Rep called the seller and told them that this means they will have to pay tax on this 'profit' amount. Is that true?

Forgiven debt is viewed by the IRS as taxable income. Whether the lender issues the 1099 or not, it is the seller's responsibility to declare the income. In the overwhelming majority of short sale situations, in order for the preforeclosure short sale to be approved the seller must not be able to bring the loan current, or bring to the table the difference between what is owed and proceeds from the sale and in most cases, the Seller is insolvent (most Americans live from paycheck to paycheck with no real savings and one bump in the road results in insolvency) If the sellers are insolvent at the time when the debt is forgiven, that 'income' may be exempt from tax. The IRS imposes several "tests" to determine insolvency. If the seller is deemed insolvent at the time the debt is forgiven all or most of the 'income' is exempt from tax. I've only had a few situations where the seller was not insolvent, and was only too happy to pay the tax instead of the total amount due.

Q. Have you ever done a short sale with Household Bank? I have a client who has a 1st and 2nd with Household, and I am wondering how difficult they are to deal with, and how flexible they are in terms of negotiating.

Each experience will be unique due to the individual circumstances. My last experience with them was horrific. The deal took 6 months to complete. I had to pay for an appraisal and title search before they would approve the proposal's terms. But I felt pretty confident that they should accept, so I risked $500 and time spent to make $5,000.

Q. I recently received a rejection from the lender on a short sale proposal I have been working on. I offered the lender $105k on a home that has an outstanding mortgage balance of $155k. Their appraisal came back at $133k. Since it's an FHA loan the lender told me that I'll need to offer at least 95% of the appraised value and that they must net $109,000. They also made the owners

list the home with a realtor in order to be accepted into the short sale program. They are giving the homeowners a period of three months to find a buyer. After that the home goes into foreclosure. I'm just a bit confused at this stage of the game and the lender is, of course, not being very responsive. The rep I spoke with (who is not the one in charge of the account) said I should be able to submit another offer to them between the $109k-$133k, but my paperwork states that any offers are between the sellers and their agent.

FHA loan servicers must make sure that any preforeclosure short sale must NET between 82% and 87% that's where the $109,000 figure comes from. Any realtor fees, costs of sale, property taxes, liens, etc, must be paid from proceeds just so long as they NET from 82% to 87% of the appraised value. There are other restrictions, too, especially in the case of junior lienholders. Any contractual negotiations must be between the Buyer and Seller, the bank can only agree to accept or reject the proposed settlement offer.

Q. I have just made an offer to buy a house thru a short sale. I have been told by the original owners that it would be accepted. My question is who does all of the title work, gets the appraisal, etc. me or the bank? What is usually paid for by each party?

The only ones who can proclaim that the terms and conditions of a proposed short sale has been approved is the mortgagee and must be in writing, and must articulate the terms of acceptance. As far as who does what just follow what is customary in your jurisdiction as you would in a typical real estate closing. Your real estate attorney (hint) should be able to guide you.

Q. I'm a newbie and I need to know can you short sale REOs that have already been foreclosed on? If so, how does this work or what are the basic steps? Thanks in advance.

The same techniques used in devising a compelling preforeclosure short sale proposal can be used when submitting an offer for the purchase of a bank owned property. Of course, the Broker who lists it will take issue with your attempts to denigrate its value.

Q. I just tried to short sale a 2nd mortgage owned by Wilshire. I contacted them and they asked me to submit the full package for short sale like the one that usually is required by senior mortgage. Before I was under the impression (reading books and mentoring materials) that usually 2nd mortgages are much easier to discount and it can be done over the phone with one or two conversations. But anyway, I have done what I was told to do and I am waiting for an answer. On $67,000.00 owed I offered them $10,000.00 . Now I am concerned that I offered too little, and they will not even want to call me back (but if I offered much more that deal wouldn't make any sense). What is the best way to approach and convince junior mortgagees or/and liens for me to get a great discount? What kind of offer should I give them? I heard from other investors that they are always able to get great discounts on 2nd. But they don't want to share their secrets.

The 'junior' lienholders are just as interested in protecting their money as are the seniors. Due to their at risk position, more 'hands-on' account servicing, and more relaxed criteria they are more likely to approve or reject a request for short sale consideration in less time than would a senior mortgagee. I suppose it's possible to negotiate a short with one or two phone calls using limited documentation but I usually provide a formal application/proposal. The "great" discount you speak of is predicated upon the lienholders' anticipated net recovery. If they feel it's to their benefit to accept $$$ now, by circumventing the foreclosure process they will. If their information suggests that they will be made whole by an executed foreclosure they will. Whatever your method of 'the ask' you've got to convince them that it's in their best financial interest to accept what you are offering as a sure thing vs. the uncertainties of the unknown.

Q. I just got a contract on a house for a great price. My problem is the young couple that is selling doesn't know what their house is worth. I asked them what the least they could accept was, and have contracted to give it to them. Am I unethical for not telling them what their house is worth? I just told them what I could afford to pay them. I haven't lied or misrepresented anything. They are moving for another job, and their house doesn't need much work at all. (5 years old). They could do a lot better with a realtor.

Congratulations. You've placed People before Profit!

Q. I am about to do a short sale with Wells Fargo. Are they hard to deal with? Easy?

That depends upon the kind of loan, who actually owns the loan, what their criteria for short sale may be, if there is PMI, and how complete and compelling your Proposal will be. Experiences within one Company can be different as night and day.

Q. When screening leads for the best paying short sales with the least amount of resistance, generally speaking, the easiest to most difficult is 1) conventional loans 1st, 2) FHA 2nd , and 3) VA last. Correct?

Despite what the seminar hucksters preach each scenario is unique. The circumstances, the physicalities, the lenders' "philosophy of the day" all require a careful review to determine feasibility.

It is a mistake to try to 'cookie cut' this dynamic acquisition technique. For some, FHA's are simple because the rules are clearly defined, while conventional loans can be anyone's guess. I would agree that VA's are more difficult than Convs or FHAs. In my experience, USDAs are the toughest.

Q. I want to do a short sale. Should I tell the lender that I already have the deed?

Telling the mortgagee that you have title is akin to shooting yourself in the foot as far as preforeclosure shorts are concerned. If the lender's criteria for short sale consideration is conditioned upon the owner's hardship and the owner no longer owns that can result in instant rejection. As I've stated before most major mortgage loan servicers require owner occupancy for short sale consideration. Most specifically state in the mortgagee short sale approval letter terms and conditions such that the mortgagor has done nothing to effectuate a change in title. So, before you go and shoot yourself in the foot better find out their criteria.

Q. I have a lead on a preforeclosure home. 1st Mortgage: $125,000, 2nd Mortgage: $15,000 , and the FMV is $170,000. The owner is 4 months behind. Can I short the 1st or 2nd? What would your strategy be for this deal?

On its face, the first has no incentive to accept a nickel less than it's due nor does it appear that the second would benefit financially from accepting less. In fact, they would both be made whole if the property were exposed to public auction. However, there is a nuisance factor. The second might consider a discount, but there has to be a compelling reason. In my opinion, as presented, this is a marginal (at best) short sale candidate.

FOLLOW UP: The compelling reason is that they are already in bankruptcy, Chapter 13, and likely to file for Chapter 7.

Sorry, but bankruptcy hardly compels a mortgagee to accept less than it's due in the scenario you have described. Mortgagees oftentimes rely upon the bankruptcy courts to act as their own, private collection servants. The exception to the rule is when the Borrower files multiple and meritless bankruptcy petitions in an effort to forestall the inevitable and that happens far less than you think. A failed Chapter 13 will result in the automatic stay lifted the foreclosure proceeds. A Chapter 7 will expedite the process for the lender. That cushion of equity is the mortgagee's buffer against loss. Denigrate the mortgagee's perception of value. Form a compelling argument as to why it's in their best, financial interest to accept a nickel less and you have yourself a real short sale proposal.

Q. Have you ever done short sales on a higher end homes? What were your experiences?

In NJ, we have thousands of the big, box McMansions that retail for $1,000,000 and up. Generally, the problem with shorting these big ticket properties is that the Homeowners have more resources available to them, are less financially distressed, and can't demonstrate a bonafide irreversible hardship. The 'hardship' is that they may have overpaid and now can't refinance their low, teaser rate mortgages. I'd think that the lenders will consider the release of a lien without payment in full, but will require the homeowner to agree to continue paying on the debt via a second mortgage.

Here is a block of 6 questions from a single email:

1. Isn't there a way to short sale prop and still allow the owner to live in it, and have them make pmts to you which helps them get their credit back up without having to kick them out of the home?

Typically, a sale and leaseback would do it. I wouldn't mention it to the foreclosing lender, though. They might see it as a benefit to the mortgagor and they don't want the mortgagor to benefit in any way.

Unless, it is incidental to the lenders' benefit. Sale Leasebacks are risky for both the Landlord, and Tenant.

2. How often will a bank take an offer at 50% or less the value for a foreclosed property?

Hardly ever. I've been doing shorts for 25+ years. 10 years ago, you could get them at 60% to 70%. Now it's more like 75% to 85% of FMV.

3. How do you determine the fixed up value of a foreclosed property to be able to negotiate a short sale price to a bank, especially if the property needs fixing up?

The ARV isn't of interest to anyone but you. The only value that matters in the negotiations is the as-is, fair market value.

4. Why can't the owner just re-negotiate a lower price with the bank?

They can. Technically, the short sale request is made by the mortgagor, and relief is granted to the mortgagor.

5. Are escrow and title companies involved in the short sale transaction?

Only if they act as closing agents.

6. Lastly, what about the tax implications of a short sale? How do you avoid getting a cap gains tax hit on a short sale?

Don't confuse capital gains with ordinary income which may result from forgiven debt. The cancellation of debt can result in an exposure to income tax liability. The IRS treats a loan as income which is offset by the obligation to repay the loan. If the debt is forgiven and the promise to repay is removed the IRS may treat the amount of the forgiven debt as taxable income, and subject to tax. However, the IRS imposes specific criteria, or a test, to determine the extent of tax liability. If a seller can demonstrate insolvency then the forgiven debt would probably be exempt from taxation. To establish insolvency, the former mortgagor (or tax professional) would provide to the IRS a letter of explanation concerning the discharged debt as indicated on form 1099C, and a schedule that demonstrates that at the time the debt was forgiven the seller had more debt than assets.

It's best to recommend that the seller consult a tax professional. IRS form 982: Reduction of Tax Attributes to Discharge of Indebtedness (and Section 1082 Basis Adjustment)

SELECTED ESSAYS

WHY DO I NEED A BUSINESS PLAN?

(Because real estate shouldn't be an impulse purchase!)

an essay by TheShortSalePro©2006

FSBO. REO. Which is better? Preforeclosure. Preforeclosure short sale. Sheriff's Sale. Which is more profitable? Sub2. SaleLeaseBack. Lease Option. What's best? Should I buy and hold, or flip? Can anyone tell me the Pros vs. Cons. Should I bird-dog? LLC? Incorporate? Do I need business cards? HELP!

What's a business plan, and why do I need one? A business plan is like a road map for you and your business. For the purpose of this essay, your business will include real estate investment, speculation, and entrepreneurialship. A well thought out plan can guide you through the identification of acquisition opportunities, and the selection of applicable acquisition techniques, helping you to avoid road-blocks and detours along the way while keeping you focused. One of the benefits of devising a business plan is the process itself since it requires you to put your goals and plans down on paper. Even if you aren't going to present your plan to an outside person (possible financial partner, hard money lender, or conventional lending institution) the exercise of writing the plan will provide direction of where the business is going, and how you hope to get there. But even the best of plans can only guide you it cannot actually take you to your destination.

Don't worry, most of you already have a business plan and an exit strategy floating around in your head, just waiting to be organized into a plan.

To coin a phrase by a former professor, "Whatever isn't written is rotten!" You really need to articulate your plan in writing. Why? Because writing the plan will actually help you to plan the business, raising questions about your competition, your capabilities, weaknesses, and the process itself. When writing your plan, you'll need to ask yourself, and answer a series of basic questions. To do that you'll need to learn about the various aspects of the business.

For example, a working knowledge in the principles of real estate would help, even if it means taking basic courses, attending seminars, or securing licenses in real estate sales, mortgage loan origination, appraisal, title insurance, &/or home inspection. You'll have to try to identify and predict obstacles that might block your success, and how best to avoid those obstacles. You'll have to assess your business and management skills, and make a realistic assessment of business potential.

Sometimes, to avoid costly mistakes, it pays to consult with an attorney, CPA, and other professionals to see if your plan is viable, financially feasible, and lawful.

What's it really all about? For most of us, it's about getting paid. To get paid, you need an exit strategy which is loosely defined as the way an investor closes out a specific investment, usually for cash. Historically, an investment in real estate has been perceived as an illiquid investment, meaning not readily convertible to cash. In recent years, however, the dynamic practice of real estate investment has incorporated a form of entrepreneurial speculation in the control (rather than ownership) of real property. Additionally, enter 'flipping' which is the buying and then reselling property for a profit within a very short holding period. Each opportunity that presents itself to the speculative investor should be evaluated with respect to that individual's or entity's business plan and exit strategy.

Like our US Constitution, your 'anticipatory' business plan will become a living document, subject to periodic review and revision. The more experiences you have, the more 'forward thinking' your plan will become the longer you are in business, the longer you will be in business. At least that's the theory. You must be open for change and learn to adapt but adapt with a careful eye to your business plan.

A business plan, like travel trip's itinerary, tells you where you are going, when you are going, how to get there, when you've arrived, what to do once you are there, and when it's time to pack up and leave.

PRE QUALIFYING A SHORT SALE CANDIDATE

An essay by TheShortSalePro©2006

A building, much like a real estate transaction, is only as viable as its foundation. If the foundation is faulty, the structure (or deal) could fall apart. If you pursue a preforeclosure short sale on firm ground, you'll have a better chance at closing the transaction.

Before anyone embarks upon a pre foreclosure short sale acquisition, the entirety of the deal and its players should first be known and pre qualified for having the potential for short sale. What sense does it make to spend time and resources on a project if probability of failure is preordained?

How does one pre qualify a short sale candidate? You must ask some questions, and do a bit of homework. You've got to learn (in no particular order):

1. the type, position, and payoff amounts of any mortgages, liens, or other encumbrances, and all owners of record;
2. the mortgage loan servicer's and private mortgage insuror's role;
3. the circumstances of the default, and mortgagors' finances;
4. if the mortgagor has made application for a workout, and what, if any, was the mortgagee's response;
5. has the mortgagor filed a petition for bankruptcy, and if so, the status of the petition;

6. the subject property's approximate as-is, fair market value;
7. if the mortgagor is willing to sell the property, and receive zero proceeds from the sale in an effort to protect/preserve their future creditworthiness; and,
8. lastly, if the short sale proposal is approved, can I complete the acquisition?

It's important to identify and estimate the payoffs for any mortgages and liens of record (property taxes, water/sewer assessments, IRS, child support, judgments, etc.) If the first mortgage loan is a VA or an FHA insured mortgage loan, the Borrower may have special consumer rights, and there may be restrictive short sale servicing criteria that would preclude short sale consideration. For example, if there is a second mortgage behind an FHA insured first mortgage, the first won't agree to a short unless the second agrees to accept $1,000 or $2,000 as payment to release their security interest. Not a dime more.

If you proceed with a short sale acquisition, later you'll need to identify the actual investor who owns the mortgage, the mortgage loan (master/slave) servicer, and any private mortgage insuror who may have an interest each capable of imposing it's own short sale criteria.

In addition to the mortgagee's ability to consider and approve a short sale request, the mortgagor must qualify for short sale relief. Had they formally sought a mortgagee approved workout? What was the status of that application? What information had they divulged to the mortgagee? Typically, an owner/occupant borrower must have experienced a financial hardship, cannot cure the default, and cannot sell the home at a price that would satisfy the mortgage(s). Additionally, the owner/occupant borrower would not have the financial capacity to pay the difference between proceeds of sale, and the outstanding mortgage balance. If the seller has illiquid assets (second home, luxury boats or cars, art or collectibles, CD's, etc.) they may be required to liquidate as a condition of short sale. The mortgagee may also require that the mortgagor agree to a cash payment, and/or an unsecured note to address the deficiency.

If the borrowers have filed a petition for bankruptcy, and are subject to a court approved repayment plan or trustee's oversight, any contract (listing agreement/purchase and sale agreement) would have to first be approved by the bankruptcy trustee, and presented for approval to the Bankruptcy Court. It's the trustee's job to administer the assets, and **maximize recovery** for unsecured creditors. Special consideration must be afforded a seller in, or close to bankruptcy.

Let's consider the property. It's key that you have a good idea as to its fair market value in its as-is condition. Ask about the condition. Ask about needed repairs, and take a look at the heating system, electrical service panel, and structural members in the basement or crawl space.

Will you be able to devise a persuasive argument in support of a short sale proposal? Will a picture be worth 1,000 words? Bear in mind that it's the mortgagee's perceived value that makes or breaks an application for short sale consideration.

A formal proposal accompanies the boilerplate (mortgagee provided) application, and includes data supportive of your argument for short sale approval. If the property has an as-is, FMV greater than the mortgage(s) balances, a short sale is not indicated. Possible, but not an indicated strategy.

Once the mortgagee approves the short sale, can you complete the acquisition in 30 days? If not, then the named purchaser should be someone/something that can complete the transaction. Generally, most mortgagee short sale approval requires that the transaction be completed within 30 days. It's best to be prepared to close, or risk a rescission of, or a modification to the terms of approval.

If, after a review of preliminary field data, you feel that a short sale could be in the best financial interest of the mortgagee, and the only non foreclosure alternative for the mortgagor, you may have a viable short sale candidate.

In my opinion, the best candidate for short sale consideration is a property whose mortgage loan is delinquent, in default, or in foreclosure that has little or no equity, in need of repairs, and whose market value could be cost effectively and dramatically enhanced such that a material profit is realized upon resale, or refinance.

SHORT SALES: CHILD'S PLAY OR NOT?

an essay by TheShortSalePro©2006

As a kid growing up in a rural area during the early 60's, the only place to buy new toys was a sparsely stocked aisle in a department store located about 15 miles away. It offered model airplane kits, model car kits, model rocket kits, and jigsaw puzzles. So, whenever anyone had a birthday party, it was no surprise that the guest of honor received several 2,000 piece jigsaw puzzles, or model rocket kits requiring an engineer's degree to assemble. So at an early age I learned to assemble model airplanes, and put together the pieces of a puzzle. Guess what? I'm still doing that today.

Short sales are very much like assembling an intricate model airplane, or putting together a jigsaw puzzle. It requires some time, forward thinking, organization, assembly, and cooperation.

First, I had to find out from Mom how long I could use the kitchen table to set up the puzzle. If dinner was to be in about an hour or two, forget it. There is no point in even opening the box. But if Mom said it's OK to use the table all day today, tomorrow, and up until Sunday dinner, then I knew that I'd probably have enough time to complete the puzzle if and only if all the pieces were included in the box, and if nobody (little sister) came along and bumped the table, or carried off a piece or two. The same holds true for a short sale. Would it be possible to structure a negotiated short sale before the anticipated completion of the foreclosure? I need to know how much time is available to effectuate a negotiated transaction. Two weeks? Probably not enough time. Two months? Probably.

I then had to visualize what the completed puzzle would look like. How big would it be? Where would I put it when it was done? How would I move it? Who would help me to move it? Would I even want it when it was done? Would anyone want it when it was done? Does this sound like a real estate deal?

Next, I had to lay out all the pieces right side up. I had to identify the straight edges, those with right angles, and by common colors. I learned that if I failed to organize the pieces early on, the assembly would be much more difficult. Just like in the short sale process, you've got to identify all the players and where they fit. Then there was the job of actually assembling the puzzle, keeping others away from the table, and assuring Mom that I would be done in time to return the table for Sunday dinner.

Isn't this what short sales are all about? Visualizing, organizing, and assembling the pieces of a puzzle in a limited period of time? Once the empowered (decision making) individual (or body of individuals) receives the written short sale proposal, you must follow that up with a series of telephone conversations the negotiations.

Just about everyone recognizes the uncertainties in negotiating creative real estate transactions, especially a mortgagee approved short sale. Despite how critical this aspect of the business has become, most 'freshman investors' lack both the skills, and sufficient understanding of the negotiating process. Negotiations are subject to constant assessment, and change as new information is introduced and evaluated. I've found that being prepared, organized, and businesslike is an absolute prerequisite to the negotiating process.

They say that you only get one chance to make a first impression, and a first impression is a lasting impression, so make sure that your written short sale proposal makes a good, first impression. I've been involved in hundreds upon hundreds of negotiated short sales in several capacities.

Here is my best advice to anyone who wants to include the negotiated short sale technique in their real estate acquisition toolbox:

Don't scrimp on pre negotiation information gathering (due diligence).

Be knowledgeable about the matter being negotiated. Know your facts!

Identify the mortgagee's essential and desired goals. Listen carefully!

Don't enter into a negotiation with unrealistic, self centered expectations.

Propose mutually beneficial, win-win situations. With cooperative goals, agreement leads to mutual gain. Be non-adversarial. Be honest. Avoid inadvertent bluffs.

Communicate calmly, politely, and effectively.

Respect your opponent's time constraints.

Be prepared to concede but have preconceived alternatives.

Build trust by volunteering to be penalized on failure to uphold a deal. (offer a nonrefundable good faith deposit)

Be prepared to act on the accepted proposal!

BLOWN AWAY BY THEIR CMA?

Submit Your Own Comparable Market Analysis To Increase Your Chances For Short Sale Approval!

an essay by TheShortSalePro©2006

Mortgage foreclosure is big business. With big business comes the opportunity for private gain, especially for lenders who impose and collect late and related foreclosure fees. And for the lawyers who represent those lenders. For title searching and insuring companies, for the forced placed homeowners insurance policy providers, for the field servicing companies who provide data in the form of drive-by inspections, mortgagor interviews, and BPOs. For real estate brokers who may list and sell preforeclosures, and, ultimately, who list and sell REOs.

A common obstacle in realty transactions, including and perhaps even more critical to successful short sales, is the perception of value. In many cases, the mortgagee's perception of value is greater than yours, and because of that, they hesitate or refuse to facilitate the seller's acceptance of your offer. How do they (mortgage loan servicers) arrive at their perception of value? What can you do to change their perception of value? I'll get to that a little later.

Mortgage loan servicers asked to consider an application for short sale rely upon opinions of value offered by others including tax assessors, real estate brokers, field inspectors, and appraisers. Their first tangible indication of value is the value on the original mortgage loan application supported by an origination appraisal.

As we know, origination values can be subjective, and are occasionally influenced by an appraiser's desire for repeat business from the hiring mortgage broker, a broker whose livelihood depends upon fees generated from loan closings. We've all read about, and some may have first hand experience with, appraisals whose opinion of value had been inflated at the direction of the Client. Even though this doesn't happen often, it happens often enough to warrant that a 'review appraisal' be performed on any property whose appraised value is challenged.

Historic values, subject to market conditions, are expected to change.

For an intelligence update, the mortgage loan servicer will rely upon a Broker's Price Opinion, or BPO. A BPO is a written estimate of the most probable sales price of a property provided by a licensed real estate broker with experience in the specific locality of the subject property. Value of the subject property is estimated by comparing like properties that recently sold and adjusted for differences. A BPO is often provided as a means to establish a listing price for a property.

Once a mortgage loan is in default (sometimes when the first payment is missed or late), the mortgagee will order a BPO, and may order that a BPO be performed every month that the loan remains in default. Who do they use to prepare the BPO? They don't simply call a real estate broker from the yellow pages and their selection is not as random as you might think. In many major mortgage loan servicing organizations, an order is placed through their corporate designated bulk BPO provider, usually a national real estate organization or clearinghouse with local (to the property) referral affiliates.

For a nominal fee upon completion ($25 to $50) the local affiliates provide the BPO as a subcontractor to the national clearinghouse who is paid by the client (mortgagee).

Not unlike political lobbyists who represent their corporate employers seeking the passage of favorable legislation, the real estate services industry lobbyists wine and dine potential clients. Clients may include VP's or operation managers of major loan servicing organizations. Think about it for a minute. BPO's can range in cost from $50 to $100, more or less depending upon your area. If each of the top 10 mortgage loan servicers have a 5% delinquency rate and each services an average of 75,000 loans that's close to $2,000,000 per month spent in BPO's. Many times, the companies that provide the BPO also get or refer the REO listing as well as the field services contracts (winterizations, lock changes, board ups, grass mowing, snow removal, evictions, etc.) So there is a lot of money at stake. It stands to reason that competition for BPO business is keen. Much like any other type of sales rep, bulk BPO providers lobby for business. And, they start at the top of the loss mit food chain, often making unrealistic claims or promises too good to be true.

The bulk BPO providers boast that their service is faster, cheaper, and better. *Better?*

If two competing, bulk BPO providers are asked to submit representative BPOs on an isolated portfolio of non performing loans, and offer essentially the same estimates of value (as it should be) then their respective promises for superior customer service and low cost should be the deciding factor to win the lucrative service contract. But, if one bulk BPO provider consistently suggests a greater value than its competition? In all likelihood, greater consideration will be given and the contract awarded to the BPO provider who indicates that the lender's net recovery in a foreclosure process would be greater.

Once the contract has been awarded to the 'clearinghouse', local affiliate brokers 'compete' for the right to perform individual BPOs for the clearinghouse. They compete by promising a quick turnaround at low cost. Why bother? Because if the property becomes an REO, the broker providing the BPO knows that he/she will likely get the listing assignment for that REO, and the commission for the eventual sale. The 'grunt work' for individual BPOs can be prepared by virtually anybody under the supervision of a broker (broker must sign the BPO) including newly licensed trainees, &/or folks with little or no knowledge or experience recognizing and/or quantifying deferred maintenance, or in assigning values to property. "Can you do it NOW?" seems to be a primary prerequisite.

My point? I suggest that the majority of BPOs are flawed in that they do not accurately reflect a property's as-is, fair market value.

Perhaps by design in that promises were made ("Our Brokers will get you top dollar for your REO!") and inflated BPOs are used to support those promises. Perhaps by brokers who aren't inclined to help the mortgagee reduce its preforeclosure inventory via 'broker less' preforeclosure, and/or preforeclosure short sales but would rather have the REO listings. Perhaps by indifference in that the broker's agent who is assigned the task of performing a BPO with little or no compensation has no interest in providing anything more than a cursory opinion. Perhaps by lack of expertise and an inability by the broker's agent to recognize conditions that can exact an adverse impact upon marketability.

Let's assume that the BPO is, or will be flawed in favor of the mortgagee's position. Part of YOUR role in the short sale process will be to influence the mortgagee's perceived value of the subject property.

To do that, always name yourself (or a member of your short sale team) as the person to contact for access to the subject premises. When you meet the broker, broker's agent, or the appraiser at the subject premises, you can introduce irrefutable information used to influence their opinion of value.

You can do that by 1) diplomatically questioning the applicability or suitability of the information contained in their BPO, and 2) providing reliable information that would not ordinarily be included in a BPO or an appraisal. Interior and Exterior photographs that indicate cosmetic and/or structural problems is essential. Estimate for repairs (worst case scenarios including termite, potable water testing/treatment, and remediation for mold, lead paint, and asbestos) can be used in support of your devaluation efforts. Empirical, comparable market data including, but not limited to original listing prices vs. closed sales prices; DOM (days on market) for comparable properties; and differences in physical condition of properties used to predict the subject's most likely sales price. Newspaper 'police blotter' reports on specific neighborhoods can suggest an area is or will soon depreciate in value or has experienced a decline in market activity. Unemployment projections/layoff notices are also used as indicators to forecast local real estate markets. All these factors can be used to suggest that the as-is value of the subject property may be less than the mortgagee has been asked to believe and accept as true. Negotiation includes the exchange of information. (I once included a videotaped walk-thru of a subject property.)

Sometimes, in the face of conflicting information and if the amount of the discrepancy warrants, the mortgage loan servicer will order a full appraisal. An appraisal is a formal, comprehensive valuation or estimation of the value of a property conducted by a disinterested person with suitable qualifications. Generally, value for single family properties is based upon a review of recent market activity using sales of comparable properties as a basis and then making value adjustments based upon the comparison of comparable property to the subject property. Commercial, income producing and special purpose properties may have their value estimated using methods other than the comparable market approach.

If an appraisal is ordered, you (or a member of your short sale team) should be the contact person, meeting the appraiser at the site and providing access. You (or a member of your short sale team) must have a handle on market data, and be able to accurately prepare your own CMA (comparable market analysis) used to influence an appraisal, &/or refute a flawed BPO, or an unfavorable appraisal.

At this point, as you hand to the appraiser the data (or report) you have devised in support of a reduced valuation, you say, "I've been through this house from top to bottom, took some pictures, and have had estimates prepared by local professionals. I've also assembled comparable sales data that I feel is appropriate. You should also know that this property is facing mortgage foreclosure and the seller must sell ASAP. I'd like to help him avoid Sheriff's Sale/Trustee Sale and buy it before he loses it. I feel this information supports, and hope you will agree that this property, in its present condition, is worth $X."

HOW TO ADDRESS THE CONCEPT OF THE SHORT SALE WITH A HOMEOWNER IN DISTRESS

an essay by TheShortSalePro©2006

Why would homeowners even consider a short sale? What's in it for them? We know that one of the conditions of short sale approval, a non-negotiable provision, is that the seller receive ZERO PROCEEDS from the sale. So if the seller gets nothing, why would they agree to do it? Why would they go through all that trouble when it would be just as easy to file bankruptcy and walk away, or, deed back the house to the bank and walk away, or simply walk away, closing the book on that portion of their lives.

If the homeowners were already resigned to the fact that they couldn't keep the house, had a mindset that they wanted to sell, and their situation just fell into place, and into the laps of the broker and the investor. Our sellers knew that they had lost their down payment, and wouldn't see a nickel (they would, but I'll get to that later on). But, they were cautiously optimistic that a short sale was in their best interest.

Most homeowners in distress have to be identified, solicited, informed, and persuaded before they agree to participate in a short sale.

It's a tough sell because you really can't promise them anything tangible yet have to warn them about the possibility that their lender would pursue a deficiency (difference between what was owed, and what was repaid) or, if the lender forgave the deficiency, the lender would likely report the forgiven debt as income to the IRS, and issue the seller an IRS form 1099, exposing them to possible liability to pay income tax on the amount of the forgiven debt. Even if the lender did not report the forgiven debt to the IRS, the seller would still be responsible for reporting the income.

What could motivate the seller to work toward a goal that would result in no monetary reward? It would have to be something worth more than money.

So, the question is, *"What's worth more than money?"*

Losing a home to mortgage, or tax foreclosure, is a process that includes a series of emotional, financial, and legal setbacks. Losing a job, or experiencing a dramatic lifestyle altering reduction of income, is a setback. Realization of one's inability to earn enough money to pay his or her bills on time is another setback.

Having collection clerks call and berate them for unpaid bills can be (and is designed to be) humiliating. Each setback takes its toll upon the homeowner, stripping away his/her self confidence while raising insecurities and self-doubt. They feel embarrassed, ashamed, and hopeful that their friends, neighbors and family don't find out.

When I meet with a distressed homeowner for the first time, we cover a lot of ground in a short time. While sipping coffee (I always accept coffee, tea, a glass of water, or, better yet, a bottle of un-opened anything) and listening carefully to their highly personal, emotionally charged story, I review their mortgage, foreclosure, and bankruptcy documents, marking them with yellow highlighter, and making notes in the margins. As the meeting draws to a close, I am frequently asked, "Can you keep this (the foreclosure/Sheriff's Sale) from the newspaper? I would just die if my mother, or father, or sister, or brother, or neighbor, or co-worker found out!"

Getting back to what would be the homeowners' motivation to voluntarily participate in a short sale. What's in it for them? To a family that's in a heightened emotional state, what's really important? Self Respect? Dignity? Integrity? Reputation? Pride? Are these feelings worth more than money? Yes, you bet they are!

How can the investor help restore their self respect, or their dignity? He/she can begin by gaining their trust. How can the investor, a total stranger who wants to purchase their property and give them nothing in return, gain the homeowners' trust? Empathy is a good

116

start. Empathy is defined as understanding, or being on the same wavelength as another.

In this case, the investor must try to empathize with the seller about the series of events leading to the mortgage foreclosure, and their pain. That could be the loss of job, loss of a spouse or child, a divorce, a predatory mortgage loan, or whatever the reason. "My cousin lost his job/health and couldn't pay the bills either. He faced losing his house and it almost cost him his marriage. It was rough." You get the idea. And make sure that you let the homeowner know that you know your stuff. If you've got credentials use them. If you've got experience let them know. Whatever is your particular area of expertise use that as a footing to establish your credibility and to link your credibility and expertise to the ability to help re-solve the homeowners' problem.

The distressed homeowner must be told that their menu of choices include allowing their home to be auctioned off at a public sale, a sale anyone could learn about, attend, and possibly become the winning bidder then endure further humiliation by being subject to a forcible eviction. Another choice would be the homeowners acting responsibly, participating in a mutually beneficial, proactive process designed to mitigate potential damages, and maintain some degree of control by moving on their own terms.

After accurately painting a worst case scenario (public auc-tion/forcible eviction/financial consequences) the investor must ar-ticulate to the homeowners that he/she is confident a successful short sale will protect their future creditworthiness, and imply that by acting responsibly and participating in a viable solution...they will experience a renewed feeling of self worth.

What's worth more than money? *Self respect!*

REALTORS™ AND SHORT SALE LISTINGS
"The Listing Appointment"

an Essay by TheShortSalePro©2006

For the purposes of this essay, I'll use the word "Realtor" to mean any licensed real estate broker, or broker's agent even though they might not actually be dues paying members of the National Association of Realtors™. I advocate the restricted use of a realtor in all short sale transactions to add credibility to the short sale proposal; to help confirm the property's as-is, fair market value and to defend that valuation; to list and (possibly) market the property in a form that clearly identifies the listing and sale as requiring mortgagee short sale approval; to pre qualify the purchaser's ability to complete the sale; to devise the basic, preliminary contract for sale; and to facilitate access to the premises for various inspections and walk-thrus. After all, that's all part of a realtor's job description. If you are a realtor, or thinking about getting a real estate license and hanging it with a broker to facilitate preforeclosure or preforeclosure short sales, then I've sorta written this essay for you.

We know that consistently successful short sales require a lot of work, and I do mean **a lot of work** and, to a lesser degree, some good luck. Those of us who have been to short sale closings know that, typically, the very first line item cost to be slashed in a pre-foreclosure short sale negotiation is found on line #700 on the HUD1. The real estate commission. Since the foreclosing lender is agreeing to take a hit the lender wants to share the pain and look to the real estate broker's commission check to impose additional reductions.

I've worked short sales across the USA, using local realtors who honor my referral fee agreement. Oftentimes, I'll provide both the seller and the buyer to a selected, local realtor and offer the listing and sale transaction conditionally. The realtor is apprised to what I'll need from the appointed realtor, and knows in advance that the contractual 5%, 6%, 7% listing fee is negotiable, and likely to be slashed by the foreclosing mortgagee whose (preforeclosure short sale) approval is essential. Some realtors decline to service the referral due to their preference/office policy to adhere to a more conventional practice, or due to preconceived stigma perhaps arising from oft repeated horror stories about a foreclosure listing gone bad. Fortunately, there are many better informed, and more receptive realtors, who hold the view that a commission earned, however large or small, is better than no commission earned at all.

I've always felt that an opportunity to advertise an office listing will make their phone ring with a chance to meet new buyers that otherwise wouldn't have called and perhaps an opportunity to sell them another property.

If you are an active real estate broker, or a brokers' agent you probably have an inkling of what's coming and in some places, already here.

A Growing Inventory Of Unsold, Overpriced, Over-Mortgaged, Preforeclosed Homes

To expand your real estate practice to include the listing, marketing and sale of properties with mortgages that are delinquent, in default, or in foreclosure that might also require mortgagee(s)'s preforeclosure short sale approval you must become familiar with special need customers, and prepare for **The List(en)ing Appointment.**

We'll fast forward past the implementation of your farming, direct mail or advertising techniques that seek out potential customers who need to sell their home quickly and without false starts. These potential customers who have already sought you out recognize you to be an authority, and well able to help solve their multifaceted problem. Bear in mind that you won't be able to solve their real estate problem without information, oftentimes confidential and perhaps embarrassing information. You'll have to ask the tough questions and hold fast to get the answers. Otherwise, you can't effectively address the situation. Pay careful attention, and take notes. Not just bold, line item notes, but the little details. For it will be those little details that will help you make or break potential for the successful resolution of the business problem at hand.

You'll have to learn about the rules and generally accepted practices that govern preforeclosure sales, and preforeclosure short sales. You should familiarize yourself with your jurisdiction's foreclosure laws and customs to be better able to identify the severity of the time sensitive problem and make sure there is adequate time to complete the sale. One of the first questions I would ask would be, " Has a Sheriff's Sale/Trustee's Sale been scheduled yet? Or about bankruptcy. "Have you filed for bankruptcy (any chapter) within the last 5 years?" You should learn the differences between Chapter 7 and Chapter 13, and how they impact foreclosure, and preforeclosure sales.

As some realtors know, homeowners currently in bankruptcy must obtain bankruptcy court's approval to enter into a listing contract, and they must get bankruptcy court's approval to enter into a contact to sell their home. Without prior approval, the bankruptcy trustee can declare the listing agreement and contract for sale void (there goes your commission.)

Ask that the homeowner provide copies of the most recent letters or court documents they've received from their foreclosing mortgagee(s), &/or their lawyers. You'll need to approximate (confirmed by a formal payoff or demand letter) the mortgage payoff(s), and the amounts for any other liens or potential liens against the property. Be certain to ask about the status of municipal property tax payments, any IRS problems, or other matters that involved the court. Ask that the homeowner provide a current copy of a credit report. available free of charge from the major credit reporting companies. The credit report might disclose judgments that would have to be addressed before the passing of clear title could occur, or indicate other potential problems, problems that will surface later on in the title report. It's best to address potential problems early on than wait until the last minute.

Most short sale criteria require that the property is offered for sale, and sold in its as-is condition allowing no credits payable to the purchaser for repairs (including termite, radon, roof, HVAC, etc.). You'll have to estimate the property's condition, and, if necessary, gather estimates for obvious repairs, helping to support a compelling short sale proposal.

You'll have to discuss the eventuality of "The Move" When. Where. How. And with what $$$.

Don't wait until the last minute to ask about the Seller's moving plan keep in contact with them. Don't simply accept their word that everything is OK. More often than not, they need help but are too embarrassed or ashamed to ask. If the (reluctant) Sellers don't have a place to go they won't leave until the very last possible moment usually under threat of eviction. Since most if not all short sale approvals specifically disallow any proceeds from sale being returned to the Seller the Seller might not have money to pay a mover or rent a truck, place a security deposit for alternative housing, or get utilities turned on.

Sometimes it becomes necessary for the realtor to help the Seller locate suitable, alternative housing and plan the move. Providing and helping to complete a rental application, registration with an affordable housing authority, or driving them to FRBOs (for rent by owner) can make the transition easier. You might also need to provide some boxes, box-packers, and a U-Haul. Sometimes, non profit organizations can provide volunteers to help. Making periodic donations to a locally active NP can't hurt and can only help especially when your need for help coincides with the NP's humanitarian mission.

Make your Client comfortable with you, their situation, and themselves.

Be ready to step in and relay an anecdote or two about other folks in situations that you've assisted to help address any of their, as of yet, unasked questions. Let them know that their situation is pretty common. More and more families today are facing foreclosure, perhaps for the first, or second or more times. If you know how many properties are sold at Sheriff's or Trustee Sales each month, or how many foreclosures are filed in your market area pass along that information. If an REO has sold on their block show them a snapshot with the address below, clearly printed. Let the Homeowners know that they are not alone. Try to help the Homeowner identify with others in his or her situation. Many other families have seen their household incomes halved, or eliminated. Many have experienced a marked increase in property taxes, making many homes and neighborhoods less affordable. Your Client may be a single Mom or Dad or grandparents who have generously taken on debt or other responsibilities for the sake of their separated or struggling children, or grandchildren, only to find the debt unbearable. The divorce rate is a proximate cause to mortgage foreclosures. (In my opinion, many foreclosure situations could be avoided if divorce attorneys would insist upon expeditious division of property, said division enforced by the Courts.) It's usually the Mom with the kids with the house. One spouse usually stops making one type of promised payment or another either a mortgage payment, **or** alimony and child support.

Sorry sorta getting off track. Make certain that ALL owners sign the listing agreement. Ask to see a divorce decree.

I usually ask the homeowner if they've received any cards or letters about the foreclosure. The typical response is to make a pained expression, and produce a plastic crate filled with letters letters and cards of all colors, sizes and shapes, many with attractive logos, many unopened. Tell them that simply because they are listing the house for sale doesn't mean that tomorrow the notices will stop or that the frequency of phone calls or the volume of mail sent by real estate and mortgage brokers, bankruptcy lawyers, and letters and offers from speculative investors will cease. They'll keep coming.

I'd ask the homeowner to show me the one letter that had painted the best scenario for his/her situation. At least you have a starting point as to what they consider to be a good exit strategy, and you'll know if their expectations are realistic. Their expectations, if overly optimistic, must be reigned in early on in the process.

Despite what the letters may say, there are no 100% LTV refi program at 2% available to people in foreclosure. it just doesn't happen.

Despite what the letters may say, a Chapter 13 Bankruptcy plan isn't a walk in the park many don't even qualify. Unless the underlying financial problem has been resolved most folks who go into a Chapter 13 to save their home fail. Etc.

Even though you've gained their confidence you'll probably have to do some amount of telephonic hand holding. Remember, you are the lifeline for these folks. Be straight with them.

The (short sale modified) listing agreement itself should contain several important clauses. Some lenders require additional, restrictive clauses, some require fewer, and some none at all.

1. <u>This listing agreement and any contract for sale is contingent upon and subject to mortgagee's written, short sale approval</u>. The listing agreement, and a subsequent contract for sale, might also need approval from a bankruptcy trustee, or a Private Mortgage Insurance company.

2. <u>The property is to be sold in it's as-is condition</u>. It's OK for the buyer to have inspections done. but the seller will not be permitted to pay for any repairs including termite treatments, radon remediation, or asbestos related problems. (These items should be disclosed early on and used to justify a reduced price offer.)

3. <u>The seller will receive zero proceeds from sale</u>.

4. <u>Mortgagee's written acceptance may take from 45 to 90 days. or more</u>. I've had FAXed approvals within a day or so after submitting a proposal, usually from junior lienholders, but I've also had deals languishing for 6 months to finally close and it depends upon the mortgagee's policies.

While you are on the listing appointment, have the seller agree to a price reduction in 30 days and ask that they sign a price reduction form. Then, let them know what they are in for. They'll have to complete and return to their mortgage lender a myriad of financial forms, and financial documents including bank statements, current paystubs, tax returns, utility bills, etc., to used by the lender to confirm their hardship, and to justify granting short sale consideration.

* If they haven't filed an income tax return for awhile, encourage them to do so at their earliest opportunity.

If a short sale facilitator brings you both parties to a transaction, you won't have to worry about finding a buyer. But if you simply have the seller you'll have to market the listing and possibly place it on an MLS.

As the listing is exposed to it's market, the short sale application process proceeds. Once the sellers are pre qualified by their lender for short sale consideration, the final documents in the short sale application process will be the Contract of Sale, and the estimated HUD1 which indicates the net proceed amount to the mortgagee(s).

Carefully screen potential buyers. They'll have to be flexible, time wise, and financially qualified. They'll need to know that the home is sold in it's as-is condition. They'll need to know that once the seller accepts the offer. it may take a month or two or three to get the approval from the mortgagee(s). Then, they'll have to close quickly usually within 30 days.

ONE TOUGH COOKIE

The Choreography Of A Short Sale

an essay by TheShortSalePro™

A while back, I got a telephone call from a woman I'll call "Cookie," who was facing the loss of her home to Sheriff's Sale. She had filed bankruptcy several times, and was in the final throes of a three year foreclosure process. Having exhausted her options from a menu of non foreclosure alternatives, she was desperate and seeking help on the Internet. Cookie's goals were not limited to simply preventing her home from being sold at an upcoming Sheriff's Sale. Not only did she want to stop the upcoming Sheriff's Sale, but she wanted to *keep* the house as her family's residence, too. What she wanted was in theory, doable. But in practice, it was anything but a simple exercise. In the immediate, she needed several things to happen. Number one, the Sheriff's Sale had to be adjourned. She would also need to devise a plan to payoff the foreclosed mortgage, and make the new housing payments affordable. Oh, and unless she could find a job, nothing would be affordable. While perusing the Internet for creative solutions to real estate problems, she came across an article or essay that I had written, presumably on pre foreclosure short sales or, sale and leasebacks. So, she sent me an e-mail describing her situation.

The History

As described, her situation was not uncommon. Recently divorced, a mother of two, trying to raise the kids, work outside the home, and maintain the roof over their heads. An interruption in her post divorce employment due to a health related temporary disability, coupled with rising property taxes, an increase in the monthly mortgage payment, and unexpected maintenance costs were each a proximate cause to the mortgage loan's delinquency, default, and foreclosure. During her period of disability and unemployment, the much needed alimony, and child support payments promised by her former husband, ceased, further compounding the financial hardship. Due to circumstance, his inability to pay was involuntary. He arranged for a "friendly" banker to give his former wife a second mortgage loan, even though they knew full well that she would be unable to make the required payments. He verbally promised the mother of his children that he would repay the loan once he had returned to the workforce. But by the time he would be able to keep that promise, it would be too late.

Cookie was, I came to learn, a very determined woman. Needing an 'angel investor' she was asking for a miracle. For me to consider accepting this challenge, I'd have to predict if the proposed transaction was feasible, or simply an exercise in futility. The steps:

1) Identify/Prequalify all facets of the proposed transaction; (2) Due Diligence; (3) Prepare the Proposal; (4) Present the Proposal; (5) Negotiate Details; (6) Anticipate all obstacles, then close

Prequalification is a constant, and dictates the scope of the due diligence process. The more we can learn, early on, the better we can predict and shape the outcome of the proposed transaction. The more experience a speculative investor has, the earlier on in the process he or she will be able to identify potential deal killing obstacles, try to navigate around them, or decide that it's not worth the effort.

Prepare the Proposal for impact! Choose your words carefully. I'm thinking about how the Proposal will be received long before I put pen to paper. It has to make a bold statement. The finished proposal will be a careful blend of facts, and compelling conjecture. Is the information at hand sufficient to shake the mortgagee from its grip on policy? Will the circumstances I choose to represent by photograph and document support the discount I seek? As I am gathering information, I am mentally preparing the Proposal for greatest impact.

Due diligence includes the gathering, organization, and analysis of all information that might impact the acquisition process and is essential to the construct of the short sale proposal. That includes confirming the Seller's hardship and eligibility to participate in a pre foreclosure short sale. Though short sale criteria has some boiler-plate commonalties industry wide, there are differences from lender to lender, loan type to loan type. And, of course, everything is sub-ject to change. The single most important variable that dictates a lenders' willingness to entertain short sales is the "market". For the purpose of this essay, the "market" includes all economic factors that influence mortgage delinquencies. The professional loss miti-gation analysts whose recommendations for mortgage loan servicing policy adjustments are based, in part, upon professional studies, and reports, including, but not limited to The National Delinquency Sur-vey, Foreclosure Diagnostics by State, and reports to government accountability offices with such titles as, Mortgage Financing: Addi-tional Action Needed to Manage Risks of FHA-insured Loans.

Know your opponent. (Reread "Parties to a Short Sale")

The skillful short sale facilitator will understand regional factors, but must have a comprehensive understanding of local market con-ditions. Local market conditions are influenced by broad brush is-sues including environmental conditions, public transportation, pub-lic recreation facilities, employment centers, schools, retail shopping districts, crime rate, and local government.

Consider how desirable it would be to live in a beautiful neighborhood within a community whose local government prac-tices eminent domain abuse, or whose police or fire departments were understaffed and under funded and unable to respond quickly to the needs of the community. Or had schools that were either overcrowded, under funded, or both, and had to cut out special sub-jects like music, fine art, or any of the industrial arts? Clip local newspaper articles, and reference them in your Proposal. These 'negatives' should be incorporated into the appraiser's opinion of value.

I once clipped a one scene cartoon from a magazine and tacked it to the corkboard next to my desk. Now curled and yellowed, not a day goes by that I don't look at it. It was a courtroom scene that depicted two lawyers, and a bewildered, black robed judge who had just been placed into custody, being led out from behind his bench in handcuffs. One lawyer remarked to the other, "Now *that's* courtroom strategy!"

What am I looking for? Physical evidence. Whether it's evidence of financial hardships, market conditions, or property condition. It's easy to document financial hardship. A current credit report. Copies of past due bills. Property tax delinquency notices. Utility shut off notices. If there is a financial hardship, it should be easy to document. Market conditions, especially a change in market conditions can be more difficult to document since most of the "evidence' is historic, and markets do not change overnight. A good indicator can be found in MLS databanks.

For example, the length of time it takes to sell a property is reflected in DOM (days on market). This indicates how long a property had been listed with its selling broker. There could be periods of time it languished on the market with another broker and that typically isn't reflected in the published DOM. Another indication as to a local real estate market can be gleaned from measuring price reductions, and from calculating the original asking prices to closed sale prices. Physical property conditions can be observed and recorded by conducting a comprehensive property inspection. An interior/exterior top to bottom look. Simply record and report on things that an informed buyer would find fault. Not every little thing, but deferred maintenance that can point to larger problems. A small burn mark on an electrical outlet. A water stained cabinet beneath a faucet. Mold on the ceiling. A bit of technical knowledge of framing, plumbing, electrical, and roofing can go along way. The ability to photograph that "problem" in such a way as to "suggest" serious problems. The photographs are supposed to get the reader to ask him/her self, "Can you imagine what's behind that wall" while casting a shadow of doubt on the accuracy of the BPO. **Doubt creates discount**.

The proposal can be compiled as more info becomes available. A financial statement, Tax returns. Pay stubs. A title report or judgment search. An appraisal or CMA. Current, local market data including newspaper articles. A property inspection, photographs, etc.

Since Cookie was out of work, I knew she would not be a good candidate for a refinance, nor would she qualify for any type of reinstatement plan with her foreclosing lender or bankruptcy. I told her to choreograph a transaction with the favorable results results that she wanted would be a very, very difficult process. She was quite persistent. Essentially challenging me to 1) accept her case, and 2) get it done. "If, in theory, what I'm asking for is possible. Than why can't you do it?" I told her that there would be costs with no guarantee of success. "But is it possible?" She asked. "Because if it's possible, I want you to try. I don't care what it costs!"

I agreed to meet her the next day at her home. About an hour's drive for me. I gathered as much market info as I could, pulling recent sales data from several sources. Before meeting with her I drove past nearby homes that had sold recently so I could mentally compare her home with those that had sold.

Cookie's House. From all outward appearances, the subject property was a well kept, 4 bedrooms, 2 bath split level on a ½ acre lot in a nice community. The rear of the property backed up to an overgrown area leading to a ravine that had formerly been a site for high tension wire towers and a railroad bed, and now was a protected nature area. As I took in the scene, I was mindful of Cookie's complaints that included water table and water runoff management/problems.

I inspected her home from top to bottom looking for any ammunition I could use in a report to 1) denigrate the lenders' opinion of value, and 2) to support a reduced payoff. I reviewed the stacks of foreclosure summonses, bankruptcy petitions, disability applications, the divorce decree, property tax notices, etc. to extract information that could support a preforeclosure short sale proposal. I copied and promised to return any documents I found informational.

I dove into the first mound of paperwork. Among several bankruptcy petitions, I found an insurance policy and learned the home's basement had flooded due to a blocked down spout. (Upon inspection, it was obvious that there was some minor water damage to the carpet, and walls. I snapped a few photos of the now dried water stains.) I also read an estimate for waterproofing the basement's cinderblock walls, which included an engineer's site report, and recommendation that the mature foundation plantings be removed, the soil around the foundation re-graded, and the area re-landscaped. That would cost somebody a few dollars. The foreclosing lender might just be that somebody, or at least I'll get them to think they are on the hook

There were bills, some paid, some unpaid, property tax bills, a copy of the deed, the property survey, the mortgage(s), the divorce decree, etc.

I usually begin the inspection in the basement. In addition to evidence of a minor flood, I inspected and photographed settling cracks in the foundation. The same cracks that were indicated in the waterproofing estimate and engineers report.

I made notes, took measurements, then set up and took pictures. For example, on the exposed cinderblock wall with the hairline foundation cracks, I tested the lone electrical outlet and found it to be malfunctioning. I took a photo of the lighted testing device which indicated a short circuit in close proximity to the crack. I used self stick pointer arrows and a tape rule to highlight/document the area. I knew that this would make a wonderful illustration in my Proposal which I had begun to mentally prepare.

I checked the rest of the house and found it to be in great condition. The garage had been converted into a 'rec room' without a building permit. Then, I revisited the back yard and peered at the distant, wooded ravine. As I walked to the rear of the property toward the ravine, I discovered in the underbrush what looked to be a "weekend warrior's" failed attempt to construct a retaining wall The deteriorating wall consisted of several courses of 8 x 8 pressure treated railroad ties. I snapped a few pictures of that, too.

The pieces were beginning to fit into the bizarre puzzle I was preparing in my head. I knew that I could weave a tale that would cast serious doubt as to the structural integrity of this dwelling. Remember, **doubt creates discount**. And this 'doubt' would be the key element to a mortgagee, pre foreclosure short sale approval.

The meeting took about 2 hours. I was able to learn a great deal from the bankruptcy petition(s) which included a MGIC distress evaluation, a property survey, and an engineering contractor's proposal to make repairs to the foundation which included a property survey.

I assured Cookie that I would consider her challenge, and I'd call her within a couple of days. On the ride back to the office I decided that I had enough ammunition to attempt to orchestrate the transaction. I devised and sent overnight to her a consulting, retainer, and scope of services contract which clearly stated: 1) the situation, 2) what I was trying to accomplish, 3) fees paid were nonrefundable, and 4) there was no guarantee. In addition to the stated fee schedule, a condition of my accepting the challenge would be that she would pay all expenses, including a present owner title/judgment search. In the overnight pack, I included a prepaid return mailer in which she could send the signed contract, and the original copies of documents I had taken from our face to face meeting.

Upon receipt, and her review of the consulting agreement, she called and hired me. By the end of the week, I had a couple rolls of film developed, and a copy of the present owner judgment search.

There was a foreclosed, FHA insured mortgage loan. There was a 2nd mortgage loan. (I still believed Cookie when she stated the second mortgage loan had been paid off, and she promised to find/produce the notice of satisfaction and I sort of forgot about it.) Other than a water and sewerage bill, and a quarter's taxes, there was not much else against the title.

Previous Chapter 13 bankruptcies had failed due to her inability to meet the hefty monthly payment. Previous workout attempts with the foreclosing lender had failed, too, since they, too, were unaffordable to her budget. Previous attempts to refinance had failed due to her lack of employment history, and income. Part of any solution would be to introduce new money into the equation. Part of the solution would be to sell the property and use the proceeds to payoff the mortgage. That would not, however, address Cookie's other problem. How to preserve affordable ownership.

Since my current business plan didn't include "buy and hold", I needed to find someone whose was. I needed to find a special buyer willing to buy the home at a discount, lease it back to the former owner at affordable rent, and give the former owner a chance to buy it back also at a discount from market value. I would have to go into contract with Cookie at terms I thought were fair, and at terms that could interest a potential buyer to step into my shoes and complete the transaction.

The construct: **preforeclosure short sale with leaseback *and* buyback option**

My primary consideration in this, and all deals, is balance. The opportunity must be both attractive to an investor, as well as fair and affordable to the homeowner. In my opinion, if a transaction is balanced to benefit all parties, it stands to have the greatest potential to close. Unless a deal closes, it's a waste of time. Usually, due to concessions and the conflict of interest, neither side is overjoyed at the terms of the agreement.

1. In order to make the construct work several events must occur, and occur simultaneously.
2. Confirm the amount of secured debt, and identify all items and amounts to be repaid from proceeds of sale.
3. Determine the home's as-is, fair market value (that manufactured data could support)
4. Contact mortgagee(s) to initiate short sale
5. Devise short sale proposal
6. Structure parameters of the deal
7. Identify transitional buyer/funding source

To make the deal attractive to the investor, the acquisition price must be considerably lower than market value, the rent paid must be at least on par with market rents, set minimal profit threshold, and create the potential for additional profit as an inducement.

In most sale leaseback situations, the objectives of the parties to the contract are in conflict. The homeowner/seller wants to keep the house, the landlord/buyer wouldn't lose any sleep if the tenant defaulted to the lease, and was degraded to simple tenancy status without the buyback option. If the Tenant defaulted and lost the option to buyback the property at a predetermined/discounted price, the investor would still have to deal with the tenancy issue, but could now sell on the open market for full market value.

Once I received the authorizations to proceed, I ordered a present owner judgment search (POJS), and a current credit profile. A POJS is performed by a title searcher who visits the local title office records, and retrieves data including current ownership and lien records, what the current owner paid, and mortgage details for all loans against the property, with lender name, amounts, and dates. Typically, the report will include a copy of the current deed showing property conveyance, along with copies of all current liens, mortgages, and recorded documents. A POJS doesn't replace a full blown title search, or the need for title insurance, but it's an inexpensive, access to vital information.

Within a few days of placing the order, the report was FAXed to me.

Cookie's previous bankruptcies had eliminated a lot of her unsecured debt. The POJS identified the first mortgage, as well as a $15,000 second mortgage with a defunct financial institution.

Although Cookie had told me that the second mortgage had been paid by her ex-husband, it was clearly listed on the POJS. I called and impressed upon her the need to find the satisfaction of mortgage document, or the check that was used to payoff the mortgage. Otherwise, this was a valid lien of record that would have to be paid off, and could be a problem.

I knew from previous FHA pre foreclosure short sales that the FHA would allow a maximum of $1,000 to payoff any junior lien holders irrespective of the total amount lawfully due them. So to make this deal work, before the first mortgagee would agree to accept less, via a pre foreclosure short sale, the $15,000 second mortgage would have to go away for $1,000.

Cookie signed all the appropriate letters of authorization, but, since they were out of the mortgage business, I had no idea where the second mortgagee was located. Assured by Cookie that the second had been paid, I pushed it to the back burner.

I was able to speak directly to the first mortgagee's FHA loss mitigation rep, and soon had their short sale application package. An FHA pre foreclosure short sale application and criteria can be more bureaucratic than a conventional first, and certainly more than a second mortgage loan short sale application. At least there are stated parameters. For example, if the borrower has a qualified hardship, and provides all the requested information, the FHA can accept a net short payoff of 82% to 87% of the confirmed by appraisal, fair market value.

DOUBT = DISCOUNT

Influencing the lender's perception of value is key. The less they think its worth, the less they'll accept as payment in full. Let's say that a given property is worth $250,000. The FHA would be willing to accept 82% of that, or $205,000. However, if the case can be made that the property isn't worth $250,000, but $210,000, the FHA would agree to accept $172,000. So the real battle to create equity in short sale deals isn't so much in the negotiations because the loan servicers have their prescribed formulas. To create equity the battle must be waged and won in the field. To win, the successful chore-ographer must identify and exaggerate problems that were unde-tected by the appraiser problems that could exact an adverse impact on marketability that once known, the appraiser (or real estate bro-ker commissioned to perform a BPO) would surely agree and factor that new information into his/her opinion of value.

Sure enough, the lender's initial, exterior drive by BPO came back at $206,000.

In this case, to cast doubt on the lender's perception of value, I used a combination of an engineer's report to an insurance company, a contractor's estimate for repairs, a topographical property survey, and photographs.

Let's say, for the moment, that the property had a retail value in an improving market of $206,000, and the FHA would accept a net payment of $168,920. That's a nice discount, especially in light of the improving market, but still the numbers were too high, I thought, to interest an Investor, and too high to facilitate the homeowner's intent upon eventual buyback.

When a mortgage loan is in default, and about to be foreclosed, the mortgage loan servicer collects and verifies information includ-ing, but not limited to confirming the value of the property. In this case, the FHA's mortgage insurance company first generated a 'dis-tressed' valuation of $156,000. When the homeowner filed bank-ruptcy, the loan servicer provided the bankruptcy court with this 'distressed' valuation. I decided to target that number in my pro-posal.

So as not to appear adversarial to the lender, or the broker who performed the BPO, I would say that I agreed that, if perfect, the subject property would have a market value around $206,000. But, I would gently raise the question as to the structure's integrity, and ask that the foreclosing mortgagee agree to order another BPO, this time an interior BPO. This time, I would be there to hand the real estate broker the results of my property inspection including my opinion of value, and market data supportive of that opinion of value. Closer to the $160,000 figure that I wanted.

As I was gathering current market data, and beginning to draft the proposal, I suggested to the homeowner that she place an ad in the local newspaper seeking an Investor to participate in a sale and leaseback. The classified ad would say something like. Investor wanted for Sale and Leaseback. Worth $206,000. Buy for $156,000, and leaseback to homeowner. Guaranteed $10,000 net profit in one year! Email for details. I composed the classified ad, and, using a designated e-mail address as the contact, she placed it in the area's largest newspaper. Within a week, I had about fifty responses to the ad. Of the fifty that responded, only about ten actually knew about sales and leasebacks. Of the ten only five were interested in seeing the house. After a couple of weeks, two of the five had seen the property. They were ready to talk numbers and go into contract. But before I went into contract with the end buyer, I wanted to make certain that I had written short sale approval. I asked each Investor to provide a mortgage pre approval, or proof that they could perform.

The FHA criteria for pre foreclosure short sale consideration included a requirement that the borrower undergo, and provide proof of financial counseling, and the property be listed for sale with a real estate broker. I scheduled the HUD approved counseling appointment (it took about three weeks) and met with the broker to list the property for sale. I asked him to list the property for $160,000.

By that time, I was reasonably sure that I could support the argument that the property's value was about $160,000 (even though it was really worth about $200,000). Working with the broker, we devised the listing agreement, and an offer to purchase in the name of an LLC for $130,000, had the homeowner sign it, and it was sent to the mortgage company as part of the complete short sale proposal. I hoped that they would counter at $131,200, and I was OK with that.

The proposal included all the documentation required by the lender, plus a comprehensive property inspection w/ photographs and repairs estimates. The seller's HUD counseling certificate was included, as well as the listing agreement, contract for sale, purchaser's pre qualifications, and an estimated HUD 1.

** the HUD1 failed to indicate the second mortgage loan payoff of $15,000.

The review/approval process was bureaucracy at its worst. The loss mitigation rep was thorough, insisted on original signatures, and required approval from her superior each step of the way. But she was consistent and helpful throughout the process and were it not for her professionalism, the deal could have died on the vine.

The search for an investor to step into my shoes was turning into an advanced on-line course on pre foreclosure sale and leasebacks. Even though the classified ad clearly stated "Experienced Investors/Principals Only!" most of the inquiries were from folks who had no idea what a SLB was, or had a distorted view, or had no money of their own and wanted to assign the contract to yet another investor.

So many late nite infomercial pitchmen tout the riches and simplicity of "no money down" real estate deals that people have the mindset that it's simple that anyone can do it in their spare time working from their kitchen table. In my 25+ years of experience, it's more an exception than the rule.

The two candidates I selected signed the contracts, and went about getting to me a mortgage pre approval.

"Pre qualification" is a lender's estimate from unverified info that the borrower provides on how much money the applicant may be able to borrow. A formal "pre approval" certification is issued after the borrower submits full financials including employment, banking verifications, and credit history. You can then be issued a certification (pre approval letter) that confirms the borrower is conditionally approved for specific loan amount. Usually, the conditions include a maximum loan to value as supported by a certified appraisal, and an update of verifications.

Once the entire proposal had been submitted for consideration, the lender's rep called and said they would approve the short sale, but that title report still indicated an open second mortgage loan with an approximate balance of $15,000.

The maximum amount the FHA permits to a junior lien holder as party to a pre foreclosure short sale is $1,000. So, as long as I had proof that the second would accept $1,000 as payment in full to release the lien the deal would proceed. But that presented a problem. I had been under the mistaken information that the second had been paid. Now, not only did this prove to be untrue, I had a major problem. To my knowledge, the second mortgagee was no longer in the mortgage business, and I had no current contact numbers, no current addresses, no nothing. Even if I could locate them, I had to convince them to accept $1,000 on a $15,000+ account.

It took a few phone calls over the course of a few days, but I was able to track down the long non performing loan. The loan had been sold a few times, and was now in the portfolio of a private investor, but serviced by a company called Fairbanks Capital. My first contact with Fairbanks didn't go too well. After I Faxed the letter authorizing them to speak with me, they acknowledged the loan, and calculated the payoff to be $15,000 plus interest, plus foreclosure fees, etc.

I told them that the property was in disrepair, scheduled for Sheriff's Sale, and the maximum payoff per the FHA senior mortgagee conditions was $1,000. After haggling for a couple of days, they agreed to release the lien for $7,500. In fact, they issued a 10 day payoff letter for $7,500, and sent it to the mortgagor.

Now I had to factor the additional $7,500 into the equation plus be able to manufacture it into an acceptable form for the HUD1. I had to make it appear that the junior mortgagee was going to accept $1,000, not the $7,500 that they had demanded. To make this deal work, the junior mortgagee would have to agree to accept $1,000 as payment in full. I would have to go back to work on the second mortgagee.

I then advised that potential buyers that they would have to pay an additional $7,500 up front, but that they would recover it on the back end plus interest. The purchaser agreed, and promised that on demand, he would issue a cashiers check to me in the amount of $7,500.

Long story short, I negotiated further and purchased the mortgage from Fairbanks. At an additional discount. For cash. They accepted. The second that I purchased the mortgage from Fairbanks (via assignment) I was the junior mortgagee, and could accept any amount as payment in full to release the lien thus complying with the FHA criteria that the junior accept $1,000 as payment in full.

Jumping forward to closing, the seller was able to payoff the mortgages and property taxes. She became a tenant, and held an exclusive option to repurchase the property from the landlord provided she paid the rent on time. Otherwise, she could forfeit the exclusive option, and her continued occupancy would be at the whim and pleasure of the landlord. At closing I walked from the table with a check payable to the real estate broker, which we split, plus $1,000 check payable to me, as junior mortgagee.

Though I had no additional contractual responsibility to her, or to the landlord, I did hear from time to time that the rent was late, but that she was making a good faith effort to exercise her option to purchase the property. When the time came for her to exercise the option, there were some discrepancies that arose due to ambiguities in the repurchase criteria, and the repurchase price was slightly greater than she had calculated.

During the pre-sale negotiations between buyer and seller, Cookie and the buyer were concerned that without 1) reestablishing her credit, and 2) without a downpayment, she would not be able to get a new mortgage loan to buy back the property. One solution would be for the landlord to agree to a rental credit. The idea of a rental credit had been discussed, but was never articulated in writing.

For example, the landlord could have extended a 100% rental credit (creating a downpayment) making it easier for the tenant/purchaser to qualify for a new mortgage loan. The landlord would simply have to increase the repurchase amount after calculating the additional capital gains tax liability that would arise from a higher sales price.

Cookie assumed the benefit of a rental credit, but failed to anticipate the extra tax that would have to be paid by the landlord/seller. How much are we talking about? The monthly rent was ($1500 x 12) $18,000. The landlord/seller would incur an extra capital gain tax on $18,000 or about $4,500.

Per the lease agreement, the landlord/seller could have 1) refused the rent, and 2) declared a breach when the rent payment was late, and 3) notify the tenant that she had forfeited her exclusive option to repurchase the property. The agreement stated that in the event of a stated default, the tenant's exclusive option would degrade to a right of first refusal. But, by accepting the late rent, the landlord did not declare that the tenant was in default, and allowed the tenant to think that her option was in full force.

Even though the landlord/seller didn't feel that his efforts and (generous) concessions were appreciated, the tenant/purchaser felt as if she were horribly exploited. However, she was able to exercise her option, and repurchase the house.

CROSSING THE LINE

To Fleece Thy Neighbor

an essay by TheShortSalePro©2006

Harvard Law School professor and bankruptcy expert Elizabeth Warren says that the majority of 'so-called' foreclosure 'rescuers' are sleazy predators offering their prey 'cement life jackets.'

How a foreclosure rescue program might work:

1. Foreclosure-rescue firms use public records, and paid data services, to gather information about homes at risk of foreclosure.

2. A company contacts homeowners and offers to help them avoid foreclosure, often with an offer like this. In exchange for ownership of the house, the foreclosure-rescue firm will make mortgage payments current, pay off the mortgage, pay $500 cash to the homeowner and allow the former owner to rent for 18 months with up to three months free.

4. The now-renter has the option of buying back the home at market value within 18 months. The renter must secure new financing.

5. If he is unable to secure financing within 18 months, the renter must move. The business is free to rent the house to someone else, or sell the property and collect equity that has built over time.

140

Most predatory practices are both sophisticated, and premeditated. However, many people who casually engage in the business of preforeclosure acquisition don't know that some of their intended activities may be considered predatory, and are oblivious to the consequences of their actions, especially if their proposed transaction falls short of the promised results.

Rest assured that there are thousands of ethical service providers in both the for profit and non profit sectors, but those ranks are being overtaken by the exponential increase in "get-rich-quick" advocates who teach people how to find and exploit desperate homeowners facing foreclosures and other hardships. These 'students' learn techniques designed to persuade the homeowners to turn over their property, and/or otherwise part with money, equity, or both. The art of 'rescuing' distressed homeowners (thinly disguised as 'creative real estate acquisition techniques) is being taught around the country in the form of infomercials, boot camps, seminars, books, tapes, teleconferences, and one-on-one mentoring.

Go ahead! Google *"creative"* real estate investment courses. Now, Google *real estate scams and fraud.* All it takes is a second to find millions of entries.

Some entries describing scams are posted by individual victims or groups of victims who are willing to share their experiences on on-line message boards and Yahoo Groups. Some entries include articles that have been published in newspapers and magazines, some are published reports prepared by mortgage loan servicing giants, government agencies, and non profit organizations, including National Consumer Law Center.

There are high profile mortgage and realty fraud cases that, over time and usually well after the fact, are discovered and reported upon. The big headlines involve institutional mortgage lenders and loan servicers who have been defrauded by other professionals, including, but not limited to, conspiring lawyers, appraisers, real estate brokers, brokers' agents, mortgage brokers, etc. Institutional losses can be in the tens of millions of dollars. These conglomerates, unlike individual victims, have the financial and political clout to both pursue the scamsters, and lobby for protective legislation and regulation. For example, in response to allegations of widespread irregularities within the appraisal industry, NJ's Governor Whitman signed into law a bill requiring criminal background checks for appraisal license applicants.

One particular, high profile, conspiracy case was dubbed, "House of Cards," and though centered in New Jersey, involved neighboring states, as well. On the surface, millions of dollars and more than two hundred properties were involved. The two-fold scheme, once exposed and unfolded, worked like this Bargain priced properties, including those that were foreclosed, and in need of repairs, some occupied, others abandoned, were purchased for cash, then illegally flipped several times within a short period (sometimes within days) to members within their cabal to record artificially inflated properties' value. Based on the inflated value, the property was marketed and sold to either a conspiratorial "straw buyer," or an unwitting purchaser lured by the dream of affordable homeownership, with 'no money down' and 'no closing costs.' The purchases were financed by a combination of high loan-to-value purchase money mortgages, silent seconds, and non existent down payments. Proceeds from mortgage loans funded the operation putting hundreds of thousands of dollars into the conspirators' pockets. The scheme was predicated on the untoward practice of manipulating information while creating unrealistic, artificially inflated values resulting in a House of Cards waiting to collapse. The appraisers, used by the conspiring mortgage broker, intentionally omitted any mention of illegal flipping activity, adverse market conditions, that many dwellings were in need of major repairs, or use appropriate comparable sales in the certified appraisals that were used to help justify the extraordinary loan amounts. Consequently, mortgage loan amounts far exceeded the property's actual fair market value. A couple of lawyers were used to preside over bogus closings who then filed false closing documents. Realtors were entangled, too.

Bonafide (unsuspecting) purchasers would go to the closing table only to be surprised by altered sales contracts and loan documents. Common alterations included an inflated purchase price, nonexistent downpayments, larger than expected first mortgage loans, and short term balloon second mortgages that the Sellers should have known would never be repaid. This process was repeated over and over, cookie cutter style, about 200 times. The framework's common denominator was distressed housing, and ethically challenged and/or financially unsophisticated participants.

When 'straw buyers' were used to obtain mortgage loans, documents were created (tax returns, paystubs, bank statements, etc.) altered, forged, and offered in the loan application to the conspiratorial mortgage broker. The broker, after funding the loan, would package the 'bad' loans with good, and sell to mortgage investors. These "undersecured" mortgages eventually fell into delinquency, default, and foreclosure.

After a while, when the house of cards showed the first signs of collapse, a distant foreclosing mortgagee would discover that the loan balance far exceeded value.

The 'legitimate' homeowners also learned that they had overpaid, and could not refinance due to LTV constraints. Those homeowners who attempted to sell soon learned that, because their mortgage loan balance exceeded the fair market value, their property became (traditionally) unmarketable. As soon as the property fell into foreclosure, the homeowners in distress were approached by an entirely new set of speculators/predators, predators who were totally unaware of the House of Cards scandal that would adversely impact hundreds of potential resales.

One June day I got to talking with another Dad who, like me, was watching his child play in a little league game. He was a self absorbed, chatty, Wall Street type and talked about the stock market, and investments in general. Getting a word in edgewise, I spoke about municipal tax liens, and casually mentioned to him I worked with people losing their homes to mortgage and tax foreclosure. His immediate response surprised me. Usually, self absorbed people are disinterested when they hear about other peoples' misfortunes. But this guy's eyes lit up and he started pumping me with questions. He posed intelligent questions which suggested to me that he knew something, not a lot, but something about the foreclosure business. I briefly explained my role in the business, and told him about several preforeclosure properties that could soon be available for sale. He continued by telling me about a 'friend of his' who was in the market for foreclosed property. Oh, and his friend was a cash buyer, and he would probably want to meet with me. Nothing new, I thought. There are always about 100 potential cash buyers in search of deals for just about every decent opportunity out there. Some are tire kickers, some are big talk do nothings, but some buyers are real. When selling distressed housing, timing is everything so it's important to maintain a pool of potential buyers. A cash buyer is King, so I agreed to meet with his friend, but I had no real expectations.

In retrospect, the meeting and events that were to follow were quite educational. His friend turned out to be a Ringleader of the as of yet unexposed conspiracy: The multimillion dollar "House of Cards" scandal.

The appointment was made to meet with the friend at my home. On the day and time I was expecting to meet with just one person, I watched with some surprise as a procession of expensive cars quickly filled up my driveway, and took up most of the on-street parking an odd mid-day site in my modest neighborhood. In all, two foursomes of men arrived. They were dressed in golf attire with expensive wristwatches, wore layers and layers of gold chain hanging from their open collared necks. They all seemed to be in their thirties or early forties and were soon sitting, fidgeting uncomfortably, in my sweltering living room. To be honest, I didn't get a warm, fuzzy feeling from them. I quickly sensed that these guys weren't all that concerned with wanting to help distressed homeowners save or refinance their homes. My gut told me that these guys were predators. Organized, slick, and impatient. And obviously well financed.

The ringleader, fidgeting and heavily perspiring, introduced himself, and everyone else in the room. As he spoke, they all were shifting uneasily in their seats looking around the room, or nervously checking their gleaming wristwatches. Of the eight, the only ones to speak were the ringleader, one fellow I was told owned a home repair business, an appraiser, and my new best buddy from Little League who set up the meeting. The rest just sat, respectfully listened, perspired, fidgeted, and scrawled a few notes in their notebooks.

"Why don't you get your air conditioning fixed?" the ringleader asked, surprising me, "what kind of money do you pull in helping poor homeowners?"

I was growing more uncomfortable. The ringleader didn't wait for an answer, but went on to say that I could easily triple what I was making if I worked exclusively with his group. My new best buddy from Little League sat there, smiling, and nodding his head in agreement. "You can make a lot of money, Dave. We can all make a lot of money. We just need access to your clients. When they call you, we want you to send them to us. We'll take care of them."

"How?" I asked.

"We'll buy their houses, and put them into houses that we've got. We have houses all over. Maybe we'll fix up their house and let them stay. Maybe they can buy their homes back from us. But we'll pay you good money for sending them to us," he said, "and you won't have to worry about them anymore."

"What have you got that we can look at in Asbury Park?" the ringleader asked, with urgency. "Or Long Branch? You know of anything vacant? We want to buy something today, and we've got cash!"

Meetings like this didn't usually happen. At least not to me. The folks I'd worked with in the past were cautious, and conservative. These guys seemed hell bent on buying something for the sake of buying. It seemed unreal and something just didn't feel right.

Then, I saw it. There it was. Plain as day. The line. These guys were asking me to sell out my clients, and cross that line.

On one side of the line, the real side, there was a never ending parade of adversarial and non-listening homeowners demanding painless solutions to their escalating problems. There was the sporadic and mediocre compensation. There was the modest house with a short driveway and a broken air conditioning system. On the other side of that line were the shiny new cars, fat wallets, and presumably a larger home with working air conditioning. And maybe a gold chain or two.

All that stood in the way was my refusal to betray my clients' trust. I knew that these guys were more about money than they were about structuring win/win deals to 'help' distressed homeowners. In retrospect, I was right.

To my thinking, the meeting was over. I stood, thanked them for coming, and told them that I would think about their offer. The ringleader seemed confused and asked, "What's there to think about?"

Aside from a few more chats with my new best buddy from Little League, I never met with them again. But I did have occasion to see, first hand, some of their handiwork.

Fast forward about six or eight months. I get a call from a homeowner who had been referred to me by his church. He said that he was losing his house to foreclosure but that he was being ripped off. Almost without exception, that's what they all say. But, as I would come to learn, this guy was ripped off. And so was his mortgagee.

"OK, come on in and bring your paperwork" I suggested. He told me that he never got any copies of the closing paperwork, including his mortgage loan... In fact, he only learned of the second mortgage because it was listed as a Defendant on the foreclosure summons and complaint. He had already asked and had been promised by the closing attorney to get copies. We agreed to meet in a few days in my office. Shortly before our appointment, however, he called and asked if I could come to his house, instead, since his wife wasn't feeling too well, and he was working in his basement trying to fix the heat. Seems that their heating system had failed, and the house was cold very, very cold.

When I got there, he was working in the basement, removing what looked like asbestos pipe wrap from an ancient hot water heating system. As I retreated up the stairs, I suggested that he wear a respirator when working with that stuff. He didn't seem to know about asbestos I apologized, told him that I was allergic to friable asbestos. He said that he didn't have a chance to pick up the files, so I looked around the house and asked him to pick up the paperwork, and meet me the next day. He agreed. As I drove back, anxious to shower, I was hoping that he would change his asbestos powdered clothing before meeting with me.

The next day he arrived, with a legal file folder stretched to about 5 inches thick which he carefully placed off to his side. Then he told me the story about how he and his family came to buy the house. They had been for years renting a small apartment in a northern New Jersey city. Though they had no savings, both had good credit, and made a good salary. He, his wife, and his children wanted out of the apartment, and decided that they wanted to live at the Jersey Shore. They scoured the newspaper, called on an ad, met a Realtor, and were shown a few houses. All but one of the houses were priced too high, and that house, a dilapidated bungalow, didn't particularly interest them or suit their needs.

Then the Realtor casually suggested another house. "It's a bit out of your price range, but you can buy it for no money down, and the Seller is willing to help out with your closing costs."

They looked at the large, empty house which was undergoing renovations. Despite the repairs in progress, they loved it.

"I never bought a house before, so I wasn't sure about the process, but to me things went fast. Too fast. The Realtor pressured me to make an offer right then and there. She called the Seller on her cell phone and negotiated the deal right then and there. The Seller offered to finish painting, put in new carpets, and upgrade the heating, plumbing and electrical systems. We agreed on a price, and, using a turned over a desk, signed all the papers. On the day we closed, we found out they didn't do what they said they would, even though the Realtor told us that everything had been done. When we saw it again on the day we moved in it was still in the same condition as when we had seen it a few weeks earlier. Just dustier. The stacks of sheetrock, the unopened paint cans, and other stuff. Still there. Untouched. In fact, our half filled coffee cups from when we signed the contracts were still there. I knew that the deal was too good to be true. We really wanted everything to work out the way we were promised, and so we believed what we were told."

He continued, "Not only did I pay more for the house than I agreed, it came with a second mortgage, too. I'm into this house for more than it's worth! Even if I wanted to, I couldn't even sell it for what I paid for it!. And it still ain't got no heat! I can't afford it! I had to fix the roof and replace the appliances. We weren't ready for that. And now I'm behind on both mortgages. They are foreclosing and I just feel like I got screwed over. I went in to see the lawyer who represented them, and who handled the closing to demand that they either fix the house, or give me my money back. I knew they wouldn't do what they promised, and I knew that I was headed for trouble so when I left, I took my file from his desk," he explained, handing me the bulging file.

"I guess you'll find what you need in here. I hope you can help me" he said. With that, I told him I would look into it, and see what, if anything, could be done.

Later that day when I opened the accordion style file folder, I was amazed at what I found. Obviously altered documents, including an appraisal, a mortgage loan application, paystubs, tax returns, a copy of a recorded deed complete with sections that had been covered up with Liquid Paper, several handwritten memos of instruction to realtors and other lawyers, and what appeared to be notes calculating estimated profits on this, and other deals in progress.

Since the entirety of the transaction appeared rife with fraud, I dove in, contacted the junior mortgagee and asked that the loan be forgiven, and the lien released. They said, "No."

I contacted the listing and selling broker (same broker's agent) and formally requested that they return the real estate commission on the sale which amounted to more than $10,000. I thought that the $10,000, if returned, could be used to fix my client's furnace, or help him get caught up on the mortgage. The VP of the 100+ office chain in 17 states said that they would 'look into the matter' but never actually did anything to help compensate my client. Later on, their (former) agent was convicted, and sentenced to prison for her role in the widespread scheme.

The first mortgagee foreclosed. My client wasn't able to bring his mortgage current to save his home, nor was he able to sell his home even via preforeclosure shortsale. Why? Because unknown to us at the time, the mortgage was now the subject of a Federal investigation, and the mortgagee needed the foreclosure to run its course to determine actual (not mitigated) damages. Once the property was sold at Sheriff's Sale actual damages/losses could be determined upon the liquidation of the property. The mortgagee intended to pursue the conspirators for fraud.

One day, I received two unusual telephone calls. The first from my (former) client who excitedly told me that the FBI was looking into the matter, and they had asked him for any papers or records that he had. He wanted to give me a heads up that he had informed the FBI that I had all his papers, and suggested that they call me.

The second call was from the local FBI office. They asked that I come in and 'surrender' the files in my possession regarding their ongoing joint investigation with the County Prosecutor and State Police.

I made an appointment for the next day to turn over the file. I had to find it, and I knew that I wanted to give it one more read before I turned it in. I was prepared to spend the next few hours reviewing that file with the precision of a magnifying glass and a fine tooth comb. But, I didn't have to pay attention to minute detail. Everything was all laid out in big, bold print.. **If ever there was a smoking gun, this was it!**

I went to the address they provided and found the non descript office building that I had driven past hundreds of times, never knowing that it was home to the FBI. My appointment was on the second floor of the two story building. The long, windowless corridor had several ceiling mounted surveillance cameras recording my movements. I was 'buzzed' though the solitary, steel doorway, and into an outer office where I was subjected to further scrutiny. Within a few uneasy minutes, I met with the burly, plain clothed, investigating Agent. We exchanged introductions, handshakes, and business cards. He invited me to sit in a chair at the side his desk. In return for the requested file, I asked for an inventory of the contents, and a receipt. He agreed, and asked me to remain seated, and wait at his huge, wooden desk for a few minutes. I looked around the multi-cubicle space loaded with small meeting rooms, file cabinets, and boxes. Lotsa boxes. Then I began to look around in the cubicle where I was waiting, and noticed a large, iron O-ring bolted through the thick, wooden desk and another bolted to the floor below presumably for those "inviteess" needing restraints and wearing handcuffs and /or leg irons.

The Agent returned without the file and explained that a clerk was preparing the receipt. We talked over coffee for almost an hour. He told me a little bit about his investigation, and I told him what I learned from my cursory review of the file's content. We discussed the basic elements of real estate fraud and predatory practices, and shared (albeit guardedly) our experiences.

I learned a lot that day. I think the Agent must have, too. Within a few months I began getting calls from the US Attorney's office asking me to help, and testify in their investigation(s) of fraudulent practices.

The scam was reported upon regularly in the local newspaper. After a couple of years, about 20 people have been indicted. Many reached plea bargain agreements, forfeiting their licenses to practice law, appraising property, or to sell real estate. A few went to/are serving time in Federal prison for their role.

At some point, each conspirator had been an honest, law abiding citizen doing good work. Then, they each took steps, gradually crossing the line, becoming more emboldened and empowered with each (undetected and unpunished) step deeper and deeper into the dark side that lay over the line.

There are many complaints and allegations of wrongdoing, both major and minor, but nothing can be done to limit questionable practices until laws are passed. Right now, the laws lag far behind the offending deeds.

Many instances of fraud and deception are unexposed and/or unpunished because homeowners may not at first realize what had happened, or when they do it's well after the fact. Informal and poorly articulated complaints either fall on deaf, uninterested ears, or are fielded and filed away by overworked and understaffed organizations. Most of the wronged individuals can't afford to hire an attorney to review the entirety of the transaction, and many are simply too embarrassed by being bamboozled, and not willing to admit culpability in the loss of their home.

Many homeowners/mortgagors, who feel victimized by predatory lending practices, have articulated their allegations and sought help from government agencies, and trade organizations, including the Mortgage Bankers Association of America located in Washington, DC. *This writer has served as an outsource resource for that organization in the investigation and reporting upon those allegations of predatory lending, and untoward realty practices.*

I've interviewed hundreds of consumers, all who felt their situation had been exploited by someone who had asked for, and with whom they had placed their trust.

Common complaints to the MBA include the conduct of mortgage brokers. In particular are the mortgage brokers whose advertisements include the offer of subprime, and hard money loans who target homeowners with bad credit who are facing the mortgage foreclosure. Their sophisticated campaigns include direct (compelling) mail, telephone pole signs (We Buy Houses) print, and now radio and television media.

Many brokers claim to fund foreclosure 'bailout' mortgage loan refinances. Generally, they do as promised and professionally facilitate high rate, short term bailout loans. In these cases where the Borrower has had the luxury of time for professional review, and decided to proceed, their complaints are, to my thinking, unfounded. But oftentimes duplicitous brokers are really wolves in sheep's clothing. By manipulating the application and underwriting progress of the proposed refinance, they intend to profit on that 'inside' information outside the scope of the legitimate business.

The scam works like this. The licensed brokers accept and/or arrange for application and appraisal fees. then drag their feet delaying the process as the distressed homeowners get further and farther along in the foreclosure process, and closer and closer to the loss of their home to Sheriffs or Trustees Sale. The brokers/speculators know that the increasingly distressed homeowners will become desperate, and willing to do almost anything to avoid the loss of their home. The brokers wait until the homeowners are days, or sometimes just a few hours away, from the scheduled foreclosure sale, then hurriedly present an excessively unfair proposal.

Usually a 'take it or leave it' proposal will require the homeowner to sign a deed as 'extra insurance' that the loan will be repaid. Loan terms and conditions, though not illegal, are oftentimes unconscionable. Desperate homeowners grab at the 'cement life jacket' disguised as a second chance at saving their home, sacrificing equity only to delay the inevitable, then drown while deeper in debt, losing their home to the very 'rescuers' who had held out a 'helping' hand.

Most of the complaints I investigated involved obviously unqualified borrowers getting approved for loans that they had no hope of repaying, but, due to the urgency of the situation, had imprudently agreed to loan terms and condition.

One example: An 84 year old woman had sought a small, temporary mortgage loan on her home to help an adult son (raise bail). Over a period of several years, she had unknowingly agreed to refinance the small loan several times. The broker would call and ask her if she wanted to skip a payment that month, or borrow a few more dollars for car or house repairs. Each time she agreed, she was actually refinancing her mortgage. Each time paying a hefty prepayment penalty. Each time paying more closing costs, costs that were rolled into the new loan amount. Soon, her modest, already stretched social security income, was insufficient to meet the increased monthly payment. The once small loan taken as a favor for her son had morphed into unmanageable debt forcing the 84 year old woman to return to work as a matron in a local post office. Soon, despite her best efforts to make the payments, the loan was foreclosed.

Should she have known better, or sought legal advice before mortgaging her home? Sure. But the self-serving mortgage broker certainly didn't act in her best interest, either. With her income what is was, she should never have been approved for anything more than the initial loan(s). But, he saw easy money and, in my opinion, he crossed the line. He had systematically sucked equity from the home, generating transaction fees for himself. Now, the woman needed to payoff the foreclosed mortgage, or lose her home.

The petite 84 year old's minimal wages as a matron, combined with her monthly social security check, wasn't enough to justify a new mortgage loan. Not fully understanding the seriousness of her situation, she remained adamant that she wouldn't sell or lose her home of 60 years. "I only borrowed a few thousand dollars" she cried. Unable to refinance, unable to afford a Chapter 13 Bankruptcy repayment plan, and unwilling to sell the house it was lost.

I'm concerned when distressed homeowners have been at best, mislead, and at worst, swindled. That's what can happen when each party's interests are in direct conflict, one of the parties is stressed out, while for the other it's business as usual.

Mortgage foreclosure can be a major, life changing event, even for those who successfully avoid the involuntary loss of their home. Homeowners facing foreclosure have a few things in common. They all have difficulties in managing their financial, and emotional stress. Stress manifests itself in many ways, including, but not limited to burnout, and an inability to prioritize, and an inability to make sound decisions.

I think it's wrong in the quest for a 'deal' that a speculative investor stretches the truth or 'puffs' when describing how he or she can "help" the distressed homeowner. Especially if the 'help' is designed to unjustly enrich the speculator at the expense of the homeowner. 'Puffing' is defined as "exaggeration by a salesperson concerning the quality of goods or services." More often than not, the homeowners are harmed, not helped, by their belief in the salesperson's puffery. Many homeowners end up paying high fees for a temporary false sense of security which contribute to their not seeking timely, *qualified* help.

Not all homeowners in distress are blameless in the process. Many are dishonest, or not totally forthcoming in their description of the problem, or in their professed ability to extricate themselves from the problem. They can be dishonest with themselves, as well as dishonest with those who offer to 'help' in whatever form that 'help' may be. By being dishonest, by withholding certain information, or failing to provide or disclose requested information in a timely fashion, they do themselves a disservice.

If a foreclosure 'rescuer' isn't well versed in the foreclosure process nor adequately prepared to respond both competently and appropriately to each newly disclosed fact, valuable time can be lost. Not only may the 'rescuer' lose control of the 'deal' due to wasted time, but the homeowner might well lose the chance to save their home. I am troubled with wannabee dealmakers who learn their craft at the expense of trusting homeowners.

I am troubled with these self serving entrepreneurs whose pretext is that they'll save the home from foreclosure by negotiating a workout with the lender (something the homeowners should be able to do for themselves) while their primary agenda is to sniff out a deal. If a deal isn't forthcoming, they'll ask outrageous fees for placing a few telephone calls or submitting some basic paperwork that the homeowner could easily do themselves. Or, they'll shrug their shoulders, and move on to the next victim.

Just because our neighbors have fallen onto hard times, does that mean that it's open season on them? Is it OK to take unjust advantage simply because they might have their backs against the wall? I don't think so. You can make a nice profit doing good work, helping people who need help by negotiating fairly.

I am troubled anytime I learn a homeowner has been tricked into deeding title to their home to an investor. They move out thinking their loan has been paid, but in fact remain obligated on the mortgage(s). A shadowy 'Investor' either rents out the newly vacated home collecting rents without paying the mortgage, or property taxes, until the home is sold at Sheriff's Sale. Or, the 'investor' brings the mortgage current (a good thing) then quickly resells the home to someone else wrapping the original mortgage into the transaction, and walking with the equity. Does the entrepreneur deserve a fee? Sure. But does he deserve every last penny of the former owner's equity? I'm not so sure about that. Not if the former homeowner was tricked into deeding away the home.

"I took the course. I made the call. I got the deed, I got the deed!" they boast to their peers on their favorite real estate message board. "Now what?" they ask.

I Am Troubled

I am troubled with these people who grab the deed, then don't know what, if anything, to do next. The foreclosure clock keeps ticking, and with each passing day the likelihood that anything good will result grows slim.

I am troubled with any practice or transaction that predictably falls short of promised results, and leaves distressed homeowners in worse shape, left to fend for themselves with less time to explore and implement viable options.

I am troubled by 'gurus' who teach (by design or by example) that distressed homeowners are deadbeats, and too stupid to save their homes.

I am troubled when apathetic speculators claim, "What difference does it make if they lose the house to the Sheriff or to me?

I am troubled when after a transparent scheme has been rejected, the rebuffed 'investor' says that the homeowners are 'in denial' and that they "deserve what they get."

I am troubled with anyone who promotes 'mortgage elimination' schemes.

I am troubled with the guys who create phony (premature) but realistic looking Sheriff's Sale notices, then tack them to the house with their contact numbers.

I'm sure we all agree that identifying and profiting from opportunity in real estate is as American as apple pie. But we shouldn't include or condone 'deception' as a legitimate tool in the pursuit of profit. Somewhere along the way, many of us have inferred that it's OK to screw our neighbor, kicking him when he's down, wounded, and needing our help the most.

There comes a point in every real estate practitioner's career when he or she must decide to do the right thing, or cross the line. Hopefully, for those who did cross the line, it was a difficult decision. But each time that line gets crossed, the easier it gets until crossing the line becomes second nature.

I think that as time goes on, and more and more people get the short end of the stick, more and more 'creative' real estate deals gone bad will be audited. Areas of concern will include the practice of law without a license (advising homeowners about bankruptcy,) and the sale of real estate without a broker's license. Certainly making false statements on loan applications, or the falsification of closing documents, will be investigated. Tax evasion, too.

You don't need to cross that line to profit in the foreclosure niche. If you have crossed it, come on back. You'll sleep better.

Mortgage Scam Snares Bank Vice President

Story by Geoff Dutton,
Reprinted with permission from The Columbus Dispatch

Property investor Richard Bird stands on the back porch of a Columbus house that he bought at 621 Gilbert St. A city code-enforcement notice on the door says no one can live inside because the house is unsafe.

Richard Bird's plans to dabble in real estate investing quickly spiraled out of control.

In a span of five months in 2002, the bank vice president racked up $1.4 million in mortgages for rental properties, based on empty promises and forged paperwork bearing his signature.

He was ripped off.

Bird's story is noteworthy not because he was scammed but because authorities eventually prosecuted and convicted the scammer. Most cases aren't prosecuted, even as mortgage fraud skyrockets.

In late October, federal law-enforcement agencies announced a joint effort to attack mortgage fraud. Ohio officials, beset by the nation's highest foreclosure rate, also vow to crack down.

Bird, who lives near Westerville, looks forward to the sentencing next month of the Cuyahoga County man who ensnared him and 15 others in the scheme. According to the federal indictment, it involved 74 Columbus and Cleveland properties financed by $4.8 million of inflated mortgages.

But the case almost wasn't investigated, much less prosecuted. And even the scammer's eventual conviction didn't free Bird from the crushing debt of the fraudulent mortgages.

Bird's ordeal shows how easy it is to fall prey to mortgage fraud and the difficulty of undoing the damage, particularly in Ohio.

The 38-year-old church deacon and former Army parachutist said he is speaking out, despite personal embarrassment, to warn others.

"You don't want anyone else to go through what we've been through," said his wife, Valerie Bird. "Short of somebody dying, I can't think of anything more painful."

For several months, Bird pleaded for help from the FBI, the state Commerce Department, the attorney general, the county prosecutor and mortgage lenders. It got him nowhere — sometimes not even return phone calls — as his finances unraveled.

"I'm looking for somebody to help me," Bird recalled, "and nobody will help me."

Everything changed when a federal agent investigating house fires in Cleveland knocked on his door.

Money pits

Bird spotted the newspaper ad four years ago: Investment properties for sale. Financing available. Earn up to $100,000 in monthly rental income.

Bird, a vice president of technology for JPMorgan Chase & Co., had less ambitious goals.

He and his wife had been looking for ways she could quit her job and stay home with their two children, who are now 5 and 7. They had toyed with the idea of buying rental properties.

"It wasn't a get-rich-quick scheme," he said.

They answered the ad and met Raymond Delacruz, 28, a bright, ambitious and charismatic salesman who drove a flashy Lotus Esprit Turbo S4 sports car. Together, Delacruz and Bird visited 45 available Columbus properties, mostly rundown houses and duplexes.

Bird bought four North Linden houses in March 2002. A week later, he closed on another house and a duplex.

Every 10 days or so, he'd close on a few more.

Signs of trouble appeared after a month or so. At one closing, Bird noticed the mortgages were refinancings, not purchase loans. He questioned Delacruz.

"He said, 'We do this all the time. We establish your ownership of the property almost simultaneously with the refinancing,' " Bird recalled. "He said, 'It's got to be legitimate because the bank approved the loan.' "

Skeptical, Bird looked to the title company's escrow officer, who reassured him. Bird signed the mortgages.

Then, Bird encountered trouble getting keys for some of the properties and rent payments from the existing tenants.

At that point, Bird had bought 11 properties, 10 of them from Donald F. Green, a landlord and property investor who buys and sells hundreds of houses a year in Franklin County. Delacruz agreed to arrange for the collection of rent payments during the transition.

Furious, Bird barged into Green's office and demanded $9,000 that he figured Green owed him. Green wasn't there, but Bird said he harangued Green's daughters out of $2,000 before storming out.

Bird also confronted Delacruz, who apologized but blamed Green.

Delacruz and Green could not be reached for comment. Delacruz's attorney didn't respond to messages seeking comment.

Delacruz calmed Bird. He showed him the properties of landlord David H. Munce. Bird toured Munce's properties and met people introduced as stable, longtime tenants.

It was an opportunity to shore up his investment.

But it only magnified the problems. Bird knew many of the properties needed major work, but repairs later exposed even more serious safety and structural defects that had been concealed.

People introduced as longtime tenants turned out essentially to be squatters who hadn't paid rent for months.

By June 2002, Bird knew he'd been conned. But by then, he held mortgages on 24 properties and had invested $100,000. Tenants quickly vanished. In his first month with all of the properties, his mortgage payments exceeded rental income by $8,000.

It went downhill from there.

"Within six months," Bird said, "half the properties I had had no tenants. Nothing."

Rejected pleas

Bird hadn't yet discovered the worst part.

Delacruz, who billed himself as a one-stop shop for investors, had conspired with an appraiser — a woman who also worked in his office — to overstate the value of the properties. They were worth a fraction of Bird's $1.4 million in mortgages, a federal investigation later revealed.

Delacruz also doctored the loan applications and purchase contracts. Between the time Bird signed paperwork and Delacruz submitted it, Delacruz jacked up loan amounts, boosted his fees and made other changes.

The loans were improper from the beginning. Delacruz duped lenders into believing that Bird already owned the properties and was refinancing them.

Bird alerted authorities.

He compiled a lengthy complaint and packet of documents for the state Commerce Department, which regulates lenders, mortgage brokers, appraisers and real-estate agents. The Commerce Department responded with a brief letter, saying there wasn't enough evidence to proceed.

A short time later, Bird learned that Delacruz had previously lost his real-estate license; Bird sent a followup letter to the department. This time, he said, Commerce told him that because Delacruz was unlicensed, it had no authority over him.

Fuming, Bird called Commerce and lashed out at a woman over the phone, demanding to know who was looking out for consumers.

"She starts whispering into the phone and says, 'Honey, I've worked here 23 years. There is no protection for the consumer. The laws protect the banks and real-estate agents.'"

Commerce generally won't investigate complaints on behalf of investors, only people buying their own homes, said spokeswoman Denise Lee.

Bird also called the FBI, which took a message and said an agent would be in touch. "I never heard back from them again — ever," he said.

FBI spokesman Michael Brooks said there were several reasons, including a lack of staffing and overlapping investigations that limited whom agents could contact without tipping off others.

"The information he gave us was already the subject of an investigation," which continues, Brooks said.

Bird also struck out with the offices of Franklin County Prosecutor Ron O'Brien and state Attorney General Jim Petro.

Of the five lenders holding Bird's mortgages, only one returned his calls. "They said, 'You signed the mortgage, right?' I said, 'Yeah.' They said, 'We look forward to receiving your payment next month.'"

Legal loopholes

Desperate, Bird stayed afloat by draining his savings, liquidating his 401(k) retirement accounts and maxing out credit cards with $40,000 in charges. At the same time, he fixed up the houses, searched for buyers and tried to refinance.

Would-be buyers and lenders balked. "People laughed at me," Bird said.

Meanwhile, he searched for a lawyer. Nobody was interested in taking the case. An acquaintance from church, Columbus lawyer Lloyd Pierre-Louis, reluctantly agreed.

It would be another risky financial gamble for Bird.

"I told him up front it's a long shot, by far, and that law was not necessarily on his side," Pierre-Louis said.

Ohio and Virginia are the only states that exempt mortgage lending from state laws prohibiting deceptive sales practices. That ruled out suing under that consumer-friendly remedy.

The mortgage-broker law, which allows people to sue brokers, also offered little hope because Delacruz wasn't a licensed broker. Other people involved in the Delacruz deals, such as appraisers and title agents, wouldn't be covered.

As for suing for fraud, it's extremely difficult for consumers in lending cases, Pierre-Louis said. Among other things, a person has to prove that he or she was personally defrauded. In cases such as Bird's, the lender — not the borrower — is the primary victim.

"We don't have the authority to stand in the shoes of the lender," Pierre-Louis said. "And often the lender doesn't care. All they know is you signed an agreement, or note, to pay what they remitted to you."

And as long as the borrower is current on payments, he said, lenders have little incentive to talk about disputed mortgages.

Bird had made all his payments. He was down to his last $1,600 and facing $12,000 a month in payments when Pierre-Louis told him to stop paying, hoping to force the lenders into a discussion.

In September 2004, Bird sued Delacruz and others under a federal racketeering law written to combat mobsters and drug dealers.

The hook: Delacruz used interstate wire transfers and the federal mail system to commit a crime, in this case mortgage fraud.

"The problem that we found," Pierre-Louis said, "is that it's extremely difficult to find any basis in Ohio to sue somebody like Delacruz."

Arson connection

Bird's first ray of hope came in September 2003.

An agent with the federal Bureau of Alcohol, Tobacco, Firearms and Explosives knocked on his door. He wanted to talk about houses in Cleveland that apparently had been torched.

He wanted to talk about Delacruz.

"Needless to say," ATF spokesman Patrick Baraducci said, "the thing started to unravel."

Local, state and federal investigators won't discuss how the dozen vacant houses that burned in 1999 and 2000 led them to Delacruz and mortgage fraud and, three years later, to Bird. They expect to charge others in the ongoing investigation.

Nobody has been charged with arson.

Ray McCarthy, an arson detective with the Cleveland Fire Division, credited neighborhood activists for helping to trace the properties and raise red flags. He declined to elaborate.

Anthony Brancatelli said he and other Slavic Village residents watched Delacruz buy and sell houses through fishy deals that caused runaway vacancy and blight in their already fragile neighborhood.

"He killed us," said Brancatelli, now a Cleveland city councilman. "He killed my neighborhood."

Bird, after months of fruitless efforts to get somebody's attention, had nearly given up hope when he found the ATF agent's note stuck in his front door.

Finally, somebody wanted to listen. If not for the fires, and a string of lucky coincidences, Bird figures he might be bankrupt by now, still viewed by authorities as a fool rather than a victim and key witness.

While acknowledging that he should have been more careful, Bird bristles when people suggest that his was a case of "buyer beware," of his own carelessness, not of criminal fraud.

"Anytime somebody says that, I want to knock the taste right out of their mouth," said Bird, who recently testified before a state Senate committee, urging reforms. "It's bull. At some point, you have to change the system. It's not enough to say it's OK because the system allows it."

Added his attorney: "You don't tell the victim of a crime it's your fault you've been victimized. But that's the attitude a lot of the lending institutions took. It's the attitude the law takes right now in a lot of senses."

Lasting damage

Though heartened by ATF's interest, Bird wasn't counting on help. He proceeded with his lawsuit.

Five months later, in February 2005, a federal grand jury in Cleveland indicted Delacruz and Laura E. Atkinson, his employee and appraiser, on 70 criminal counts including bank fraud, wire fraud and moneylaundering.

The scheme began in Cleveland. When code-enforcement officials there bore down on Delacruz — in 2001, a judge sentenced him to live in one of his ramshackle properties for a month — the pair moved to Columbus.

By the time of their indictment and arrest, they were living in southern California.

Delacruz pleaded guilty to 10 counts with penalties ranging from probation to 145 years in prison, although the plea bargain specifically requires some prison time. He's free pending sentencing on Jan. 20.

His lawyer, Thomas H. Bienert Jr. of San Clemente, Calif., didn't return repeated messages.

Atkinson, 56, who declined comment, pleaded guilty to bank fraud and mail fraud.

The criminal convictions didn't cancel the fraudulent mortgages that Bird signed.

A series of victories in Bird's racketeering lawsuit also didn't undo the debt. Bird won a $2 million judgment against Delacruz in August, 2½ years after reporting the scam. Bird hasn't been able to collect.

Others have settled, without admitting wrongdoing: sellers Green and Munce; Conestoga Title (also known as AmeriTitle); and Erin O'Keefe-Nehring of AmeriTitle. Bird and his attorney wouldn't discuss the settlements, citing confidentiality agreements.

Munce said he settled with Bird for $10,000 to avoid a costly legal fight, and denied wrongdoing. O'Keefe-Nehring couldn't be located.

When Bird stopped making mortgage payments in October 2004, the lenders began calling, as he'd hoped. He's still negotiating.

"All of these properties will be foreclosed on. They have to be," he said.

Bird said he has reached tentative agreements with four of the five lenders.

The deal: He won't fight the foreclosures, and the lenders will help him repair his credit. The lenders also have vowed not to sue him; when properties sell at a public sheriff's auction, lenders can go after the borrower if the sale doesn't fetch enough to cover the delinquent loan.

Despite the criminal convictions, ongoing investigation and $2 million judgment against Delacruz, Bird faces an uncertain financial future.

"I don't know if I'll ever be made whole."

Foreclosure 'Rescue' Can Be Risky, Costly

By Joseph Barrios
ARIZONA DAILY STAR
Tucson, Arizona | Published: 10.02.2005
Reprinted with permission.

How foreclosure rescue works

1. Foreclosure-rescue firms use public records and paid data services to gather information about homes at risk of foreclosure.

2. A company contacts homeowners and offers to help them avoid foreclosure, often with an offer like this: In exchange for ownership of the house, the foreclosure-rescue firm will make mortgage payments current, pay off the mortgage, pay $500 cash to the homeowner and allow the former owner to rent for 18 months with up to three months free.

3. The now-renter has the option of buying back the home at market value within 18 months. The renter must secure new financing.

4. If he is unable to secure financing within 18 months, the renter must move. The business is free to rent the house to someone else or sell the property and collect equity that has built over time.

In danger of losing her Green Valley home to foreclosure, Linda Carstensen thought the solution to her problems had arrived in the mailbox. The letter promised she could fix her credit and save her home. She picked up the phone - and ended up losing $750, and nearl losing her house.

Carstensen had turned to a foreclosure-rescue firm, which buys houses at a discount from homeowners at risk of foreclosure and then sells them at a profit if the former owners can't afford to buy them back later.

Tucsonans have filed at least 19 complaints in the last three years in court or with the state against foreclosure-rescue firms, and the list of unhappy customers has caught the eye of state Attorney General Terry Goddard, whose office is investigating several complaints. He wouldn't say how many, but Tucson bankruptcy attorney Eric Sparks says he has talked with Goddard's office about questionable transactions involving a half-dozen businesses.

Goddard stops short of saying Arizonans should avoid foreclosure-rescue firms, but he advises financially troubled homeowners to first seek help from a nonprofit financial-counseling organization. His office has sued one foreclosure rescue firm, a Tucson bankruptcy judge has shut down another, and a third is getting out of the business because defending itself against complaints from customers is proving too costly.

In Tucson, as many as 10 foreclosure-rescue firms are soliciting people in danger of losing their homes to foreclosure, said Sparks, who has filed complaints in Bankruptcy Court against three such businesses. Complaints against two are pending; a third, Foreclosure Rescue Services, agreed to stop doing business in Arizona after admitting to improper filing of bankruptcy cases. There are enough customers to keep the companies in business. In the second quarter of this year, nearly 10,000 Arizona homeowners had mortgages classified as seriously delinquent, according to the Mortgage Bankers Association.

That number could grow if mortgage rates continue to rise, pushing homeowners struggling to keep up with adjustable-rate and interest-only loans beyond their ability to make monthly mortgage payments. Consumer advocates say such homeowners often put down little or no money when they buy their houses, so they find it easier to walk away if they get into financial difficulty.

Most people would be better off selling their homes than turning to a foreclosure-rescue firm - especially in today's hot market, said Cris Poor of Family Housing Resources, a nonprofit Tucson organization that offers financial counseling

Even homeowners who wait until the last minute could sell their homes, said Judy Lowe, president of the Tucson Association of Realtors Multiple Listing Service. Homes here stay on the market an average of 26 days - and some sell in a day

"Why would anyone not put their home on the market and sell it at market value and protect their credit? I can't imagine how these other companies put their foot in the door," Lowe said. "If it's under $200,000 and it's priced right within the marketplace, there's no reason why it couldn't be sold in two weeks."

Promises made, cash offered

Foreclosure-rescue businesses find potential clients by perusing lists of homeowners in danger of foreclosure.

They make contact through letters, e-mails or phone calls. They also post signs offering quick sales with the option of buying homes back.   And   they   promise   free   rent   and   cash   bonuses. Foreclosure rescue provides a valuable service, said Tucson attorney Scott Gibson, whose firm represents Tucson-based Deed and Note Traders. It offers a chance for financially troubled homeowners to stay in their homes and to eventually own them again, he said. But it also can generate hard feelings. Deed and Note Traders' foreclosure rescue arm has bought 45 houses at risk of foreclosure in the last 10 years; seven clients have sued the company, claiming it violated the sale agreement.

The company has successfully defended its business practices in six of those cases. In the seventh, a judge ordered the company to return ownership of a house because paperwork was improperly prepared and there wasn't "fair consideration" for the deed transfer under bankruptcy law. There was no finding of fraud. "For many people in a foreclosure, saving the possession of their home and keeping the same neighbors totally outweighs whether their name will be on the deed or another company will be on the deed," said David Kinas, chief executive officer of Deed and Note Traders. Kinas writes an "Ask the Expert" advice column about residential real estate for Tucson.com, the Web site for the agency that handles the joint business functions of the Arizona Daily Star and the Tucson Citizen. Gibson said Deed and Note Traders pays a fee to run the "advertorial" column on Tucson.com .

In some cases, families buy back their houses. Deed and Note Traders bought a house in danger of foreclosure near East 22nd Street and South Wilmot Road for $83,500 in August 2003.

In August of this year, the family repurchased the house for $121,000 - a difference of $37,500.

That was not necessarily pure profit. Owners-turned-renters generally are allowed to stay in their homes and get two to three months' free rent as well as cash bonuses. And they're sometimes allowed to buy back their homes below market value.

Job loss, illness

Carstensen, the Green Valley resident, received a letter from Utah-based Foreclosure Rescue Services in January 2003.

A "foreclosure specialist" with the company said she could help Carstensen save her house and urged her to check out the company with the Better Business Bureau.

"That's what we did, we couldn't find anything wrong," Carstensen said. She signed on, eager for some relief after being laid off from a call-center job and then suffering through an illness. She paid the company $750 to design a custom program and "go to bat" for her with creditors. The company agreed to work with her to prevent a scheduled March 12, 2003, foreclosure sale, according to a complaint against the company that was part of her eventual bankruptcy case.

Carstensen became concerned when an appointment with a Tucson lawyer was canceled because it required a $500 fee she had not been told she would have to pay, according to her complaint. On March 11, the day before her home was to be auctioned, Carstensen called the company and was told she would have to file for bankruptcy herself, she said. With papers prepared by the company, Carstensen sped to Tucson and made it to bankruptcy court about 10 minutes before the office closed. It was just enough time to save her house, although she lost her new sport utility vehicle and is still about $22,000 in debt with medical and credit-card bills. She hired Sparks to represent her in the bankruptcy case. The company eventually admitted in a court order that it had improperly prepared bankruptcy petitions. U.S. Bankruptcy Judge Eileen W. Hollowell ordered it to stop conducting business of any kind in Arizona. The company later closed.

In a recent interview, Karl Hartley, a Utah resident and former owner of Foreclosure Rescue Services, denied any wrongdoing. He said the company became involved in a "little spat" with Sparks, and he said he agreed to shut the business here because of legal costs. "I don't live in Arizona. I didn't have the money to defend myself against all of his accusations," he said. His lawyer said it would cost roughly $50,000 to prepare a case, he said.

The Better Business Bureau - of Idaho - issued a warning in November 2003 about the company's mail solicitations. The same release warned consumers about the risk of losing their homes to companies offering help in avoiding foreclosure. The warning was posted on the BBB's Web site about eight months after Carstensen filed for bankruptcy. Virtual Realty faces lawsuit other foreclosure-rescue companies have faced scrutiny in recent years. The state Attorney General's Office filed a lawsuit in June against Virtual Realty Funding Co., a Phoenix company that conducted business in Tucson. The lawsuit, which claims an unspecified number of homeowners facing foreclosure were pressured into signing over their homes, is pending.

In an administrative order filed in July suspending the company's license, the state Department of Real Estate lists seven homeowners - two of them in Tucson - who claim employees misrepresented details of their agreement. The company promised but failed to get homeowners loans or failed to tell them their houses would be deeded to third parties, the order said.

Deed and Note Traders, which also renovates and resells houses, is shutting down its foreclosure-rescue arm because it has been challenged in court so frequently and CEO Kinas is worried the negative publicity will harm other parts of the business, Gibson said. Even so, Kinas says he has helped customers who needed a financial life raft. He pointed to the free financial advice on his company's Web site and to testimonials from customers who say they avoided foreclosure and later repurchased their homes. When asked last week, the company did not provide the name of a satisfied customer willing to be quoted.

Customers usually get two months' free rent and cash in their pockets, Gibson said. That leaves them better off than in a foreclosure, when they lose the house anyway and have to move out in two weeks.

"Are they really any worse off? At least they can hope they can purchase the house back - maybe get a better job or a second job," Gibson said. "People that have pursued claims against Deed and Note and others say, 'This is just terrible. You stole their equity.' We did them a favor. We let them stay in the house."

http://www.azstarnet.com/dailystar/dailystar/95926.ph

A (Complicit) Victim's Story

The allegations articulated within the following US Department of Justice press release are the basis for the following section. Seeking help, an as of yet un-indicted "co-signer" or "strawbuyer" contacted this forum, and in the course of trying to explain her unwitting participation in the scheme, provided a letter from her (then) attorney, which had been sent to one of her three foreclosing lenders, and the FBI. Per the co-signer's request, some names have been changed. The story is real.

Pair Indicted in LA Foreclosure Rescue Scheme

Martha Rodriguez, 33, Downey, California and Edward Seung Ok, 39, Torrance, California were indicted by a Los Angeles grand jury in connection with allegations that they falsely promised dozens of homeowners in Los Angeles County, California that they could stop foreclosures, according to media reports. The pair promised that co-signers on new loans would help the homeowners refinance their mortgages until they could clean up their credit and get their own new loans. Instead, according to media reports, the indictment alleged, Rodriguez and Seung used falsified mortgage applications to defraud lenders and the homeowners, causing losses of at least $8 million.

U.S. Department of Justice

Debra Wong Yang
United States Attorney
Central District of California

United States Courthouse
312 North Spring Street
Los Angeles, California 90012

PRESS RELEASE

FOR IMMEDIATE RELEASE
November 30, 2005

For Information, Contact Public Affairs
Thom Mrozek (213) 894-6947

TWO ARRESTED ON FEDERAL FRAUD CHARGES IN FORECLOSURE SCAM TARGETING HOMEOWNERS AND COMMERCIAL LENDERS

Los Angeles, CA - Two individuals operating real estate and escrow agencies in Downey and Seal Beach were arrested this morning for allegedly victimizing dozens of homeowners through misrepresentations and fraudulent transactions, and eventually robbing them of the equity in their homes.

In an indictment filed yesterday in United States District Court in Los Angeles, Martha Rodriguez and Edward Seung Ok were charged with 10 counts of mail fraud by operating a foreclosure scheme that targeted commercial lenders and homeowners in the cities of Lakewood, Wilmington, Carson, West Covina, La Puente, El Monte, Wilmington, Downey, Los Angeles and Asuza. The scheme allegedly caused losses of at least $8 million.

According to the indictment, the defendants would locate homeowners whose loans were in default by scouring databases that list pending foreclosure sales. The defendants would then pay others to visit the identified homeowners and convince them they could avoid forfeiture of their homes. When homeowners expressed interest, Rodriguez and Ok would meet with them and tell the homeowners that they could stop the foreclosure of their homes. Rodriguez and Ok explained that they would provide short-term loans to cover their debts. The victims were told that their homes would eventually be refinanced by "co-signers" with good credit, and that would help the homeowner qualify for a new loan. The defendants promised the homeowners that their credit would be improved within a period of 6 to 12 months.

The indictment further alleges that homeowners were asked by the defendants to sign various documents including loan applications, trust and grant deeds, while being assured they would not lose title to their homes. The defendants promised the deed would either be held in escrow or that the title would be returned to them once their credit was fixed.

The defendants continued the scheme by applying for loans, in some cases using straw buyers, who never intended to reside in the home. The straw buyers were paid a fee of up to $5,000. The loan applications included information relating to their income, bank account and employment. In other cases, the defendants would submit applications using the information and forged signatures of past clients, without their knowledge. The defendants would instruct the banks to wire the loan proceeds directly to their escrow accounts, and only a small portion of the loan proceeds would go to the homeowner. The majority of the loan proceeds would go to Rodriguez and her family members, Ok, and other unindicted coschemers, according to the indictment.

Rodriguez, 33, was taken into custody at her Downey residence this morning. Ok, 39, of Torrance, was arrested simultaneously at a probation office in Arcadia. Both are scheduled to make their initial appearances this afternoon in federal court in Los Angeles. If convicted on all counts of the indictment, Rodriguez and Ok each face a maximum possible penalty of 200 years in prison.

An indictment contains allegations that a defendant has committed a crime. Every defendant is presumed innocent unless and until proven guilty beyond a reasonable doubt.

This case is the result of an investigation by the Federal Bureau of Investigation.

Here is our initial e-mail conversation:

Strawbuyer / Co-Signer: (Editor's Note: hereafter "S")

Hi, I stumbled upon your website after finding out that I'm a victim of a mortgage fraud scheme. Just a little background, it was an "investment property" scam where people in foreclosure sold their homes on a temp basis until they fix their credit. I was one of the straw buyers and now I'm left with 3 properties totaling $1.5M. I've received notices of foreclosure on 2 of 3 properties and all the lenders are aware of the situation, along w/a FBI investigation. The sellers are currently living in the properties as tenants, but they haven't paid anything towards the loans. Can you assist with how to proceed w/the lenders? Thanks for all your help.

TheShortSalePro replies: I can assist you. I had a similar situation like this in Atlanta, Georgia, and also in New Jersey I would need for you to provide some documentation. Once you provide and I review the requested information, I would devise a list of questions you would need to answer. Then, we could proceed. What would be your "best case" desired result?

S says: Thanks for your quick response. My best case would be to remove my name from the properties and work on cleaning up my credit. I am willing to do all the foot work and talk to the banks myself. Would I be able to get some advice if I posted on the forum?

TheShortSalePro replies: If you are in financial distress, we could intervene and negotiate for their acceptance of a Deed-In-Lieu of foreclosure, which could allow you to walk away. or, we could assist in a preforeclosure sale. Are all three properties mortgaged with different lenders?

S says: I am currently working with three different banks on three different properties for a deed in lieu but I'm at the early stages and they haven't accepted at this point. They've only sent a pkg w/requested documentation. A few things though, I don't live in the properties and don't have access to them for the broker to do an appraisal. My loan app was forged and falsified so it'll show that I can't afford any of the mortgages. Do you think the DIL is the best approach? Otherwise for the sale, I would have to evict all the tenants and I don't know how long that process would take. I just want to get my name off of them ASAP. What happens if they deny the DIL?

TheShortSalePro replies: You don't have to evict tenants to list the property to sell. and if you are already speaking to the lenders about a DIL, you are on the right track. You are 1) the owner of record, and 2) the landlord of record, correct? You indicated that the mortgage lenders are "aware" of the situation. Being aware and being agreeable to let you off the hook are two different scenarios. Why did you feel it necessary to have an attorney when speaking to the FBI? Is the lawyer still working on your case?

S says: The lawyer is no longer working on the case but I wanted representation because the articles in the paper were identifying strawbuyers as co-conspirators. I asked him to stop all services after the meeting but prior to that, he was building up the entire situation like I was going to get indicted and have to possibly do time or pay fines. He handled my case like I was being convicted for homicide! Then when we met w/the FBI, he didn't say a word. My family was totally freaked out that I may end up in jail so I thought that was my best alternative since it was a criminal investigation. Now that the FBI has gotten the information they need to build their case, they're saying I have to deal w/the banks myself. Even though the banks are aware of fake loan docs, they're saying that I'm still responsible for everything. They say they deal w/fraud every day. Now I'm just trying to un-do this entire mess. I am the owner of record but none of the tenants are paying anything towards the mortgage and neither am I. I don't want to keep the properties as rental properties. I went the DIL route because I thought it would be the path of least resistance. I assumed w/a pre-sale, I would have to evict the tenants, find a realtor, etc. Do you think this may be a better approach? Since you're the expert, would you mind helping me devise a game plan?

TheShortSalePro replies: Please send overnight to me copies of the contracts for sale, the mortgage/notes, leases, foreclosure notices, and your requests for DIL consideration.

S says: What are the contracts for sale? Is that the purchase agreements or loan docs? What is the mortgage/notes? Is that the mortgage stmt I receive every month showing bal due? What are the leases? Lease agreements between me and seller/tenant? There was nothing in writing. I have foreclosure notices. The DIL requests were made on the phone. I did not make a written request. Sorry for all the questions. I know nothing about real estate, which is why I shouldn't have even gotten myself in this mess!

TheShortSalePro replies: I'll need, or anyone who may be able to help you, will need copies of the documents of the transactions. You were a straw buyer? Let's see the written agreements between you, and the sellers. You made application for mortgage loans? Did you keep copies of the applications, or any of the documents that were signed by you? Leases? Leases are the agreement between buyer/landlord and seller/tenant who were to pay rent to you..

S says: That's the big problem. I was brought into this as a straw buyer by a now ex-boyfriend. They said I would be a property investor. His friend and his friend's brother own the company that scammed everyone. Because of the "relationship," everything was verbal. There is no documentation of any agreement. I spoke w/one of the seller/tenants and she said she also didn't have anything in writing. I only have purchase agreements (w/my sig), loan docs (w/my sig), mortgage statements, and notices of intent to foreclose.

I just requested copies of the loan apps yesterday. I should get them by next week. I never filled one out so I'm assuming the were falsified and forged. The FBI also provided me a copy of the indictment against the escrow company.

I am 30 yrs old. I originally retained the same attorney as my ex, under his persuasion that we would save money by using the same guy. He requested a $3000 retainer from each of us and said that amount would cover cleaning up our credit entirely and representing us w/the FBI. Anything after the FBI meeting would be extra or referred if he couldn't handle it. A month later, I get an invoice for $4500, less retainer and I was still in the same situation as the day I hired him. 2 foreclosures and still haven't talked w/the FBI. I wasn't confident w/his abilities so far and no longer wanted to deal w/my ex so my family hired a criminal attorney. Of course, this attorney said my civil attorney was unqualified to handle this type of case. My bill after meeting w/the FBI was $8000. No promises from either attorney were made in writing. In the end, I feel like I paid $11,000 to tell my story 4x to different people.

I've attached the letter my original attorney sent to all 3 lenders and the FBI.

December 16, 2005

Ms. XXX, Manager
Risk Management Department
New Century Loans
1610 E. St. Andrew Place, Suite B150
Santa Ana, CA 92705

RE: *S (trawbuyer / Co-Signer)* :

Dear Ms. XXX:

As we discussed on the telephone on December 7th, I have been retained to represent *S* with regard to the aforementioned loans. You indicated in our telephone conversation that you would forward a copy of this correspondence to Mr. BS, an attorney in the Loss Mitigation Department of New Century Loans. Please provide me with the contact information for Attorney BS, including his telephone and facsimile numbers and his mailing address. I also request that both you and Attorney BS separately confirm that you have received this correspondence via letters addressed to me.

I have enclosed a copy of an article which appeared in the Los Angeles Times on December 6, 2005. Unfortunately, that article mischaracterizes the situation of the people whose credit was used to obtain these fraudulent loans. These unfortunate borrowers, including my client, were also defrauded by Mr. X and Madame Y. This letter will set forth the process by which : *S* was defrauded. Marvin Lee, the boyfriend of: *S*, has been a casual acquaintance of Wes Ok, the younger brother of Edward Ok, for about ten years. In the past two years, Marvin and Ed started spending more social time together. In early May 2005, Wes invited Marvin out to dinner at a Korean restaurant in Torrance. Wes arrived in his new Porsche. At the dinner Wes explained that his brother Ed had opened a real estate business, Deko, Ltd., that Wes was working with Ed and they had been very successful. In fact, they were so successful that Wes had just purchased his Porsche and was looking into purchasing another one and Ed had just purchased a Lamborghini. Wes asked whether Marvin had good credit and Marvin replied that he did. Wes said Deko, Ltd. locates own-ers with homes in foreclosure who want to keep their homes but cannot do so because they have bad credit. Deko, Ltd. buys these properties using investors and holds the properties for one year. During that year, the sellers fix their credit and reapply for a loan to buy their house back. All parties are protected through utilizing the services of Bellasi Escrow. Bellasi would protect the sellers by holding their titles, so the buyers could not sell their homes. Bellasi would also protect the buyers by holding one year's worth of mortgage payments in an escrow account, thereby insuring payments are made and the buyer's credit is protected. This escrow account was to be created by pulling equity out of the homes at closing. Should the sellers be unwilling or unable to make the monthly payments, Bellasi would make the payments. In the event that the entire escrow account had been used be-fore the end of one year, the sellers understood they would be evicted and their homes would be sold. The sellers want to keep their homes, so they are motivated to and will make the payments. Wes said in the worst case scenario, where the sellers had to be evicted, Deko would do the eviction. After the eviction, the investor would sell the prop-erty directly to Deko, which would pay all additional mortgage and renovation costs and keep all of the profits from the sale of the property or the investor could pay a portion of the additional costs and share in the profits from the sale. Wes asked Marvin if he would be interested in purchasing investment properties. Each investor would be able to purchase from four to eight investment properties. When Marvin stated that he did not earn enough income to support any properties, Wes said it did not matter because payments would be made by the sellers, with the escrow accounts held by Bellasi Escrow as a safety net. Wes said there are many advantages to being an investor. The first advantage is getting a tax break because you are able to write off all the interest on your taxes. The second advantage is building your credit. The final advantage is getting an upfront management fee for each property. Investors are paid management fees of $6500-7500 for properties over $500,000 and management fees of $4000-5000 for properties under $500,000. In exchange for the management fee, Deko, Ltd. requires that the investors call each bank each month for payment status. If payments had not been made by the 10th of each month, investors were to contact Sheila Milstead at Bellasi Escrow to make the payments. It should be noted that Wes, Ed and Marvin are all Korean. In the Korean community, it is quite common for business deals to be done based upon a handshake, with no written documentation at all. Many Koreans are very trusting of other Koreans. Relying on their friendship and Wes and Ed's apparent success, Marvin thought this was a good investment. Marvin is organized and never late on payments but was still concerned about being able to afford multiple properties. Wes assured Marvin that his good credit would be enough and it did not matter how much he earned because these were investment properties, meaning the tenants pay-ments would cover the mortgage and Bellasi Escrow would be his insurance. After the dinner, Wes and Marvin went drinking. As usual, Wes paid for the dinner and the drinking. About a week later Wes, his brother Ed, and Ed's two-year-old son met with Marvin at the same Korean restaurant in Torrance. Ed reassured Marvin by going over the whole invest-ment process again, also adding that he has been so successful that he had purchased a $5,000,000 home in Huntington Harbour. Ed said stocks are too risky and real estate is the only way to make money. Marvin decided to go forward with the offer. Marvin believed Ed and Wes because they said they had been doing this for a while, they had friends who had done it, and everyone was making money. They were driving nice cars and throwing money around, so they appeared to be successful entrepreneurs. Although Marvin owns his residence, he has no prior experience with investment real estate. Marvin was grateful that Wes was giving him an opportunity to learn about real estate investing. Shortly thereafter, Wes and Ed started faxing Marvin purchase agreements for multiple properties and Marvin was working with Sheila Milstead at Bellasi Escrow to get the paperwork completed. Wes explained that Marvin would be signing multiple purchase agreements at one time because Bellasi did not want to hurt his credit by running credit checks too many times. They would batch the properties and just run the credit one time. Marvin signed the purchase agreements and faxed them back. A notary named Troy Folk came to Marvin's office and Marvin signed two sets of loan documents. About a week after signing the two sets of loan documents, Marvin met with Wes and Wes gave Marvin a check for $7500 from Bellasi Escrow and another check for $5000, which was a personal check from Wes.

Wes had told Marvin that if he knew anyone else with good credit, he should give Wes their name and they could do the same deal with them. After Marvin received the two checks, he thought it was a good investment and introduced his girlfriend, , S to Wes to become an investor. This is how S got involved in late July, 2005. S also has no knowledge of real estate nor does she own her residence. S went through the same process as Marvin, signed four sets of loan documents, was approved for three properties, and received two checks, each for $6500 from Wes' personal checking account. By the time the third loan for a property on Hadden Avenue in Los Angeles was approved, Bellasi was under investigation and no check was received for that property. S never received closing statements on any of these properties so she had no idea how the proceeds of the loans were disbursed at the time of the closing. After S was approved for her investment properties, the first payments were due on October 1, 2005. After dutifully calling the banks and finding out that the payments were not received, S called Bellasi Escrow. Sheila explained that all accounts held by Bellasi were frozen and under FBI investigation and she had no idea why. Sheila assured S that they were doing everything in their power to resolve the situation and to be patient. By October 7, 2005, S was getting nervous because she was already receiving collection calls from the lenders. S told that the payments must be received by the following week and her credit would be affected if the payments were not made. A meeting was arranged on October 10, 2005 between Ed, Wes, Marvin, and S said he was working with Bellasi to resolve the problem and this had never happened before. Ed urged S to make the payments to save her credit and said he would reimburse her with 10% interest. Ed promised that if funds at Bellasi were not released by November 1st, he would make all of the payments himself. Ed just needed his attorneys to draft the agreement. S made payments on two first mortgages and two second mortgages at Fremont Investment & Loan and People's Choice Home Loan on October 16th. November 1st arrived and Ed and Wes were now avoiding all calls from S . Bellasi Escrow closed their doors and Sheila Milstead left the company. The few times S was able to speak with Ed or Wes, Ed and Wes responded that everything was on hold pending approval from their attorneys. The lenders were aggressively calling for payment and threatening Notices of Intent to Foreclose. At this point, S could not make the multiple mortgage payments and her only hope was that Deko, Ltd. would help when they could since the Bellasi funds were frozen. On November 30, 2005, S saw on Fox 11 O'clock News that Edward Ok and Martha Rodriguez were arrested for mortgage fraud. She then found articles in the LA Times uncovering the scam. S first learned through these sources that she had been victimized along with the homeowners. S was fraudulently induced into entering into three purchases via this scam. The first property loans are with Fremont Investment & Loan. The first mortgage is for $504,000 at $3528.00 per month and the second mortgage is for $126,000 at $1070.99

per month. The second property loans are with People's Choice Home Loan, Inc. The first mortgage is for $405,600 at $2630.72 per month and the second mortgage for $101,400 at $889.11 per month. The third property, on which you made the loans. The first mortgage is for $308,000 at $2008.42 per month and the second mortgage is for $77,000 at $713.00 per month. *S* was told that the sellers, who remained on the property as tenants, would make the payments on the loans. Failing that, Bellasi Escrow was to make the payments out of the seller's escrow account and, failing that, Wes and Ed said that they would make the payments. *S* cannot afford to make payments on these three properties and wants to deed them back in lieu of foreclosure.

Subsequent to our telephone conversation, I discovered some disturbing information. I was told by reliable sources that New Century Loans has known about these fraudulent loans for several months. When you and I spoke on December 7th, you appeared to be unaware of the fraud committed by Bellasi Escrow. Perhaps you were made aware of this fraud in connection with one of the other names used by Martha Rodriguez and Edward Ok, which was Silvernet. In spite of the fact that your company knew that these loans were fraudulently obtained, New Century Loans continued aggressive collection activities against *S* and has now filed notices of default against her credit, damaging the credit of my client. Such activities on the part of New Century Loans when it had knowledge that these loans were fraudulently obtained constitute unfair and deceptive trade practices and are prohibited by Business and Professions Code Sections 17200 – 17210.

In any event, if you were personally unaware of this fraud prior to our telephone conversation, you have now been informed about the fact that *S* was defrauded by Martha Rodriguez, Bellasi Escrow, Edward Ok and Deko, Ltd. Any further collection or foreclosure action and any further reporting against the credit of *S* is a continuing violation of the Unfair Practices Act and is prohibited by Business and Professions Code Sections 17200 - 17210.

We would like to work with you to resolve this situation in an amicable manner. *S* wants to repair her formerly excellent credit and wants to deed back to New Century Loans in lieu of foreclosure the property. *S* hereby requests that all collection and foreclosure action cease with regard to these loans, that no negative credit information regarding *S* be transmitted to the credit reporting agencies and that any negative credit information already transmitted to the credit reporting agencies regarding *S* , including, but not limited to, notices of default and notices of intent to foreclose, be removed from her credit reports.

Please confirm to me in writing within ten days of today's date that all collection and foreclosure action has ceased with regard to the loans of *S*, that you have initiated the deed in lieu of foreclosure process, that no further negative credit information regarding *S* will be transmitted to the credit reporting agencies and that any negative credit information already transmitted to the credit reporting agencies regarding *S*, including, but not limited to, notices of default and notices of intent to foreclose, has been removed from her credit reports. Should you fail to respond, we will have no choice but to bring an action against New Century Loans for violation of the Unfair Practices Act. Thank you very much for your cooperation.

Sincerely,
Attorney for the Strawbuyer *(S)*
Enclosure

CC: Strawbuyer / Co-Signer

As of this writing, the Strawbuyer has discontinued her relationship with her lawyer. She is cooperating with law enforcement officials, considering the voluntary return of her ill-gotten gain, and has offered to convey title to the mortgaged property to the foreclosing lenders via a Deed In Lieu of foreclosure. Of course, this might help her escape prosecution, but does nothing to help the homeowners who were scammed and, consequently, lost their homes.

Coincidently, thinking there might be some Truth In Lending and Regulation Z violations that could help extricate *S* from the mess, I referred her to a Rhode Island based company that "specializes" in such matters. The next day *S* called to tell me that the "company" was less interested in helping her to resolve her problem and more interested in snatching the deeds from her presumably to further exploit the situation. Go figure.

HONESTLY, WHAT <u>ARE</u> THEIR OPTIONS?

an Essay by TheShortSalePro ©2006

Method salesmen, and creative real estate seminar pitchmen will try to convince you that homeowners in foreclosure have little choice but to hand you their deed and keys. They'll tell you that many homeowners don't know what their homes are worth, and are resigned to losing their home without so much as a passing, backward glance. In fact, they'll say, many will be grateful for an opportunity to simply walk away from their mess allowing you to profit from their misfortune by using this technique or that technique. Once in a while, that may be true. But not with the frequency implied. In 25+ years, working with hundreds upon hundreds of families facing foreclosure seeking help, I've never met with a single homeowner willing to walk away from their equity. Never. So often their equity was initially a down payment gift or inheritance from a deceased parent or grandparent. Oh, at first they may pretend not to care, that losing their home doesn't matter that much, but when pencil hits paper they will.

In my experience, the majority of distressed homeowners profess to know what their home is worth. What they mean is they think they know what their neighbor's homes are worth. They'll know the asking or listed price, and they'll know if the house was smaller or larger than their own. But, they might not appreciate upgrades that had been installed, its general condition, or what the final sales price had been. When comparing their home to their neighbor's homes, most overlook functional obsolescence and deferred maintenance, and fail to consider the time factor of foreclosure.

I'd agree that most distressed homeowners think their homes are worth more than they really are worth. That mistaken assumption can become a problem when the success of a non foreclosure alternative is contingent upon the property's value. If its worth what they've stated, they might qualify for a refinance. If its worth a little less, or a lot less, their hopes are dashed.

During the lead-up to declaration of default and foreclosure, the mortgagee will usually present the mortgagor a menu of generic, non foreclosure alternatives, and a list of local non profit credit or housing counselors. Conventionally recommended non foreclosure alternatives which may be available include assumptions, compromised or short sale, deed-in lieu of foreclosure, deferments, forbearance, modifications, preforeclosure sale, partial claim, recast, refinancing, and streamline refinance.

Conventionally recommended non foreclosure alternatives include:

REFINANCE. With adequate equity, homeowners can try to pay off their old loan with a new loan from a new lender. A streamline refinance option would be offered by your existing lender.

FORBEARANCE. Qualified homeowners may be able to convince their lender to temporarily reduce or suspend payments until the hardship has been resolved, allowing the homeowner the chance to catch up on the delinquent amount.

MORTGAGE MODIFICATION. The terms of the loan agreement may be permanently changed to extend the length of repayment, reduce the interest rate, re-amortize, or any combination that will result in long term affordability.

PARTIAL CLAIM. HUD might intervene, and provide a small, interest free, second mortgage loan to bring the first mortgage loan current.

BANKRUPTCY. An attorney's advice might result in an affordable repayment plan.

PREFORECLOSURE SALE. The homeowner might be able to salvage equity and protect future creditworthiness by selling the home before the forced, public foreclosure sale.

PREFORECLOSURE SHORT SALE. If the sellers owe more than their homes are worth, their lender(s) can permit the sale by accepting less than they are contractually due.

DEED IN LIEU OF FORECLOSURE. The homeowner may be able to 'give back' the property to the lender.

Despite several requests that the homeowner contact their lender to discuss possible workout options, why do so many delinquencies result in foreclosure? One reason might be that when the home-owner calls for help as directed, the mortgagee representative isn't properly trained to identify situation appropriate workout options. Additionally, homeowners may be distrustful of their lenders' actions. Many homeowners believe, mistakenly, the lenders' real objective is to take their home.

When homeowners' loans are foreclosed, the foreclosure lawsuit documents may become public knowledge, and 'listed' by information providers. These entrepreneurs sell these lists to subscribers seeking such information (leads). Homeowners' mailboxes soon overflow with solicitations from lawyers, mortgage brokers, real estate brokers, consultants, etc., all offering simple solutions to their complex problem. From these slick solicitations, many homeowners glean a basic, but false idea, as to what their options might be, and mistakenly presume that all options they've read or heard about are available to them.

During early stages of default, homeowners aren't too receptive to the idea of probative credit counseling, selling their home, or filing bankruptcy. They want a quick fix. Why do so many distressed homeowners hesitate to implement a proactive solution? It isn't so much that they are in 'denial' and aren't willing to face the facts as is commonly parroted by disappointed, speculative investors whose proposals have been rejected. While they know they have a problem, they lack of understanding as to the seriousness of the problem. To their thinking, all they need is a little 'catch-up' loan. They are looking for a short term fix to a long term problem. While they think they may 'know' what the short term fixes are, they might not be ready to pursue conventionally accepted options until it's too late.

For example, let's consider the idea of *foreclosure bail-out/refinance loans*. Newspaper classified ads and direct mail solicitations suggest foreclosure bailout loans are as commonplace as if ordering a pizza. Homeowners believe the hype, but eventually realize that approvals, rates and terms are conditioned upon loan to value, and creditworthiness. They learn, too, about loan application fees and appraisal fees which are payable at their door at the time of appraisal. They also learn about rigid underwriting criteria, and only after their 'competitive' rate loan application has been rejected, do they learn about alternative 'loan to own' programs designed to separate a procrastinating owner from his home, and his equity.

The fact is that folks with lousy credit, but with sufficient equity can still refinance their foreclosed mortgage, replacing it with a loan that carries a higher rate of interest, shorter term, and loaded with more default triggers. These 'subprime' loan programs offer a win/win scenario to the new lender. If the borrower makes the payments, the lender, having already pocketed big upfront fees, continues to collect big interest. If the borrower fails to make the payments, there is an adequate cushion of equity that anticipates foreclosure, and full net recovery.

When seeking a *forbearance* the homeowner must demonstrate to the lender that their hardship, proximate cause to the default, was temporary and will be resolved shortly, or has already been resolved. They can do this by presenting a 'back to work' letter from a physician or employer, or paystubs that establish additional income. The forbearance, if granted, suspends collection activity for a specific period of time allowing the financially distressed homeowner to regain financial stability. The homeowner should seek a forbearance only when they see real light at the end of the tunnel. I woulda, shoulda, coulda (got that job) simply won't fly.

Homeowners seeking *mortgage modification* must have already resolved their financial hardship. The lender must be convinced that the homeowner can now afford a regularly scheduled payment, even if that payment is less than the amount of the previous payment. The lender will then consider the cost to foreclose, vs. the cost to modify the terms of the loan agreement. If it makes financial sense to reduce the interest rate, &/or extend the term of the loan rather than devote resources to foreclose, they will.

If the *partial claim* program is available, homeowners seeking the HUD partial claim must have an FHA insured loan, and qualify for specific relief. Information on HUD loss mitigation programs is available on line at www.HUD.gov. Information on VA insured loan loss mitigation programs may be found on line at www.homeloans.va.gov.

For homeowners who cannot afford the mortgage lender's reinstatement program, *bankruptcy* may offer an affordable repayment plan designed to help the borrower to keep the home. Typically, a Chapter 13 Bankruptcy plan will 'force' the lender to begin accepting the previously rejected, regularly scheduled, monthly payment. The homeowner will make additional, predetermined payments to the bankruptcy trustee which represent a portion of the amount of missed payments, including fees, costs, etc. The trustee will distribute the additional payment to creditors, including the mortgagee. Chapter 13 repayment plans may be devised and completed from within 36 to 60 monthly installments.

If the homeowner successfully completes the plan, the bankruptcy is discharged and the mortgage loan is considered current. Even though bankruptcy laws have recently changed, this still affords a viable option for the qualified, distressed homeowner.

Some property owners facing the loss of their home to foreclosure decide to sell their property via a *preforeclosure sale*. Some attempt to sell the home without using a real estate broker, instead, relying on a yard sign and placing ads in local newspapers. Some will list their home with a full service real estate broker, or one which offers a scaled down version of professional help in exchange for a discounted fee. These homeowners are reluctant, but resigned to sell to avoid foreclosure. They hope by marketing their home early on in the foreclosure process, they'll sell at close to full retail value. Unfortunately, at this point, those homeowners who utilize the services of a real estate broker fail to disclose the pending foreclosure to their broker, and consequently the property is introduced to the market with an inflated asking price. As a result, their property often languishes unsold as foreclosure costs continue to accrue. Ill-informed real estate brokers, thinking they have ample time to implement price corrections, often learn, too late, that a foreclosure sale has been scheduled, and rapidly approaches. This presents a two fold problem for the seller. Firstly, prospective buyers now know that the sellers are between a rock and a hard place, and will be inclined to accept any reasonable offer, and, secondly, it sharply reduces the available time to market, secure a buyer, and close. Instead of having months and weeks, they now may have but weeks and days.

In the case of homeowners resigned to sell, who face foreclosure but have several months or more before the foreclosure auction, the best advice I could give would be to 1) make sure they understand and respect the foreclosure timeline, 2) determine their home's actual as-is, fair market value, 3) list with an established real estate broker at a competitive price.

When circumstances dictate the need for an expedited sale, and/or if the property is in poor physical condition, the seller should be introduced to speculative investors who purchase properties, for cash, in as-is condition, but often at a steep discount.

If the homeowner is resigned to sell, but owes more than the property is worth, a preforeclosure sale is still possible. If the property is in poor physical condition, this may be an excellent opportunity for a speculative investor to pursue a preforeclosure short sale.

As a last resort, a homeowner, unable to refinance, sell, or otherwise avoid the loss of the home to foreclosure, may ask the lender to accept a deed in lieu of foreclosure. In theory, under certain conditions, the homeowner would execute a special deed, hand over the keys, and in exchange for a release of liability, simply walk away.

That option is included in just about every mortgagee provided boilerplate, menu of non-foreclosure alternatives I've seen. Just about every homeowner I've counseled believes this is a common practice. Truth be told, I haven't seen that option employed very often. Maybe once or twice over two decades by first mortgagees. I have been told, though, that nowadays many junior mortgagees are willing to accept a DIL rather than go through an expensive foreclosure process. But, I haven't seen it.

The majority of families who face mortgage foreclosure will solve their problem before losing their home. There are those who procrastinate, or experience additional hardship(s), and may be inclined to accept a lowball offer, or participate in a creative technique that they think is to their advantage.

I'd like to take this opportunity to describe the foreclosure process as it exists in New Jersey, a judicial mortgage foreclosure jurisdiction, then an examination of their non-foreclosure options.

A judicial mortgage foreclosure begins with the lender filing a lawsuit, and unless or until the debt is repaid, will result with the property sold at a public Sheriff's Sale.

The New Jersey Foreclosure Process And Timeline

- **Pre FORECLOSURE/COLLECTIONs**
  Courtesy reminder calls, late notices, threats implying foreclosure.

- **Letter of Intent to FORECLOSE**
  Written notice giving Borrower 30 days to cure default and avoid further legal action.

- **FORECLOSURE**
  Lender files lawsuit in FORECLOSURE, Lender seeks and is awarded final judgment, Sheriff authorized (Writ of Execution) to conduct public sale.

- **SHERIFF'S SALE**
  Sheriff advertises sale in local papers, highest bidder is awarded your HOUSE

- **ROR (Right of Redemption)**
  Former homeowner has 10 days to 'redeem' and buy back the house.

- **Eviction**

New Jersey Mortgage Foreclosure, And The NJ Fair Foreclosure Act Of 1995

This essay will define several key terms that relate to the foreclosure process, the Fair Foreclosure Act of 1995, and its impact upon both Borrower, and Lender.

Assuming the foreclosure is uncontested, and there are no delays, the timeline from the date the foreclosure file is first received, to expiration of Right of Redemption to the recordation of Sheriff's Deed, will take less than one year. As you can imagine, politically influential lending giants are working hard everyday to reduce the time it takes to foreclose. A perfect example of this influence is the recent bankruptcy legislation that makes filing bankruptcy problematic for the distressed homeowner.

A mortgage is a security instrument that pledges property in exchange for repayment of a loan. The Borrower gives the mortgage to a Lender/Investor in exchange for the loan of money. A lender/investor can be anyone or anything including a Corporate Conglomerate, a local or National Bank, an Investment House, an Insurance Company, a Pension Fund Manager, or a rich Uncle.

Most Lenders engage mortgage loan servicing companies (Chase, CitiMortgage, GMAC, Washington Mutual, Countrywide, Greentree, MTG Electronic, etc.) for the administration of the mortgage loan including the collection of monthly payments of principal and interest, penalties on late payments, acting as an escrow agent for collected funds to pay property taxes, insurance, and if necessary, to cure defaults and initiate foreclosure when a homeowner's payments are seriously delinquent.

Mortgage Loans are to be repaid according to the terms and conditions indicated in a Mortgage Note, a document that accompanies the mortgage and details how the loan will be repaid, and what consequences the Borrower may face if the loan isn't repaid according to the terms of the note.

If the Borrowers default, or fail to make payments as agreed, the Lender may initiate an expensive and complicated legal process that can result in the forced, public sale of the property, and displacement of the former homeowner. This process is called mortgage foreclosure, and is the Lender's remedy of choice. Let me repeat that: **Foreclosure is the lender's remedy of choice!**

Despite rosy economic forecasts, evidence suggests that more people are facing mortgage default and foreclosure today than at any time since the Great Depression. In NJ, there are approximately 1200 new foreclosure filings each month, and not surprisingly, NJ leads the nation in bankruptcy filings. Soon, distressed homeowners seeking to file a petition for bankruptcy will find it more difficult, and more expensive. With limited awareness, few people understand this growing trend, or related legislation that may prove to exact an adverse impact upon us all.

Lenders anticipate that a certain number of Borrowers will default, and that a certain number of loans will be foreclosed. Historically, foreclosure would only benefit lenders during good economic times. But when real estate markets have excessive inventories of unsold homes, and a buyer pool whose employment is largely unstable foreclosure might not be in the best financial interest for lenders seeking to recover money were it not for PMI (private mortgage insurance).

Many mortgage lenders, as a condition of making a loan, require that the Borrower purchase (for the lender's benefit) an insurance policy insuring against losses sustained by the Lender arising from Borrower default. PMI is a Lender's safety net. When and if the Borrower defaults to the terms of the loan, the Lender forecloses, liquidates but doesn't recover enough to satisfy the debt (called a deficiency) the PMI will pay a claim to the Lender in an amount represented in a percentage up to the Lender's actual out of pocket losses in some cases, depending upon the limits of the policy, up to 100%. But that doesn't help you, the Borrower, or let you off the financial hook. You could still owe money long after you've lost your home!

For this essay, "equity" may be defined as the value in a home remaining after debt after all liens are paid, and after all costs of sale are considered.

The portion of the amount a homeowner borrows for either a purchase or refinance compared against the value of the home is called Loan To Value, or LTV, for short, and expressed as a ratio. The maximum allowable LTV is determined by several factors of risk including the value and condition of the home, and the Borrower's creditworthiness. LTV ranges from 60% for a poor credit Borrower with a home needing some TLC, to 100% or even 125% for some well qualified Borrowers whose homes are picture perfect.

Risk also plays a factor when a lender decides at what interest a loan will be made. The greater the risk (or perceived risk) the higher the interest charged. A poor credit Borrower will pay a greater interest rate than a Borrower with a better credit history.

A loan payment is considered to be late if the lender has not yet received and applied payment by the due date. Though the Servicer may or may not may not charge a late fee during a complimentary 'grace' period the payment is still considered to be late, and the Borrower in breach. Typically, once a payment is 'late' a data based, computer generated letter is sent that advises the Borrower of a late fee, and reminds the Borrower to send in the payment and accompanying late fee. Other "preliminary" procedures that the Servicer implements include, but is not limited to placing a call or calls to the Borrower's home, place of work, a neighbor's home, or another family member's home with a "friendly" reminder. If passive collection techniques don't work, the account is transferred from the first tier collection clerks to 'default collection specialists' who threaten the Borrower with foreclosure, eviction, and homelessness (hoping to coerce the Borrower into sending a payment) but simultaneously preparing to foreclose.

In response to the public's fears of dramatic increases in mortgage foreclosure, the Fair Foreclosure Act of 1995 was initially intended to protect consumers by introducing legislation that would enact a set of uniform rules and practices which foreclosing lienholders would observe. However, pressure from financial giants GE Capital, Ford Consumer Credit, CitiCorp, GMAC and others threatening to withdraw from the NJ market while demanding self-serving legislation caused the original draft to be revised several times over several years.

How the Fair Foreclosure Act actually 'protects' distressed homeowners, or how "fair" it really is for Borrowers is open for debate. and that is the subject for another essay. But here is a statistic. Before the Fair Foreclosure Act took effect, the average time needed to complete a mortgage foreclosure in NJ was 610 days. Now, ten years later, it's closer to 290 days. Clearly a win for the major mortgage lenders.

The Fair Foreclosure Act (hereafter FFA) applies only to residential mortgages on property of less than four units, where one unit is occupied or will be occupied by the Borrower or the Borrower's immediate family at the time the loan is made. Though it was FFA's intent to protect Borrowers from huge, corporate lenders, in practice the FFA benefits foreclosing lenders' recovery process by insuring consistency in preliminary notification, thus reducing the number of (expensive and time consuming) challenges resulting in a more expedient, uniform process.

The Foreclosure Clock Begins To Tick..

The FFA's first requirement for lenders is that they provide the Borrower with a <u>30 day notice of the lender's intent to foreclose</u>. A written notice must be sent by certified or registered mail to the property address, and to the Borrower's last known address. The Borrower has 30 days to pay the amount in default to avoid further legal action (and costs) imposed by the Lender.

The Notice of Intent (NOI) must include:

1) A description of the obligation or real estate security interest;

2) The nature of the default;

3) The right of the Debtor to reinstate the loan;

4) The amount of money needed to fully reinstate the loan;

5) The date by which the reinstatement must be tendered, which shall not be less than 30 days from the date the notice is effective; the name, address and telephone number of the individual to whom the reinstatement should be sent;

6) What actions the Lender will take, such as foreclosure, if the reinstatement does not occur;

7) The Borrower's liability for the payment of all attorney fees and courts costs if reinstatement occurs subsequent to the commencement of foreclosure;

8) The Borrower's right, if any, to transfer the property subject to the security instrument;

9) The Borrower's right to be represented by legal counsel, and who to contact in the event he/she is unable to afford legal counsel;

10) The possible availability of financial assistance from state, federal or nonprofit groups, if any. This requirement is satisfied by attaching a list of programs promulgated by the Commissioner of Banking; and

11) The name, address and telephone number of a lender representative who the Borrower can contact if the Borrower disagrees with the mortgagee's assertions of the debt or defaulted amount.

(This Notice does not replace HUD or VA notification requirements. The FFA allows the Borrower to cure the default, subsequent to the expiration of the NOI, and prior to entry of final judgment, once every 18 months. After entry of final judgment, the Lender may or may not accept reinstatement at it's discretion.)

After the NOI expires, and the Borrower neither challenges or cures the default, the Lender can move to foreclose the mortgage, and force the public auction (Sheriff Sale) of the property to repay the debt.

Now, the Borrower's financial problem has been compounded into a financial *and* legal problem.

The Lender (Plaintiff) begins by filing a Complaint and a lawsuit is born. All parties having an interest in the property (Borrowers, junior lienholders, tenants, etc.) must be named and included as Defendants, and served a copy of the Summons and Complaint.

Usually, the service of the complaint is made to the Defendant, or any member of the Defendant's household over the age of 14 by a process server or a Sheriff's Deputy. The Defendant has 35 days to Answer the Complaint.

If NO Answer is forthcoming, the Lender must send a "notice of intention to take final judgment" to the Borrower, giving the Borrower a chance to reinstate the mortgage. If the Borrowers respond to the notice within 10 days that they intend to reinstate with 45 days the Lender must wait 45 days before entering the judgment.

On the 46th day, the Lender will move to enter the Default Judgment which consists of the amount due, plus all costs including attorneys' fees, and a Writ of Execution directing the sale of the mortgaged property.

Following Entry of Final Judgment and the Court's issuance of the Writ of Execution, the Lender will forward it's request to schedule a Sheriff's Sale. The Sheriff will advertise the Sale once a week for four consecutive weeks. The Borrowers are entitled to two adjournments, each for 14 days.

Redemption. If within 10 days following the Sheriff's Sale, the former Homeowner can pay all amounts due, he can redeem the house. This doesn't mean that the loan will be reinstated. But that the former Homeowner has an opportunity to 'buy back' the house for what was owed plus any costs, fees, penalties, commissions, or premiums owed to the successful bidder at Sheriff's Sale.

If there are no bidders at the Sheriff's Sale, and the former Homeowner cannot 'redeem' the property within the statutory 10 days, the Lender is awarded a Sheriff's Deed, and takes back the property. The Lender can now list the home with a real estate broker and sell the property. If the property isn't sold such that proceeds are enough to satisfy the debt.. The Lender may pursue a deficiency judgment in the amount between the full amount of the debt, less what was recovered at sale. Sometimes the former homeowner must continue to pay for a home that they no longer own.

Eviction. Evictions are horrible to witness. I've seen a few, and the gut wrenching and tear jerking experience still haunts me to this day. But the dissolution and splintering of a family, the destruction of "home", the physical eviction of clothes, toys, books, food, and memories, homelessness, and years of post foreclosure credit problems are a natural consequence of failing to make timely, proactive decisions when facing mortgage foreclosure.

Following mortgage foreclosure and Sheriff's Sale, there are two main types of eviction proceedings: (former) mortgagor eviction, and tenant eviction. In (former) mortgagor eviction, the Clerk of the Superior Court forwards a Writ of Possession (an order) to the Sheriff. The Sheriff demands that the former owners vacate the premises within a prescribed period (about two weeks). If the former owners do not leave voluntarily, they are physically evicted on the date set forth by the Sheriff. A locksmith changes the locks, a moving company empties the premises.

A foreclosing mortgagee who acquires tenant occupied property can evict by showing 'good cause' including, but not limited to: the failure to pay rent; failing to maintain/destruction of the leased premises; failure to enter into a new lease when asked to do so following Sheriff's Sale; or failure to vacate if the tenant had been notified that the new owner wanted to use the property as a personal residence. Only a court of competent jurisdiction can order the eviction of a tenant.

Deficiency. The amount a Borrower still owes a Lender *after* the home is seized and sold, if it's sold for an amount less than the amount of debt.

Method salesmen, and creative real estate seminar pitchmen will try to convince you that homeowners in foreclosure have little choice but to hand you their deed and keys. They'll tell you that many homeowners don't know what their homes are worth, and are resigned to losing their home without so much as a passing, backward glance. In fact, they'll say, many will be grateful for an opportunity to simply walk away from their mess allowing you to profit from their misfortune by using this technique or that technique. Once in a while, that may be true. But not with the frequency implied. In 25+ years, working with hundreds upon hundreds of families facing foreclosure seeking help, I've never met with a single homeowner willing to walk away from their equity. Never. So often their equity was initially a down payment gift or inheritance from a deceased parent or grandparent. Oh, at first they may pretend not to care, that losing their home doesn't matter that much, but when pencil hits paper they will.

In my experience, the majority of distressed homeowners profess to know what their home is worth. What they mean is they think they know what their neighbor's homes are worth. They'll know the asking or listed price, and they'll know if the house was smaller or larger than their own. But, they might not appreciate upgrades that had been installed, its general condition, or what the final sales price had been. When comparing their home to their neighbor's homes, most overlook functional obsolescence and deferred maintenance, and fail to consider the time factor of foreclosure.

I'd agree that most distressed homeowners think their homes are worth more than they really are worth. That mistaken assumption can become a problem when the success of a non foreclosure alternative is contingent upon the property's value. If its worth what they've stated, they might qualify for a refinance. If its worth a little less, or a lot less, their hopes are dashed.

During the lead-up to declaration of default and foreclosure, the mortgagee will usually present the mortgagor a menu of generic, non foreclosure alternatives, and a list of local non profit credit or housing counselors. Conventionally recommended non foreclosure alternatives which may be available include assumptions, compromised or short sale, deed-in lieu of foreclosure, deferments, forbearance, modifications, preforeclosure sale, partial claim, recast, refinancing, and streamline refinance.

REFINANCE. With adequate equity, homeowners can try to pay off their old loan with a new loan from a new lender. A streamline refinance option would be offered by your existing lender.

FORBEARANCE. Qualified homeowners may be able to convince their lender to temporarily reduce or suspend payments until the hardship has been resolved, allowing the homeowner the chance to catch up on the delinquent amount.

MORTGAGE MODIFICATION. The terms of the loan agreement may be permanently changed to extend the length of repayment, reduce the interest rate, re-amortize, or any combination that will result in long term affordability.

PARTIAL CLAIM. HUD might intervene, and provide a small, interest free, second mortgage loan to bring the first mortgage loan current.

BANKRUPTCY. An attorney's advice might result in an affordable repayment plan.

PREFORECLOSURE SALE. The homeowner might be able to salvage equity and protect future creditworthiness by selling the home before the forced, public foreclosure sale.

PREFORECLOSURE SHORT SALE. If the sellers owe more than their homes are worth, their lender(s) can permit the sale by accepting less than they are contractually due.

DEED IN LIEU OF FORECLOSURE. The homeowner may be able to 'give back' the property to the lender.

Despite several requests that the homeowner contact their lender to discuss possible workout options, why do so many delinquencies result in foreclosure? One reason might be that when the home-owner calls for help as directed, the mortgagee representative isn't properly trained to identify situation appropriate workout options. Additionally, homeowners may be distrustful of their lenders' actions. Many homeowners believe, mistakenly, the lenders' real objective is to take their home.

When homeowners' loans are foreclosed, the foreclosure lawsuit documents may become public knowledge, and 'listed' by information providers. These entrepreneurs sell these lists to subscribers seeking such information (leads). Homeowners' mailboxes soon overflow with solicitations from lawyers, mortgage brokers, real estate brokers, consultants, etc., all offering simple solutions to their complex problem. From these slick solicitations, many homeowners glean a basic but false idea as to what their options might be, and mistakenly presume that all options they've read or heard about are available to them.

During early stages of default, homeowners aren't too receptive to the idea of probative credit counseling, selling their home, or filing bankruptcy. They want a quick fix. Why do so many distressed homeowners hesitate to implement a proactive solution? It isn't so much that they are in 'denial' and aren't willing to face the facts as is commonly parroted by disappointed, speculative investors whose proposals have been rejected. While they know they have a problem, they lack of understanding as to the seriousness of the problem. To their thinking, all they need is a little 'catch-up' loan. They are looking for a short term fix to a long term problem. While they think they may 'know' what the short term fixes are, they might not be ready to pursue conventionally accepted options until it's too late.

For example, let's consider the idea of *foreclosure bail-out/refinance loans*. Newspaper classified ads and direct mail solicitations suggest foreclosure bailout loans are as commonplace as if ordering a pizza. Homeowners believe the hype, but eventually realize that approvals, rates and terms are conditioned upon loan to value, and creditworthiness. They learn, too, about loan application fees and appraisal fees which are payable at their door at the time of appraisal. They also learn about rigid underwriting criteria, and only after their 'competitive' rate loan application has been rejected, do they learn about alternative 'loan to own' programs designed to separate a procrastinating owner from his home, and his equity.

The fact is that folks with lousy credit, but with sufficient equity can still refinance their foreclosed mortgage, replacing it with a loan that carries a higher rate of interest, shorter term, and loaded with more default triggers. These 'subprime' loan programs offer a win/win scenario to the new lender. If the borrower makes the payments, the lender, having already pocketed big upfront fees, continues to collect big interest. If the borrower fails to make the payments, there is an adequate cushion of equity that anticipates foreclosure, and full net recovery.

When seeking a *forbearance* the homeowner must demonstrate to the lender that their hardship, proximate cause to the default, was temporary and will be resolved shortly, or has already been resolved. They can do this by presenting a 'back to work' letter from a physician or employer, or paystubs that establish additional income. The forbearance, if granted, suspends collection activity for a specific period of time allowing the financially distressed homeowner to regain financial stability. The homeowner should seek a forbearance only when they see real light at the end of the tunnel. I woulda, shoulda, coulda (got that job) simply won't fly.

Homeowners seeking *mortgage modification* must have already resolved their financial hardship. The lender must be convinced that the homeowner can now afford a regularly scheduled payment, even if that payment is less than the amount of the previous payment. The lender will then consider the cost to foreclose vs. the cost to modify the terms of the loan agreement. If it makes financial sense to reduce the interest rate, &/or extend the term of the loan rather than devote resources to foreclose, they will.

If the *partial claim* program is available, homeowners seeking the HUD partial claim must have an FHA insured loan, and qualify for specific relief. Information on HUD loss mitigation programs is available on line at www.HUD.gov. Information on VA insured loan loss mitigation programs may be found on line at www.homeloans.va.gov.

For homeowners that cannot afford the mortgage lender's reinstatement program, *bankruptcy* may offer an affordable repayment plan designed to help the borrower to keep the home.

Typically, a Chapter 13 Bankruptcy plan will 'force' the lender to begin accepting the previously rejected, regularly scheduled, monthly payment. The homeowner will make additional, predetermined payments to the bankruptcy trustee which represent a portion of the amount of missed payments, including fees, costs, etc. The trustee will distribute the additional payment to creditors, including the mortgagee. Chapter 13 repayment plans may be devised and completed from within 36 to 60 monthly installments. If the homeowner successfully completes the plan, the bankruptcy is discharged and the mortgage loan is considered current. Even though bankruptcy laws have recently changed, this still affords a viable option for the qualified, distressed homeowner.

Some property owners facing the loss of their home to foreclosure decide to sell their property to via a *preforeclosure sale*. Some attempt to sell the home without using a real estate broker, instead relying on a yard sign and placing ads in local newspapers. Some will list their home with a full service real estate broker, or one that offers a scaled down version of professional help in exchange for a discounted fee. These homeowners are reluctant but resigned to sell to avoid foreclosure. They hope by marketing their home early on in the foreclosure process, they'll sell at close to full retail value. Unfortunately, at this point, those homeowners that utilize the services of a real estate broker fail to disclose the pending foreclosure to their broker, and consequently the property is introduced to the market with an inflated asking price. As a result, their property often languishes unsold as foreclosure costs continue to accrue. Ill-informed real estate brokers, thinking they have ample time to implement price corrections, often learn, too late, that a foreclosure sale has been scheduled, and rapidly approaches. This presents a two fold problem for the seller. Firstly, prospective buyers now know that the sellers are between a rock and a hard place and will be inclined to accept any reasonable offer, and secondly, it sharply reduces the available time to market, secure a buyer, and close. Instead of having months and weeks, they now may have but weeks and days.

In the case of homeowners resigned to sell who face foreclosure but have several months or more before the foreclosure auction, the best advice I could give would be to 1) make sure they understand and respect the foreclosure timeline, 2) determine their home's actual as-is, fair market value, 3) list with an established real estate broker at a competitive price.

When circumstances dictate the need for an expedited sale, and/or if the property is in poor physical condition, the seller should be introduced to speculative investors who purchase properties, for cash, in as-is condition, but often at a steep discount.

If the homeowner is resigned to sell, but owes more than the property is worth, a preforeclosure sale is still possible. If the property is in poor physical condition, this may be an excellent opportunity for a speculative investor to pursue a preforeclosure short sale.

As a last resort, a homeowner, unable to refinance, sell, or otherwise avoid the loss of the home to foreclosure, may ask the lender to accept a deed in lieu of foreclosure. In theory, under certain conditions, the homeowner would execute a special deed, hand over the keys, and in exchange for a release of liability, simply walk away.

That option is included in just about every mortgagee provided, boilerplate, menu of non-foreclosure alternatives I've seen. Just about every homeowner I've counseled believes that this is a common practice. Truth be told, I haven't seen that option employed very often. Maybe once or twice over two decades by first mortgagees. I have been told, though, that nowadays many junior mortgagees are willing to accept a DIL rather than go through an expensive foreclosure process. But, I haven't seen it.

The majority of families that face mortgage foreclosure will solve their problem before losing their home. There are those who procrastinate or experience additional hardship(s) and may be inclined to accept a lowball offer, or participate in a creative technique that they think is to their advantage.

TYPES OF LETTERS I USE:

Don't get too hung up on having or needing boilerplate forms or letters. Get used to writing your own letters and preparing your own forms in your own style that will get the job done. What works for me may not work as well for you. My writing tends to be less conversational, and not very reader friendly.

A Letter of Authorization is little more than a note from the Borrower to the Lender in which the Borrower gives its permission for the Lender to discuss their loan account with a named third party. The named third party could be a real estate broker, a mortgage loan broker, a credit counselor, an attorney, a family member, a neighbor, or a potential Purchaser. It can be printed, handwritten, typed, or scrawled on a napkin with a crayon. Be advised that neither pencil or crayon drafted letters FAX very well. I usually request from the foreclosure lender as much info as possible, including a loan workout request application, a loan status and terms (interest rate, amount of monthly payment, a loan payoff statement, and any preliminary title work their files may contain. I don't always get what I've asked for, but it sets the stage for how I will approach the proposal.

An **Introduction to the Seller** into the short sale process helps me to set the pace of what's expected. The Seller's cooperation is greatest early on in the process, and tends to wane as the process drags on, so it's best to get as much information from them (appointments for inspections, too) in the first few days after they have agreed to sell. I like to have the Seller initial and return a copy of this letter just to have in case they say, "You didn't tell me that I needed THAT!" It's important the Seller is fully aware of what we are trying to accomplish, and be able to participate in the process. I like to follow up a face to face meeting with a letter making sure that the Homeowner understands the process, and what will be expected of him/her.

Dear Seller:

Preforeclosure "Short Sales" are **negotiated** workout programs wherein the Mortgagee, having considered a formal proposal in form and supportive content consistent with their internal criteria, agrees to accept less than the full payoff amount due from You (Borrower). A "Short Sale" workout program permits a qualified homeowner to sell a property irrespective of the amount owed. The Mortgagee may accept, reject, or make a counteroffer to our Proposal. If the request is approved, appropriate documents will be forwarded for your signatures. Terms must be agreeable to You, (the Seller) and the decision to proceed will be Yours.

A successful "Short Sale" requires extraordinary professionalism from your real estate broker; and cooperation from the Seller, The Buyer, and the Mortgagee. Please notify me if you are contacted by your Lender (telephone, mail, or a face to face visit). Promptly advise your Lender that you are seeking a "Short Sale" workout, that you have listed the property for sale with a licensed real estate broker, and request that a "Short Sale" workout application be sent to you immediately.

I have provided several financial worksheets and schedules that you must complete, sign, and return to me within the next three days. Your prompt attention to this will help to assure a smooth transaction, and expedite a favorable solution to your problem. After you assemble all the needed information, I'll be happy to help you complete the forms, or draft the Letter of Hardship.

Pursuant to our preparation of your "Short Sale" application for mortgagee(s) consideration, kindly assemble the following information:

  * copies of two most recent months of pay stubs and/or

 disability, unemployment, or social security payments;

- 2 most recent bank statements (checking and savings)

- last 2 years income tax returns (all schedules), true copy of request for extension, or letter describing why you are not required to file a tax return; &/or a profit & loss statements (if self employed)

- concise but detailed letter explaining hardship (chronology);

- copy of property tax statement; a statement of any liens or judgments filed against the property;

- a Letter describing any physical problems with your home leaking roof, damp basement, insect infestation, etc.);

- if possible, provide a few photographs of your home's exterior (front and back) & interior, showing areas in need of repair or replacement. Show worn flooring, peeling paint or water stains, leaking pipes, holes in walls, etc.

- copy of Broker's Listing Agreement

- copies of recent property survey, appraisals, or CMAs

- copy of any deed, mortgage, divorce decrees, bankruptcy petitions, discharges, or dismissals

An **Introduction to the Broker** is really a set of instructions the broker should follow to insure the likelihood of success. Some-times, once the listing is signed, they forget about what's needed from them market data, photographs, BPO, etc. so I also ask that they initial and return a copy of the checklist provided.

In my opinion, the real estate broker is an essential element to any short sale transaction. More and more mortgage loan servicers are now requiring that a property be listed with a licensed real estate broker as a condition for considering a short sale proposal. Most real estate brokers consider a short sale listing as "problematic, and too much work." For the most part, they are right. That's why you, as the Purchaser/Facilitator must convey your expertise to the broker, assume the responsibility for devising the Proposal, and to proactively negotiate an acceptable payoff based upon an offer of offers to purchase produced by and resulting from the broker's efforts.

Here are my "Words to Broker"

A Preforeclosure "Short Sale" workout program permits a qualified homeowner to sell a property irrespective of the amount owed. Preforeclosure "Short Sales" are **negotiated** workout programs wherein the Mortgagee, having considered a formal proposal in form and supportive content consistent with their internal criteria, agrees to accept less than the full payoff amount due from the Seller. Mortgagee may accept, reject, or make a counteroffer to the Proposal. A successful "Short Sale" requires extraordinary professionalism from the real estate professionals, and cooperation from the Seller, The Buyer, and the Mortgagee.

Specific, restrictive language must be included in the listing agreement, and in any Offers to Purchase. No Offer to Purchase should be considered or presented to the Seller unless the specific language has been included.

Preforeclosure Sale Process:

Once the broker to broker referral arrangement is devised, the listing broker immediately contacts the seller, and lists the property at its as-is, fair market value. The broker will FAX a copy of the listing agreement, and any offer to purchase to *TheShortSalePro* prior to presenting the offer to the seller. If the offer is consistent with listing instructions, *TheShortSalePro* will recommend the seller accept the offer. *TheShortSalePro* will prepare short sale request application, present to the mortgagee, and initiate negotiations for preforeclosure, short sale approval.

The listing broker will provide to *TheShortSalePro*:

- Signed listing agreement via FAX and regular mail;
- Comparables (BPO/CMA) used to determine subject's FMV via E-mail, & regular mail;
- Photographs of the subject property that demonstrate adverse conditions;
- An estimated HUD 1 settlement statement; typical costs to the seller;
- Any offer to purchase, via FAX, prior to presentation to seller;
- Accepted and signed Contract of Sale (FAX and hard copy via regular mail)
- Purchaser's mortgage prequalification statement (FAX and hard copy via regular mail)

Language to be included in listing agreement:

- The sale of this property is subject to mortgagee(s)'s written, short payoff approval at terms acceptable to the seller.
- Mortgagee(s)'s written approval or rejection may take from 45 days to 90 days, or more.
- The property is to be sold in an as-is condition; the seller will effect no repairs.

Specific Language to be included in Contract for Sale:

- Includes listing clauses, plus
- There will be NO financial concessions to purchaser for compliance &/or repairs at closing.
- The seller will receive ZERO proceeds from sale.

REMARKS...

The information contained herein this manual is not intended to be a substitute for legal or financial advice. Before making any decisions with respect to any real estate transaction, you should consult with an attorney and tax professional.

"Not every default, or foreclosure scenario will lend itself to the short sale acquisition technique."

"Foreclosure laws, customs, or practices can vary from state to state, and county to county."

"An understanding of the specific foreclosure laws and customs in the applicable jurisdiction is crucial to the demonstration of the foreclosure time lime."

"The only numbers that really matter are the mortgagee's perception of the subject's as-is, fair market value and their maximum recovery from proceeds of the sale."

"Frequently, troubled mortgage loans are transferred from one mortgage loan servicer to another..."

"The preforeclosure short sale acquisition technique is not an exact science and it's as much an art as science. A picture is worth 1,000 words and a picture supported by words and numbers is an invaluable component to any short sale proposal."

IS THERE AN END IN SIGHT?

The increase in numbers of formal complaints against predatory lending and realty practices, the increase in the scope of illegalities and in actual dollars involved are causing lawmakers to propose laws to curtail such activities. California, Illinois, Maryland, Missouri, and New York are among those states.

Even though California has very strict laws regarding preforeclosure transactions, the laws apparently don't yet prevent Californian based companies from reaching out beyond their borders.

For example:

A NJ woman called my NJ based office at four o'clock yesterday afternoon. She explained she had just learned her home was to be sold at Sheriff's Sale the next morning. She went on to say she had already used the Sheriff's two, discretionary, adjournments and wanted to know how long she would have to move out after the Sheriff's Sale. At risk was about $80,000 in equity.

I asked a few questions, and learned that months earlier she had executed the deed to her home to a Californian based "foreclosure rescue" company who promised to buy the house, stop the foreclosure by curing the default, rent the house back to her, and give her an opportunity to buy the house back with a year or two.

She also learned that in an attempt to stop the Sheriff's Sale, the "company" had prepared and filed a bankruptcy petition in her behalf without her knowledge, or consent.

Red flag? You bet!

Despite this illegal act on the part of the company, the woman still had hope the company would deliver on their promise to solve her foreclosure dilemma.

The immediate dilemma was how to stop the sheriff's sale which was scheduled for the next day.

Historically, the distressed homeowner had the option to file an emergency petition for Chapter 13 Bankruptcy. But, the recently enacted bankruptcy laws have made filing for bankruptcy, even an emergency petition, more difficult by requiring the petitioner first undergo HUD approved, preforeclosure, counseling. At this late hour, there was no time for that.

I asked the woman to FAX to me the agreement(s) she had signed with the foreclosure rescue company. Of course, when it arrived, the boilerplate forms were barely legible. I was able to do a Google search and found the company's two fold web site. On one hand they offered 'rescue' programs for distressed homeowners. On the other hand they solicited investment capital from speculative investors, to be secured by mortgage. The investment capital would be used to effectuate 'rescue' activities including the purchase of foreclosed real estate, collection of heavy, front end fees, equity stripping, and possible assignment to other realty speculators.

The immediate dilemma was how to stop the sheriff's sale which was scheduled for the next day. Without any remaining discretionary adjournments, to stop the sale a judge would have to intervene and order the sheriff's sale adjourned.

The woman would have to speak with the Judge, present a compelling argument, and "beg" the sale be adjourned.

I devised the following letter, portions of which have been deleted or disguised herein, addressed it to the sitting Judge, and told the woman to present it to the Judge first thing the next morning.

New Jersey Superior Court,
Chancery Division

Re: mortgagee v. mortgagor   docket #
        property address

Judge:

My name is David Petrovich. I am Executive Director for Society for the Preservation of Continued Homeownership (www.SPOCH.org). We offer help to low and moderate income homeowners with mortgage or tax foreclosure related, and, income tax matters.

Learning her home is scheduled for Sheriff's Sale tomorrow, "Theresa" called our office seeking counseling and explained that she may have been swindled by a California based, "foreclosure rescue" company, and faces the loss of her home, tomorrow, to Sheriff's Sale. Upon a review of the boilerplate agreement between "Theresa" and the **"predatory, foreclosure rescue"** operator, I believe that she may have been deceived. She, and her family, stand to lose $80,000 in equity.

Upon listening to her set of circumstances, I believe that "Theresa" should be able to save her home... were it not for the tactics employed by the "predatory, foreclosure rescue" operator, and the scheduled Sheriff's Sale. Assured by the "predatory, foreclosure rescue" operator that her housing problem had been solved, she did not exercise her right to pre-foreclosure counseling.

I'd ask that you order the scheduled sale adjourned for 30 days, and permit "Theresa" to participate in HUD approved, credit and pre-bankruptcy counseling. Due to the excessive equity in the property, the Plaintiff would certainly be made whole in the event of a forced, foreclosure sale even if the process is delayed by 30 days.

Thanking you in advance for any consideration offered to Theresa, I remain,

Sincerely

David M. Petrovich

Early the next day, the woman went to the courthouse to wait for the Judge to arrive at his office. She advised the Judge's assistant that her home was scheduled, that day, for sheriff's sale, and she urgently needed to speak to the Judge. An hour or so later the assistant approached her and told her the Judge was too busy to see her. She handed the letter to the assistant that I had provided, in addition to her copy of the agreement she had with the predatory, foreclosure rescue operator. With emotion, she implored the assistant to give the documents to the Judge. The Judge's assistant, recording her cell phone number, told her to go home, nothing more could be done.

Shortly afterward, driving home, her cell phone rang. It was the Judge's assistant who informed her the Sheriff's Sale would be adjourned for an additional 30 days.

The woman called to discuss the strategy to save her home which now included preforeclosure, and prebankruptcy counseling. She has an additional 30 days to obtain the counseling certificate, then meet with an attorney to discuss a Chapter 13 repayment plan. Hopefully, she will qualify and be able to keep her home. If not, she still has the option of selling her home.

As of this writing, as I prepare to submit this manuscript to the publisher, the phone is ringing. Odds are it is someone who was thrown a cement life jacket.

GLOSSARY

THIS COMPLIMENTARY GLOSSARY HAS BEEN COM-
PILED FROM VARIOUS SOURCES AND IS PROVIDED AS A
GENERAL REFERENCE AND SHOULD NOT BE A SUBSTI-
TUTE FOR LEGAL, ACCOUNTING, OR BUSINESS ADVICE.

IF YOU CANNOT FIND THE WORD OR TERM YOU NEED,
OR IF YOU IDENTIFY AN ERROR IN MEANING OR
SPELLING, PLEASE CONTACT ME AT SHORTSALE-
BLUE@AOL.COM

Abandonment A process in bankruptcy wherein the court releases a property from it's control when it is deemed to have no value to the estate.

Abstract A succinct summary; (e.g. an abstract of judgment; an abstract of title, etc.)

Abstract of Judgment The essentials of a money judgment obtained via an adjudicated lawsuit. When an abstract is recorded in the recorder's office the judgment becomes a general lien on all the debtor's property located in that particular county.
Comment by JohnMerchant "The reason for an AJ is that a J itself is NOT recordable, so an AJ is drafted and recorded to show the details of the J. If you'll go to your county recorder and ask to see their AJ records, you

can see the exact form that's used in your state and you can also see the existent, current, outstanding Js by date the AJs were recorded."

Acceleration Clause Clause in a deed of trust or mortgage which "accelerates" the time when the indebtedness becomes due. For example, some mortgages or deeds of trust contain a provision that the note balance shall become due immediately upon the resale of the land or upon the default in the payment of principal and interest.

Acknowledgment A formal declaration before a duly authorized officer (such as a notary public) by a person who has executed an instrument that such execution is his own. An acknowledgment is necessary to entitle an instrument (with certain specific exceptions) to be recorded, to impart constructive notice of its contents, and to entitle the instrument to be used as evidence without further proof. The certificate of acknowledgment is attached to the instrument or incorporated therein.

Acquisition An act or process, such as foreclosure, by which one procures ownership of property

Addendum An addition or change to a contract.

Adjournment A putting off or postponing of business or of a session until another time.

Adjudication A judicial determination

Adjustable Rate Mortgage (ARM) A loan with an interest rate that fluctuates based on a specified financial index.

Administrator If a person dies without a Will (Intestate) the Court will appoint a person, or Administrator to handle the Estate, whose functions are similar to those of an Executor

Ad Valorem Tax A tax based on the value of the property as a percentage of that value.

Advances Moneys paid, on behalf of an owner, by a junior interest holder. Done to temporarily cure a delinquency on a senior encumbrance that threatens to extinguish the junior's position. Thereafter the junior lien holder can start their own foreclosure if they are not immediately reimbursed for the advances paid out.

Adverse Possession A means of acquiring title where an occupant has been in actual, open, notorious and continuous occupancy of a property under a claim of right for the required statutory period.

Affidavit A sworn, notarized statement that's signed by the affiant before witnesses

Agency The relationship of trust that exists between sellers and buyers and their agents. The agency is formed through a written contract.

Agent A person who is authorized by another to represent him/her. (real estate agent) A person licensed by the state to conduct real estate transactions.

Agreement of Sale Also known as an agreement to convey. A signed, written contract entered into between the seller and buyer for sale of real property under certain specific terms and conditions.

Alienation The transfer of an interest in or title to property to another.

Amortization The gradual repayment of a debt in a series of equal periodic amounts until the total debt, including interest, is paid in full. Senior loans are typically amortized over 30 years, whereas junior loans are generally amortized over a much shorter time period.

Appraisal A statement of value or estimation of the value of a property as of a certain date conducted by a disinterested person with suitable qualifications. Generally, value for single family properties is based upon a review of recent market activity using sales of comparable properties as a basis and then making value adjustments based upon the comparison of comparable property to the subject property.

Appreciation Increase in value or worth. The difference between the increased value of property and the original sales price.
Annual Percentage Rate (APR) The cost of the loan expressed as a yearly rate on the balance of the loan.

Answer In a lawsuit, this is a legal document that the defendant must file in response to the claims alleged in the complaint.

Anticipatory Breach A communication that informs a party that the obligations of the original contract will not be fulfilled.

Appurtenance A right, privilege, or improvement belonging to, or passing with, the land.

Arm's Length Transaction A transaction between relative strangers, each trying to do the best for himself, or herself.

As-Is Condition The purchase or sale of a property in its existing condition

Assessment A bonded tax imposed to pay for public improvements (e.g. street/alley paving, curbs, sidewalks, etc.) beneficial to a limited area . Paid semiannually over a 10 year period to the Bond Division of the city or county treasurer's office where the property is located.

Assessed Value Assessed Value applies in ad valorem taxation and refers to the value of a property according to tax roles. Assessed value may not conform to market value, but it is usually calculated to a market value base. A tax assessor's determination of the value of a home in order to calculate a tax base.

Assignee One to whom a transfer of an interest is made (i.e. assignee of a deed of trust).

Assignor One who transfers property by assignment.

Assignment Written document by which property, other than real property, is transferred from one person to another. Assignment of mortgage, assignment of deed of trust, assignment of lease, assignment of rentals, etc. are common assignments. The "assignee" receives the property assigned.

Assumability When a home is sold, the seller may be able to transfer the mortgage to the new buyer. This means the mortgage is assumable. Lenders generally require a credit review of the new borrower and may charge a fee for the assumption. Some mortgages contain a due-on-sale clause, which means that the mortgage may not be transferable to a new buyer. Instead, the lender may make you pay the entire balance that is due when you sell the home. Assumability can help you attract buyers if you sell your home.

Assumption Clause A provision that allows a buyer to take responsibility for the mortgage from a seller.

Assumption of Mortgage A formal agreement with a lender in which a new property owner agrees to be personally liable for the repayment of a preexisting lien. Generally entails paying the lender an assumption fee and sometimes a higher interest rate. Doesn't release the original borrower from further liability unless the agreement specifically provides for it.

Attorney-in-Fact An agent authorized to act for another. Commonly evidenced by a recorded Power of Attorney. Holder of the power can exercise it only as long as it has not been revoked and the grantor remains alive and competent enough to act on their own behalf if need be.

Automatic Stay A bankruptcy case automatically prevents continuation of creditor collection activity. Filing bankruptcy is the only way to get this protection. (mortgagees may petition the Court to **"lift"** the stay and permission to resume collection activity (usually foreclosure).

Backup Offer A secondary bid for a property that the seller will accept if the first offer fails.

Balloon Payment A lump sum final installment payment of a promissory note that is much larger than the regular installment payments.

Bankrupt A person who is insolvent; one whose total property s legally declared insufficient to pay his/her debts.

Bankruptcy A proceeding in U.S. District Court wherein debtors who can not meet the claims of their creditors may be adjudged bankrupt by the court. There are three different types (and many chapters) of bankruptcy proceedings: (see Cramdown)
    Chapter 7 - "Debtor Wipeout". The court oversees the liquidation of the debtors' nonexempt assets, distributing the cash proceeds proportionally amongst their creditors. Most of the time this is not the bankruptcy proceeding mortgagors/trustors will choose since their real objective is to stall off the trustee's sale as long as they can rather than liquidate everything.
    Chapter 11 - This is a business reorganization proceeding.
    Chapter 13 - "Debtor Workout". This is the almost-automatic choice of most mortgagors/trustors seeking to use a bankruptcy filing to delay the inevitable sheriff's sale or trustee's sale as long as they can. It's hypothetically possible to drag out a Chapter 13 proceeding for several years. The purpose of this proceeding is to give a "wage earner" time for rehabilitation a temporary respite free from the collection efforts of creditors. But a sharp mortgagee's &/or beneficiary's attorney can usually cut the delay down to about 90 days by persuading the court to grant relief from the automatic stay when the debtors are unable to keep current with their post-petition payments on their property.

"Bare Bones" Petition Initial, tentative filing of a bankruptcy petition that qualifies the petitioner to the benefits of the automatic stay pending the filing of the full petition within the following 15 days. Failure to complete the filing of the full petition will result in the dismissal of the "face sheet filing" and a bar to any subsequent refiling for the next 180 days.

Bargain and Sale Deed A deed that carries with it no warranties against liens or other encumbrances but that does imply that the grantor has the right to convey title.

Bargain and Sale Deed w/Covenant A deed in which the grantor warrants or guarantees the title against defects arising during the period of his or her ownership of the property, but not against defects existing before that time.

Bargain Sale The sale of property for less than market value.

Basis The cost of an asset increased by the cost of a allowable improvement and reduced by depreciation and amortization deductions to calculate gain or loss on sale.

Bootleg Improvement Building, expanding, or modifying a structure without benefit of a required permit.

Breach of Contract The failure to perform provisions of a contract without a legal excuse.

Broker A person licensed by the state to work in a specific field including real estate, mortgage loans, insurance, securities, etc.

Broker Price Opinion (BPO) A written estimate of the most probable sales price of a property provided by a licensed real estate broker with experience in the specific locality of the subject property. Value of the subject property is estimated by comparing like properties that recently sold and adjusting for differences. Often provided as a means to establish a listing price for a property.

Bullet Mortgage A mortgage that requires monthly payments of interest only until the final mortgage payment when full payment of principal is due.

Business Plan is a written document used to describe your business, and summarizes an organized sequence of predetermined actions to complete future objectives.

Buy Down An upfront payment to a lender to reduce a loan's interest rate, either temporarily (the first year or two) or permanently

Buyers' Broker A real estate broker who exclusively represents the buyer's interests in a transaction and whose commission is paid by the buyer rather than the seller.

Buyers Market A market with a lot fewer buyers than there are sellers. Indicated by a prolonged marketing time of more than 90 days and generally high mortgage interest rates of more than 12%.

By-Laws The internal rules of management by which an entity conducts it's business.

Cancellation Clause A clause that details the conditions under which each party may terminate the agreement.

Cap A negotiated upper limit the interest rate on a variable rate mortgage can rise, both annually and over the life of the mortgage.

Capitalization Capitalization occurs when items owed on a loan are treated as part of a new, principal balance. When *arrears* are capitalized, the amount of the arrears is included in the principal before the interest is applied. Also a mathematical process for estimating the value of a property using a proper rate of return on the investment and annual net income expected to be produced by the property. [Income ÷ Rate = Value]

Capital Gains Profits an investor makes from the sale of real estate or investments.

Capital Gains Tax A tax placed on the profits from the sale of real estate or investments.

Cash Flow The surplus left over out of the rents after paying out all operating expenses and mortgage payments.

Certificate of Occupancy (CO, or CofO) Document issued by a local governmental agency that states a property meets the local building standards for occupancy.

Certificate of Reasonable Value (CRV) An appraisal issued by the VA approved appraiser which establishes the property's current market value.

Chain of Title A chronological list of documents that comprises the title record history to a specific parcel of real property.

Charge Off The process of writing off sums that have been deemed uncollectible.

Chronic Delinquent A payment pattern wherein the borrower habitually violates the terms of the note by paying late.

Clear Title Title that is not encumbered or burdened with defects.

Closing The final procedure in which documents are signed and recorded, and the property is transferred.

Closing Costs The miscellaneous costs that the buyer and seller incur to complete or "close" a real estate transaction. These costs are in addition to the price of the property. Expenses incidental to the sale of real estate, including loan, title and appraisal fees. The agreement of sale negotiated previously between the buyer and the seller may state in writing who will pay each of the above costs.

BUYER'S EXPENSES	SELLER'S EXPENSES
Documentary Stamps on Notes	Cost of Abstract
Recording Deed and Mortgage	Documentary Stamps on Deed
Escrow Fees	Real Estate Commission
Attorney's Fee	Recording Mortgage
Title Insurance	Survey Charge
Appraisal and Inspection	Escrow Fees
Survey Charge	Attorney's Fee

Closing Statement A document which details the final financial settlement between a buyer and seller and the costs paid by each party.

Clouded Title Any claim, encumbrance or defect that contradicts the title record as understood by the property owner. Intractable disputes are re-solved judicially (*quiet title action*).

Code A collection of laws relating to a certain topic, such as real property, patents, etc.

Codicil A change to a will that adds or subtracts provisions or clarifies portions of the document.

Collateral Anything of value, like real property, pledged as security for a debt.

Collateralized Mortgage Obligation (CMO) A multiple class pay-through bond which is structured using prioritized classes of securities and divided into different maturity terms. The issuer pays cash inflows from the collateral to the holders of the class or classes or securities which holders are then entitled to payment in accordance with the trust indenture. The creation of classes of securities reduces the prepayment risk on each holder's investment.

Commission A fee paid to a real estate agent/broker by a principal as compensation for finding a buyer or seller and completing the sale. Usually a percentage of the sale price and commonly amounts to 6 to 7 percent on houses and 10 percent on raw land.

Commitment A promise or firm agreement; a lender's contractual obligation to make a loan to a qualified borrower

Community Property Some state's laws provide that where a couple acquires any asset during marriage, the husband and wife will be considered to have one-half interest in the property.

Comparables (Comps) Similar properties (situated near the property you're interested in) that are currently listed for sale or have recently sold.

Comparable Market Analysis (CMA)/Competitive Market Analysis (CMA) A study, intended to assist an owner in establishing a listing price, of recent, comparable sales, properties that failed to sell, and property presently on the market.

Complaint A document commencing a lawsuit.

Comprehensive Environmental Response, Compensation and Liability Act of 1980 CERCLA The Act that establishes the potential for lender liability for environmental clean up on a mortgaged property.

Compromise Sale A VA approved short sale.

Conditional Commitment A promise by a lender to make a loan if the borrower meets certain conditions

Conduit The financial intermediary that sponsors the conduit between the lender(s) originating loans and the ultimate investor. The conduit makes or purchases loans from third party correspondents under standardized terms, underwriting and documents and then, when sufficient volume has been obtained, pools the loans for sale to investors in the CMBS market.

Confirmation Hearing (Bankruptcy) A hearing where the Debtors proposed Chapter 13 plan is reviewed and either approved or denied by the bankruptcy judge.

Confirmation Hearing (Foreclosure) A hearing held subsequent to the Sheriff's Sale to confirm the sale and transfer title to the successful bidder.

Contingency A condition specified in a purchase contract, such as the perspective buyer making an offer contingent on his or her sale of a present home, or such as a satisfactory home inspection.

Contract An agreement entered into by two or more legally competent parties by the terms of which one or more of the parties, for a consideration, undertakes to do or refrain from doing some legal act, or acts. Essential elements of a valid contract are parties competent to contract, a proper subject matter, consideration, mutuality of agreement, and mutuality of obligation.

Contract for Deed A contract for the sale of real estate wherein the purchase price is paid in periodic installments by the Purchaser, who is in possession of the property even though title is retained by the seller until the final payment. Also called an installment contract, or a land contract.

Contract to Purchase A contract the buyer initiates which details the purchase price and conditions of the transaction and is accepted by the seller. Also known as an agreement of sale.

Controlling Party A party designated in a CMBS that has the right to approve and direct certain actions of the Special Servicer with respect to specially serviced loans.

Constructive Notice Notice imparted by the public records (e.g. the county recorder's records). The law presumes that one has knowledge of instruments that are properly recorded.

Conventional Mortgage A mortgage loan not insured by HUD or guaranteed by the Veterans' Administration. It is subject to conditions established by the lending institution and State statutes.

Conversion (Bankruptcy) The change to a case under a chapter different that the one originally filed under, The court may convert a case on the request of the debtor or the request of a party in interest.

Corporate Guarantee A guarantee made by the issuer (issuer guarantee) or a third party to cover losses due to delinquencies and foreclosures up to the guaranteed amount. The rating of the guarantor is commonly required to be, at minimum, equal the highest rating of the securities. This is a form of credit enhancement.

Corrected Mortgage Loan A Mortgage Loan that had previously incurred a default or related event, had been transferred to the Special Servicer for handling and becomes a Specially Serviced Mortgage Loan, had cured the default by any of a number of avenues available to the Special Servicer and thus became a Corrected Mortgage Loan returned to the Master Servicer for administration.

Cosign Agreeing to be responsible for someone else's debt.

Cost Approach The process of estimating the value of property by adding to the estimated land value the appraiser's estimate of the reproduction or replacement cost of the building, less depreciation.

Cramdown A controversial procedure in bankruptcy wherein the court reduces a secured debt (i.e. trust deed or mortgage) to the current value of the property. The court actually splits the mortgage debt into two parts. The amount equal to the current value of the home is treated as a secured claim that the debtor must continue to pay. The portion of debt in excess of the property's current value becomes an unsecured claim that's usually not repaid in full.

Credit The money a lender extends to a buyer for a commitment to repay the loan within a certain time frame.

Credit Bureau A company that receives information about a consumer's credit history, and keeps records that are available to others seeking information on that consumer.

Credit History A record of an individual's current and past debt payments.

Credit Rating The degree of credit worthiness assigned to a person based on credit history and financial status.

Credit Report A credit bureau report that shows a loan applicant's history of payments made on previous debts. Several companies issue credit reports, but the three largest are Trans Union Corp., Equifax and Experian (formerly TRW).

Cure a Default With respect to delinquent mortgage loans, all missed payments have been made and loan payments are current.

Days on the Market (DOM) The period of time a property is listed for sale until it is sold or taken off the market.

Dealer A repeat buyer whose intent to resell quickly rather than holding for investment. There are no tax breaks for those who make money with quick turnover properties. The income, or gain is taxed as ordinary income.

Debt Collector The term 'debt collector' applies to collection agencies and lawyers that are collecting debt for others.

Debtor's Examination This is normally a court ordered proceeding in which a debtor must answer questions about current income and assets from which a judgment may be collected.

Decree A judgment by court (a divorce decree)

Deed A written document that transfers ownership of land from one party to another. The seller is called the "grantor" and the buyer is called the "grantee". Deeds may be of many kinds. For example, there are grant deeds, quitclaim deeds, gift deeds, guardians' deeds, administrators' deeds, warranty deeds, etc. depending upon the language of the deed, the legal capacity of the grantor, and other circumstances.

Deed-in-Lieu of Foreclosure (DIL) Used by owners to voluntarily convey the title of their property to the mortgagee/beneficiary (lender) to avoid the negative credit consequences of a foreclosure. Lenders are generally re-luctant to accept a "deed in lieu" unless the title is free and clear of any other encumbrances junior to theirs and the owners execute an estoppel affidavit acknowledging that they are acting volitionally, with informed consent.

Deed of Trust (Trust Deed) A three party security instrument conveying the legal title to real property as security for the repayment of a loan. The owner is called the "trustor". The neutral third party to whom the bare legal title is conveyed (and who is called on to liquidate the property if need be) is the "trustee". The lender is the "beneficiary". When the loan is paid off the trustee is directed by the beneficiary to issue a deed of reconveyance to the trustor, which extinguishes the trust deed lien.

Default Failure to make the loan payments as agreed in the promissory note.

Default Judgment A judgment in a lawsuit against a defendant who did not meet the legal requirements in connection with the case (failure to appear, failure to file an answer, missing deadlines, etc.).

Defendant In a lawsuit, the person(s) or business(s) being sued.

Deferred Interest When the amount of interest a borrower is required to pay on a mortgage loan is less than the amount of interest accrued on the outstanding principal balance. This amount is usually added to the out-standing principal balance of the mortgage loan.

Deferred Maintenance Any repair or maintenance of a piece of property that has been postponed, resulting in a decline in property value.

Deficiency The amount a debtor owes a creditor on a debt after the creditor seizes and sells the collateral. A deficiency arises when the collateral is sold for less than the amount of the debt.

Deficiency Judgment A personal judgment against a debtor for the amount remaining due after a judicial foreclosure of a mortgage or a trust deed.

Delinquency A loan payment that is at least 30 days past due. Usually after 90 days delinquency, the lender has the right to initiate foreclosure proceedings against the loan which is in default.

Delinquent Mortgage A mortgage that involves a borrower who is behind on payments. If the borrower cannot bring the payments up to date within a specified number of days, the lender may begin foreclosure proceedings.

Demand The payoff amount necessary to retire a secured debt
Depreciation A decline in the value of property. Usually due to the obsolescence or wear and tear of the improvements on the land or adverse changes in the neighborhood.

Discharge A document that ends a debtor's legally enforceable obligation to pay a debt.

Disclosure Regarding real estate, it is revealing all known facts concerning the property being transferred such as the presence of high levels of radon gas, or lead paint.

Disposition Fee "Workout fees" paid to a special servicer for making a loan current or liquidating a problem loan or foreclosed property. Can also include late fees, modification fees and loan administration charges. These fees are negotiated with each CMBS.

Distressed Property Property that is in poor physical or financial condition.

Documentary Stamps A State tax, in the forms of stamps, required on deeds and mortgages when real estate title passes from one owner to another. The amount of stamps required varies with each State.

Down Payment The upfront cash commitment paid by the buyer. It makes up the difference between the sales price of a property and the loan amount obtainable.

Due Diligence The legal definition: due diligence is a measure of prudence, activity, or assiduity, as is properly to be expected from, and ordinarily exercised by, a reasonable and prudent person under the particular circumstances; not measured by any absolute standard but depends on the relative facts of the special case. In CMBS, due diligence is the foundation of the process because of the reliance securities investors must place on the specific expertise of the professionals involved in the transaction. It is physically and financially impossible for most CMBS investors to perform the many duties required to prepare, analyze, deliver and service commercial mortgages. Due Diligence protects these investors from unethical improprieties and unprofessional practices. Prevailing industry standards are used as the primary benchmark from which prudence is judged. Due diligence is said to be the cornerstone of securities law.

"Due on Sale" Clause (DOS) Provision in a mortgage or deed of trust calling for the total payoff of the loan balance in the event of a sale or transfer of title to the secured real property. A contract provision which authorizes the lender, at its option, to declare immediately due and payable sums secured by the lender's security instrument upon a sale of transfer of all or any part of the real property securing the loan without the lender's prior written consent. For purposes of this definition, a sale or transfer means the conveyance of real property of any right, title or interest therein, whether legal or equitable, whether voluntary or involuntary, by outright sale, deed, installment sale contract, land contract, contract for deed, leasehold interest with a term greater than three years, lease-option contract or any other method of conveyance of real property interests. Standard language which states that the loan must be paid when a house is sold.

Duress Unlawful constraint or action exercised upon a person who is forced to perform an act against his or her will.

Earnest Money An advance payment towards the purchase price of property that binds the parties to a purchase contract for property. It is usually not refundable if the purchase doesn't go through as a fault of the buyer, unless specified otherwise. Also known as Good Faith Deposit.

Emergency Petition See "Bare Bones" petition.

Encumbrance A legal right, claim or lien upon real property that diminishes the owner's equity or the land's value. Typical encumbrances are mortgages, trust deeds, judgments, assessments, mechanic's liens, easements, etc.

Environmental Risk Risk of loss of collateral value and of lender liability due to the presence of hazardous materials, such as asbestos, PCB's, radon or leaking underground storage tanks (LUSTS) on a property. CERCLA (Comprehensive Environmental Response, Compensation Liability Act) of 1980 discusses potential liabilities due to environmental problems.

Equal Credit Opportunity Act Prohibits discrimination in any aspect of a credit transaction on the basis of race, religion, age, color, national origin, receipt of public assistance funds, sex, or marital status.

Equity (in property) The property's current value minus the sum of all liens against it.

Equity Line of Credit (HELOC) A mortgage loan that works much like a charge card, wherein a homeowner borrows money as needed, up to a pre-negotiated limit. Interest is paid only on the amount of the loan used and the borrower can pay off the balance as quickly or as slowly as they like.

Equity of Redemption A right of the owner to reclaim property before it is sold through foreclosure by the payment of the debt, interest, and costs.

Escheat The reversion of property to the state or county, as provided by state law, in cases where a decedent dies intestate without heirs capable of inheriting or when the property is abandoned.

Escrow Amounts set aside for a particular purpose. For example, one type of escrow would be money paid to your mortgage company for payment of property taxes, and insurance.

Escrow Analysis A lender's periodic examination of an escrow account to determine if the lender is withholding enough funds from a borrower's monthly mortgage payment to pay for expenses such as property taxes and insurance.

Estoppel A bar to the assertion of a right or a defense in consequence of a previous position, act or representation.

Estoppel Certificate A document in which a borrower certifies the amount he or she owes on a mortgage loan and rate of interest.

Exclusive Agency Listing A listing contract under which the owner appoints a real estate broker as his or her exclusive agent for a designated period of time to sell the property, on the owner's stated terms, for a commission. The owner reserves the right to sell without paying anyone a commission.

Exclusive Right to Sell Listing A listing contract under which the owner appoints a real estate broker as his or her exclusive agent for a designated period of time, to sell the property on the owner's stated terms, and agrees to pay the broker a commission when the property is sold whether by the broker, the owner, or another broker.

Executory Contract A contract under which something remains to be done by one or more of the parties.

External Obsolescence Reduction in a property's value caused by factors outside the subject property such as social or environmental forces or objectionable neighboring property. Also called locational obsolescence or economic obsolescence.

Eviction A legal procedure to remove a tenant (including former homeowner) for reasons including failure to pay rent.

Exempt Property Property that the law allows you to keep when you are faced with collection on an unsecured debt.

Exit Strategy The way in which an investor closes out a specific investment, usually for cash.

Fair Debt Collection Practices Act A federal law passed in 1977 which outlaws debtor harassment and other types of collection practices. The act regulates collection agencies, original creditors who set up a separate office to collect debts, and lawyers hired by the creditor to help collect overdue bills. An original creditor--the company or individual that originally granted the credit--is not covered by the act, but may be covered by similar measures approved by state governments.

Fair Market Value The highest price a property in it's as-is, where-is, with all faults condition, will bring on the open market, given an informed and freely willing buyer and seller.

FANNIE MAE (FNMA) Federal National Mortgage Association the largest secondary-market investor in residential mortgages in the United States. Provides a constant and orderly market for banks to go to when they need to sell mortgages in order to keep their loan portfolios in balance with government-mandated liquidity ratios.

Federal Home Loan Mortgage Corporation (FHLMC, Freddie Mac) A stockholder-owned corporation chartered by Congress to create a continuous flow of funds to mortgage lenders in support of homeownership and rental housing. Freddie Mac purchases single-family and multifamily residential mortgages from lenders and packages them into securities that are sold to investors.

FHA (FHA Loan) Federal Housing Administration (formed in 1934). It's now a branch of H.U.D. It's basic function is to spur housing in the directions that Congress mandates by issuing mortgage insurance to institutional lenders on the loans they make under the 47 different loan programs that FHA now sponsors. With such loan insurance lenders are willing to lend with smaller down payments and at lower rates of interest. A loan insured by the Federal Housing Administration open to all qualified home purchasers. Interest rates on FHA loans are generally market rates, while down payment requirements are lower than for conventional loans. FHA loans cannot exceed the statutory limit.

Fiduciary A person serving in a position of trust.

Fiduciary Duty The relationship of trust that buyers and sellers expect from a real estate agent. The term also applies to legal and business relationships.

Financial Institutions Reform, Recovery and Enforcement Act of 1989 FIRREA This Federal Act was passed for the primary purpose of facilitating the "bailout" of the savings and loan industry in the wake of the insolvency of its insurer, the Federal Savings and Loan Insurance Corporation. Title XI of FIRREA sets forth appraisal guidelines which are frequently followed in the appraisal of commercial real estate assets for CMBS.

Flipping Buying and then reselling property for a profit within a very short holding period.

Flipping the Contract occurs when a contract to purchase a property is assigned to another before the first contract is closed.

Forced Sale When one sells or loses his property without actually wanting to dispose of it.

Forbearance A course of action a lender may pursue to delay foreclosure or legal action against a delinquent borrower.

Forbearance Agreement A formal agreement between a borrower and a lender to temporarily postpone an ongoing foreclosure.

Foreclosure The process by which a lender takes back a property on which the mortgagor has defaulted. A servicer may take over a property from a borrower on behalf of a lender. A property usually goes into the process of foreclosure if payments are more than 90 days past due.

For Sale By Owner (FSBO) The owner markets and sells the home without using a licensed real estate broker to avoid paying a sales commission.

Fraud Deception that causes a person to give up property, or a lawful right.

Fraudulent Transfer Giving away property to keep it from creditors.

Free and Clear Ownership of property free of all indebtedness. When an owner's equity is equal to the fair market value of her property.

Friendly Foreclosure A foreclosure that is actually instigated by the mortgagor/trustor for some ulterior reason - generally to clear up clouded title, etc.

Functional Obsolescence A loss of value to an improvement to real estate due to functional problems often caused by age, or poor design.

Funding Money that someone loans, invests in, or gives you because they believe in the plan you've submitted.

Garn-St. **Germain Act** Sec. 1701j-3. - Preemption of due-on-sale prohibitions. Exempt from DOS includes a transfer into an inter vivos trust in which the borrower is and remains a beneficiary and which does not relate to a transfer of rights of occupancy in the property

Garnishment A creditor's seizure, to satisfy a debt, of property belonging to the debtor that is in possession of a third party. An example would be the seizure of money from your bank account, or your wages (wage garnishment).

Good-Faith Estimate An estimate from an institutional lender that shows the costs a borrower will incur, including loan-processing charges and inspection fees.

Government Sponsored Enterprise GSE Agency, such as GNMA, FHLMC, etc., formed by the Federal government to provide a secondary market for residential real estate loans.

Grace Period A period of days during which a debtor may cure a delinquency without penalty (before triggering a late charge, a foreclosure or an acceleration of the balance due).

Grantee The person acquiring title to real property by a deed.

Grantor The person transferring title to real property by a deed.

Guilty Knowledge Where a broker was aware of his or her salesperson's wrongdoing, but did not report the activity to the applicable authority.

Hard **Money Loan** A loan made based primarily upon the collateral's equity, rather than the creditworthiness of the Borrower.

Highest and Best Use That possible use of land that would produce the greatest net income and thereby develop the highest land value.

Holdover Tenancy A tenancy whereby a lessee retains possession of a leased property after his or her lease has expired and the landlord, by continuing to accept rent, agrees to the tenant's continued occupancy.

Home Equity Loan HEL Loan made to provide homeowners with access to excess built-up equity in their residence. Typically, secured by a junior lien mortgage where a superior lien mortgage exists.

Homesteading A document that protects some of a home's equity from lawsuits.

HUD-1 Uniform Settlement Statement A closing statement or settlement sheet that outlines all closing costs on a real estate transaction or refinancing.

Index A published measure of economic conditions usually relative to other financial instruments such as Treasury notes or Treasury bills. The lender uses a particular index to calculate the interest rate on an adjustable rate mortgage (ARM) by adding a fixed margin to the index. The most common indexes are:

    Constant Maturity Treasury (CMT)
    Treasury Bill (T-Bill)
    12-Month Treasury Average (MTA)
    11th District Cost of Funds Index (COFI)
    London Inter Bank Offering Rates (LIBOR)
    Certificates of Deposit (CD) Indexes
    Prime Rate

Interest Rate Cap Limits the interest rate or the interest rate adjustment to a specified maximum. This protects the borrower from increasing interest rates.

Institutional Lenders Banks, savings & loan associations, and insurance companies who lend out depositors' money as contrasted with private individuals lending out personal funds.

Insolvent A person or business that does not have sufficient assets to pay it's debts.

Illiquid (an investment) Not readily convertible to cash.

Insurable Interest An interest in property substantial enough to cause the owner of it an actual loss if it were damaged or destroyed. The beneficiary of any insurance policy, even a title insurance policy, must show an "insurable interest" in order to be covered by it.

Interest The cost of using borrowed money. It's quoted as an annual percentage of the loan amount. The rate can either be fixed or fluctuate ("adjust") over the life of the loan.

Inter-Vivos Trust A trust created during the Decedent's lifetime, also called a living trust.

Involuntary Lien A lien imposed upon property by the operation of law rather than at the will of the owner. Property taxes, federal income taxes, bonded assessments and abstracts of judgment are examples of involuntary liens.

Involuntary Prepayment Prepayment on a mortgage loan due to default

Joint Tenancy An estate owned by two or more parties in equal shares that is created by a single transfer document. Upon the death of a joint tenant the surviving joint tenants take the entire decedent's share of the property, so nothing passes to the heirs of the deceased.

Judgment The decision of a court or law. If a court decides that a person must repay a debt, a lien may be placed against that person's property.

Judgment Lien A general lien (good for 10 years) created by a court ordering a debtor to pay a certain amount of money to the judgment creditor. The lien will bind to the debtor's real property once an abstract of the judgment is recorded. Thereafter the debtor won't be able to resell, refinance or buy any other property in the county without paying off the lien.

Judicial Foreclosure A foreclosure that's processed via a court action. Usually limited to a collection action on an involuntary, judgment lien that automatically attached against a debtor's real property by operation of law (such as a recorded abstract of judgment).

Judgment Proof People or businesses with property of minimal value, which can be entirely protected by exemptions, making it difficult or impossible for any creditor to force you to pay a debt.

Junior Bene Buyout The purchase of a junior mortgagee or beneficiary's mortgage or trust deed position via an assignment at a steep discount because of an impending foreclosure on a senior mortgage or trust deed. If done correctly the new mortgagee/beneficiary will be paid in full via the resale or refinancing of the real property.

Junior Lien A lien that does not have first claim on the property it is secured by because it was recorded later than a competing lien secured by the same property.

Junior Mortgage A mortgage loan that is subordinate to the primary, or senior loan(s).

Late Charge A fee imposed on a borrower when the borrower does not make a payment on time.

Late Payment A payment a lender receives after the due date has passed

Lease Option A lease that contains the right to purchase the property for a specific price within a certain time frame.
Letter of Credit (LOC) An obligation by a third party to cover losses due to delinquencies and foreclosure. The rating of the third party is commonly required to be, at minimum, equal to the highest rating of the securities. A form of credit enhancement

Lien A claim against real property. Also called a 'security interest' or an 'attachment'.

Liquidation The sale of a defaulted mortgage loan or of the REO property that previously secured the loan.

Liquidation Fee That portion of the Special Servicer's compensation that is payable when the Special Servicer obtains a full or discounted payoff with respect to any Specially Serviced Mortgage Loan or obtains any Liquidation Proceeds with respect to any Specially Serviced Mortgage Loan or REO property. The fee is calculated by applying the Liquidation Fee Rate as set forth in the Pooling and Servicing Agreement to the related payment or proceeds.

Lis Pendens (LPs) A recorded notice of pending litigation, the outcome of which could affect the title to a particular piece of property.

Listing Agreement A limited-time agreement with a licensed real estate broker that authorizes the broker to represent the seller in the sale of their property.

Lock A lender's promise to hold a certain interest rate and points for you, for a given number of days, while your loan application is processed.

Loan-To-Value (LTV) The relationship between the dollar amount of the loan and the value of the property. For instance, a loan with a $70,000 loan balance on a property with a $100,000 value would result in an LTV of 70%. Lenders require a protective equity cushion between their loan positions and the fair market value of a secured property. Nonguaranteed lenders generally require that their loans amount to no more than 75% to 85% of their appraiser's estimate of the market value of the encumbered property.

Lock-Out Period A period of time after loan origination during which a borrower cannot prepay the mortgage loan.

London Interbank Offered Rate LIBOR The short-term (1 year or less) rate at which banks will lend to each other in London. Commonly used as a benchmark for adjustable rate financing.

Loss Severity Rate of loss on a liquidated mortgage; defined as the ratio of (a) the outstanding principal on the mortgage loan(s) minus the realized loss over (b) the outstanding principal on the mortgage loan(s).

Low-Ball Offer An offer made to a seller that is substantially below their asking price, and/or market value.

Low Income Housing Tax Credit Tax credit given to owners for the construction or rehabilitation of low income housing.

Marketable Title A title that is free and clear of objectionable liens, clouds, or other title defects. A title which enables an owner to sell his property freely to others and which others will accept without objection.

Market Conditions Factors affecting the sale and purchase of homes at a particular point in time.

Market Value The highest price which a buyer, willing, but not compelled, would pay, and the lowest price a seller, willing but not compelled to sell, would accept. The current value of property as determined by exposure to offers from willing buyers in the open market.

Master Servicer Required to service mortgage loans collateralizing a CMBS on behalf of, and for the benefit of, certificate holders. Responsibilities vary according to the servicing agreement. Common responsibilities include a) collection of mortgage payments and delivery of the funds to the trustee; b) advancement of any late payments to the trustee; c) provision of mortgage performance reports to bond holders; and d) transfer of all loans that become non-performing to the special servicer.

Mechanic's Lien A non-voluntary, statutory lien recorded against a specific property in favor of contractors/materialmen for unpaid improvements made to the property. A mechanic's lien priority is established when the improvements were begun *(visible to the eye* test) rather than when it was recorded. The lien must be coupled with a court action to be perfected

Memorandum of Agreement A writing meant to memorialize the essentials of a transaction or act as an actual contract.

MLS Multiple Listing Service An exclusive listing with the additional authority and obligation on the part of the listing broker to distribute the listing to other brokers in the multiple listing organization.

Modification A change in any of the terms of the loan agreement.

Mortgage A written pledge of property that is put up as security for the repayment of a loan. The lender is the mortgagee and the property owner is the mortgagor.

Mortgagee Approved Preforeclosure Short Sale see short sale

Mortgage Banker A loan originator that uses its own funds to make real estate loans which it then resells to long term mortgage investors.

Mortgage Broker An agent that matches borrowers with lenders in exchange for a referral fee that amounts to part or all of the "loan points" being charged the borrower.

Mortgage Insurance Premium The payment made by a borrower to the lender for transmittal to HUD to help defray the cost of the FHA mortgage insurance program and to provide a reserve fund to protect lenders against loss in insured mortgage transactions. In FHA insured mortgages this represents an annual rate of one-half of one percent paid by the mortgagor on a monthly basis.

Mortgage Servicer A bank, mortgage company, or similar business that communicates with property owners concerning their mortgage loans. The servicer usually works for another company that owns the mortgage.

A mortgage servicer may accept and record payments, negotiate work-outs, and supervise the foreclosure process in the event of a default.

Motivated Seller Any seller with a strong incentive to make a deal.

Multifamily Property A building with five or more residential units. Usually classified as a high rise, low rise or a garden apartment. There are three rating types for multifamily properties: Class A, B, and C. Class A Properties are above average in terms of design, construction and finish; command the highest rental rates; have a superior location in terms of desirability and/or accessibility; and generally are professionally managed by national or large regional management companies. Class B Properties frequently do not possess design and finish reflective of current standards and preferences; construction is adequate; command average rental rates; generally are well- maintained by national or regional management companies; and unit sizes are usually larger than current standards. Class C Properties provide functional housing; exhibit some level of deferred maintenance; command below average rental rates; usually located in less desirable areas; generally managed by smaller, local property management companies; tenants provide a less stable income stream to property owners than Class A and B tenants.

Multiple Listing Service (MLS) The combined property listings of local real estate brokers, /members that are pooled together in an MLS book and computer network for the widest marketing exposure to their membership at large.

Negative Amortization Occurs when interest accrued during a payment period is greater than the scheduled payment and the excess amount is added to the outstanding loan balance. For example, if the interest rate on an ARM exceeds the interest rate cap, then the borrower's payment will not be sufficient to cover the interest accrued during the billing period. The unpaid interest is added to the outstanding loan balance.

Net Operating Income (NOI) Total income less operating expenses, adjustments, etc., but before mortgage payments, tenant improvements and leasing commissions.

Net-Net Lease (NN) Usually requires the tenant to pay for property taxes and insurance in addition to the rent.

Non-Assumption Clause A loan provision that prohibits the transfer of a mortgage to another borrower without lender approval.

Nonconforming Loan Loans that do not comply with FNMA or Freddie Mac guidelines. These guidelines establish the maximum loan amount, down payment, borrower credit and income requirements, and suitable properties. Loans that do conform to these guidelines may be sold to Fannie Mae or Freddie Mac.

Notary Public A bonded officer licensed by the state to "acknowledge and attest" to the validity of signatures of others. Notarized signatures are required of the general public for any documents that individuals record in order to prevent the perpetration of fraud by forgery.

Notice of Default (NOD) To initiate a non-judicial foreclosure proceeding involving a public sale of the real property securing the deed of trust, the trustee under the deed of trust records a Notice of Default and Election to Sell ("NOD") the real property collateral in the public records.

Offer and **Acceptance** Two essential components of a valid contract; a "meeting of the minds," when all parties agree to the exact terms.

Optional Termination A legal provision in a CMBS that defines when and who can liquidate a CMBS prior to the last payment on the mortgages in the pool.

Option A legal right to purchase property at some future date for a specified price and terms. The right is forfeited if not exercised in time.

Oral By mouth; not written; verbal; spoken; parol.

Other Real Estate Owned (OREO) A term used primarily by commercial banks to identify real estate on the books that was taken back through foreclosure of a mortgage loan. The term "Other" REO is used by banks to distinguish foreclosure real estate from bank real estate owned (REO) which is corporate real estate assets. Typically, the real estate industry uses the term REO for foreclosed real estate.

Overbid That amount of money bid in excess of the trustee's or sheriff's minimum bid. It is distributed, pro tanto, to the succeeding equity holders.

Per-Diem Interest Interest charged or accrued daily.

Personal Property Property that is movable or harvestable, i.e. securities, furniture, cars, promissory notes, clothing, intangibles, etc.

Physical Deterioration Loss of value due to wear and tear or action of the elements.

P.I.T.I Refers to the monthly housing expenses of: Principal, Interest, Taxes and Insurance

Plaintiff The person or business that initiates a lawsuit.

Points A charge made by a lender that's part of the borrower's cost of obtaining a loan. Each point equals one percent (1%) of the loan amount. Points increase the effective yield on the loan above the nominal interest rate being charged.

Pooling and Servicing Agreement A legal contract defining the responsibilities and the obligations for management of a CMBS particularly for the Master Servicer and the Special Servicer. This primary document governs and controls much of the CMBS process. Also abbreviated as PSA, not to be confused with the Public Securities Association which is also known as PSA.

Portfolio Loan A loan that a lender intends to hold in inventory rather than resell in the secondary market. Such a loan only has to satisfy the lender's guidelines rather than the arbitrary rules of the secondary mortgage market.

Posting Giving notice by physically attaching it to a prescribed bulletin board and/or attaching it to the affected property itself.

Postponement An oral announcement, made in lieu of a scheduled sheriff's or trustee's sale, that reschedules the pending sale.

Power of Attorney (POA) A document that authorizes an individual to act on behalf of someone else.

Pre-Approval Letter A letter from a lender that informs a seller about the amount of money that a potential buyer can obtain.

Preliminary Title Report ("Prelim") A title company report showing the open title record of a property prior to the issuance of a title insurance policy.

Prepayment Penalty A fee charged by a lender if a loan is paid off earlier than required.

Present Owner Judgment Search A credit/lien search for municipal liens, a search for civil judgments, bankruptcy, and other docketed matters resulting in a lien on real property.

Prepayment Premium A penalty paid by the borrower for any prepayments made on a mortgage loan if required under the loan documents. The premium is usually set at a fixed rate which, at times, decreases in steps as the loan matures. For example, a mortgage loan can have a premium of 5% for the first seven years and during the next five years the premium decreases at a rate of 1% per year (4% in year eight, 3% in year nine); after year twelve, there is no prepayment premium.

Prepayment Risk The risk that a borrower will repay the remaining principal or an amount other than the scheduled payment on a mortgage prior to maturity, thus shortening the life of the loan. In order to reduce prepayment risk, commercial mortgages commonly have lockout periods and/or prepayment premiums or yield maintenance.

Presale Sale of property in anticipation of foreclosure or repossession, usually with the lender's consent.

Principal The amount of money owed on a loan, excluding interest and other charges.

Priority The superiority of an interest relative to other interests on the same property. Generally, the first to record is first in right.

Priority Clause A clause in a subordinate lien (such as a 2nd trust deed) which states that it is subject to a prior lien.

Private Mortgage Insurance (PMI) Insurance against a loss by a lender, due to a default in payments from a borrower. Often required when a buyer is paying a small down payment (less than 20% of the appraised value of the secured property)

Probate The process by which a court changes the title to a deceased person's real property. The property is from a decedent to either: 1) his or her heirs (as determined under the laws of intestacy), called an "intestate estate"; or 2) pursuant to the terms of his or her will or trust, called a "testate estate". All techniques which "avoid probate" involve changing title to the decedent's real property without court involvement.

Promissory Note An unconditional instrument of indebtedness between borrower and lender (containing all of the terms of the loan) that is commonly secured by a mortgage (mortgage note) or deed of trust.

Promoter One who conceives, develops and organizes a business or real estate project and is the motivating force that brings it to fruition.

Prospectus A printed statement disclosing all material aspects of a real estate project.

Puffing Exaggerated or superlative comments or opinions not made as representations of fact and thus not grounds for misrepresentation.

Purchase-Money Mortgage (PMM) A mortgage that a borrower gives in exchange for a loan to acquire a property.

Qualifying Ratios Lenders compute qualifying ratios to determine how much a potential buyer can borrow.

Quiet Title An action at law to remove an adverse claim or cloud from the title of property. The court decree obtained is a "Quiet Title" decree.

Quit Claim Deed A form of deed containing no warranties as to the quality or validity of the title being transferred. It's frequently used to remove a cloud, claim, or ambiguity in the title record.

Rate Step-Ups An increase in mortgage rates with respect to balloon mortgages, if the borrower fails to show progress towards refinancing, such as an appraisal, engineering report, or environmental study, or is unable to obtain a signed commitment or sales contract on the underlying property.

Ready,Willing, and Able Buyer One who is prepared to buy property on the Seller's terms and is ready to take positive steps to consummate the transaction.

Reaffirmation An agreement in the bankruptcy process to pay back a debt that would otherwise be discharged in bankruptcy.

Real Estate Broker Any person, partnership, association, or corporation who sells (or offers to sell), buys (or offers to buy) or negotiates the purchase, sale, or exchange of real estate, or who leases (or offers to lease) or rents (or offers to rent) any real estate or the improvements thereon for others and for a compensation or valuable consideration.

Real Estate Investment Trust (REIT) A business entity formed to invest in real estate, mortgages and/or securities backed by real estate. REITs are required to pass through 95% of taxable income to their investors and are not taxed at the corporate level. The three major types of REITs are equity, mortgage and hybrid, with equity being the dominant type.

Real Estate Mortgage Investment Conduit (REMIC) A vehicle, created by the Tax Reform Act of 1986, which permits the sale of interests in mortgage loans in the secondary market. It is a pass-through entity that can hold loans secured by real property and issue multiple classes or investors without the regulatory, accounting and economic obstacles inherent with other forms of mortgage-backed securities.

Real Estate Owned (REO) The term used to describe real property collateral to which title has been taken back by the mortgagee (trust by way of beneficial ownership) through foreclosure or deed in lieu of foreclosure.

Real Estate Settlement Procedures Act (RESPA) A federal law designed to make sellers and buyers aware of settlement fees and other transaction-related costs. RESPA also outlaws kickbacks in the real estate business.

Realized Loss The amount of principals, interest and fees that is not realized (unrecovered) from the sale of a defaulted mortgage loan or sale of foreclosed REO property. It is equal to the amount of (a) the outstanding principal balance of the loan plus (b) all unpaid scheduled interest plus (c) all fees applied to the sale of the property minus (d) the amount received from liquidation.

Realtor ™ A designation for a broker, or broker's agent who is a member of the National Association of Realtors, a trade group. A real estate broker, or the broker's agents may, or may choose not to be a member of Realtor™.

Recording Filing a document with the county recorder to have it entered into the public record, giving constructive notice to the public at large of its contents. Establishes priority amongst competing claims.

Redeem Recovering collateral from a creditor by paying the entire amount you owe. In bankruptcy, property can be redeemed in some situations by paying the collateral's value even if that amount is less than the entire amount owed.

Redemption Period A period of time established by state law during which a property owner has the right to redeem his or her property from a forced, public foreclosure sale.

Redemptive Right Generally refers to a debtor's right to reacquire title to property lost via a judicial foreclosure (germane to mortgage states) within a year or so afterward. It also refers to IRS's right to redeem property that had secured a federal tax lien prior to a non-judicial foreclosure by a senior lien. IRS's right is limited to 120 days after the sheriff's sale or trustee's sale and requires reimbursement to the winning bidder of the trustee's sale.

Refinancing The process of paying back old debts by borrowing new money.

Regulation Z The federal code issued under the Truth-in-Lending Act which requires that a borrower be advised in writing of all costs associated with the credit portion of a financial transaction.

Reinstatement The process of remedying a default so that they lender will treat you as if you had never fallen behind.

Relief from Automatic Stay An order from the bankruptcy court allowing a lender to proceed with his default remedies (e.g. sheriff's sale/ trustee's sale) against a debtor exempt from the automatic, protective shield of the bankruptcy court.

Repayment Plan When a borrower falls behind in mortgage payments, many lenders will negotiate a repayment plan rather than go to initiate foreclosure proceedings..

Replacement Cost The construction cost at current prices of a property that is not necessarily an exact duplicate of the subject property, but serves the same purpose or function as the original.

Reproduction Cost The construction cost at current prices of an exact duplicate of the subject property.

Repossession When a house is repossessed, it is taken back by the lender holding the mortgage.

Rescission The cancellation of a contract. When you use your home as collateral for a loan, you generally have the right to cancel the credit trans-action within three business days. This is called your "right of rescission," and it is guaranteed by the Federal Truth in Lending Act

Right of First Refusal An agreement by a property owner to give another person the right to buy or rent the property before it goes on the open market.

Right of Redemption (ROR) In certain states, the Trustor under the deed of trust, or mortgagor under the mortgage, and/or junior lien holders have the right to redeem the real property following foreclosure sale. The period of time during which the property may be redeemed, if right of redemption is permitted and whether it is applicable to non-judicial and/or judicial fore-closure, varies significantly by state and can be as little as three months or more than a year.

Risk Based Capital (**RBC**) The amount of capital (or net worth) an investor must identify as allocated to absorb a potential loss in an investment or investment class. This requirement was established by institutional regulatory bodies in the last few years because of losses in this last recession.

Sale-Leaseback A transaction in which the buyer leases back the property to the seller for a specified period of time.

Sale-Leaseback w/Exclusive Option to Repurchase The Tenant enjoys an exclusive option to purchase the property at a predetermined price within the term of the Lease.

Sales Comparison Approach The process of estimating the value of a property by examining and comparing actual sales of comparable properties.

Seasoning The length of time since origination of a mortgage loan. The longer a loan has been outstanding and performing to its terms, the better "seasoned" it is. A loan that has been outstanding, for say three years, but shows a poor pay history, i.e., several late pays, particularly beyond 30 days, is not considered seasoned because of its performance.

Secondary Market Most lenders sell the loans they originate to large-scale, national investors such as "Fannie Mae" and Freddie Mac". The reason they do is to recycle their money to create more loans (on which they collect loan origination fees, points, etc.). In order to sell their loans originating lenders have to adhere to Fannie Mae's underwriting guidelines.

Second Mortgage A mortgage in addition to the first mortgage. Home equity loans, credit lines, home improvement loans are second mortgage loans. Second mortgage is subordinate to the first one. Second mortgage loans are nonconforming loans, so, they usually carry a higher interest rate, and they often are for a shorter time.

Section 8 A federal, rental (and purchase) assistance program under HUD for very-low-income families. The money is funneled to local housing authorities who pay (directly to landlords) the difference between market rent and what eligible families can afford to pay. The housing "voucher" program is a more flexible variant where the recipient families freely rent whatever they want for whatever rental amount they choose to pay.

Section 1031 Under section 1031 of the IRS, owners or real estate held for investment or for use in a trade or business can exchange their property tax-free for "like-kind" real estate.

Self-amortizing Loans Loans for which the full amount of the principal sum borrower will be completely paid off at the loan's termination pursuant to the loan's payment schedule.

Sellers' Broker sellers' broker represents the interest of the seller

Servicer Institution acting for the benefit of the certificate holders in the administration and servicing of mortgage loans in the CMBS. Functions include reporting to the Trustee, collecting payments from borrowers, advancing funds for delinquent loans, negotiating workouts or restructures (as permitted by the PSA), taking defaulted loans through the foreclosure process, and liquidating defaulted loans and REO.

Servicing Advances Generally defined as a customary, reasonable and necessary out of pocket costs and expenses incurred by the Master Servicer or Special Servicer in connection with the servicing of a mortgage loan after an event of default, delinquency or other unanticipated event or in connection with the administration of an REO property. These advances are paid by the Master Servicer or sometimes the Special Servicer and are generally reimbursable from future payments and other collections. In all cases, the requirements to make servicing advances are detailed in the Pooling and Servicing Agreement.

Servicing Tape A loan tape, more commonly now a diskette, maintained by the loan servicer and containing the current and historical loan payment characteristics of a mortgage loan. The detail and calculation methods utilized to maintain this information have historically varied widely across servicers. One of CSSA's primary objectives is to promote consolidated streamlined information criteria, and definitions to be used by servicers in an effort to increase CMBS liquidity and marketgrowth.

Servicing Transfer Event With respect to any mortgage loan, a servicing transfer event occurs when the borrower has defaulted or, in the reasonable judgment of the Master Servicer, certain circumstances have occurred that make it likely that the borrower will default and not be able to cure within a reasonable time. In the event, the Master Servicer can transfer the day to day handling to the account to the Special Servicer until such time as the Special Servicer determines the default has been cured and that the loan is now a Corrected Mortgage Loans.

Settlement Statement A document that details who has paid what to whom.

Sheriff's Deed The deed issued by a sheriff to the highest bidder at a sheriff's sale.

Sheriff's Sale The sale of property by the sheriff under authority of a court's judgment and writ of execution in order to satisfy an unpaid judgment, mortgage, lien, or other debt of the owner.

Short Sale A type of preforeclosure sale in which the mortgagee agrees to let you sell the property for less than the full amount due, and accept the proceeds as payment in full.   The sale of property at a fair market price that's lower than the loan balance(s).

Soldier's and Sailor's Relief Act Protects certain military personnel from losing their homes to foreclosure while on they're on active duty.

Special Lien A lien that binds a specified piece of property, unlike a general lien, which is levied against all one's assets. It creates a right to retain something of value belonging to another person as compensation for labor, material, or money expended in that person's behalf. In some localities it is called "particular" lien or "specific" lien.

Special Servicer Some transactions have a separate special servicer which assumes servicing responsibilities when a loan goes into default and conducts the "workout" or foreclosure process. There are various types of special servicers: (1) those retaining first-loss pieces; (2) those investing in "B" pieces in return for special services rights and (3) those appointed solely because of their asset-management expertise.

Special Servicing Fee That portion of Special Servicer's compensation that accrues with respect to each Specially Serviced Mortgage Loan and each Mortgage Loan which has become REO, as per the applicable Pooling and Servicing Agreement. This fee is calculated on a loan-by-loan basis on the basis of the same principal amount and for the same period respecting which any related interest payment due or deemed due or deemed due is computed and is payable from general collections on Mortgage Loans and REO held by the Master Servicer.

Specific Performance Suit A legal action brought in court of equity in special cases to compel a party to carry out the terms of a contract.

Speculator One who buys or inventories goods, currencies, etc. or develops, packages real estate, etc. with the intent to resell for a profit.

Standby Fee That portion of the Special Servicer's compensation which accrues with respect to each Mortgage Loan, including Specially Serviced Mortgage Loans and Mortgage Loans which been converted to REO, as applicable per the Pooling and Servicing Agreement. This fee accrues at the Standby Fee Rate, is calculated in the same manner as the Master Servicing Fee and is payable by the Master Servicer from its Master Servicing Fee.

Straw Man A person acting as a front or a dummy buyer for another.

Stress Test A series of tests performed by the rating agency which test projections of the mortgage pool under varying levels of "stress-related" assumptions. These stress tests to which the pooled loans are submitted include analysis of the mortgage documents, real property collateral, tax structure, geographical distribution, loan servicing and administration is- sues. The rating agency determines the likelihood of timely repayment using historical loan experience for the collateral type and its own statisti- cal database concerning probability of default and severity of loss.

Subject To (Sub2) The purchase of a property with an existing lien against the title without assuming any personal liability for its payment.

Sub Servicer A servicer that contracts with Master and Special Servicers to perform some of the specific functions required under the servicing agreement. This may include real estate services such as property in- spections, foreclosure services or individual loan administration. The Mas- ter or Special Servicer is legally responsible for the activities of their sub- servicers.

Sub-performing Loan A loan that is making payments but not the full principal and interest payments that the Mortgage Note demands. Many investors also classify a loan as sub-performing even if monthly payments are current but when the loan to value ratio or other primary value indicator is such that it is unlikely that the loan will be unable to pay off in full at ma- turity.

Suit to Quiet Title A court action intended to establish or settle the title to a particular property, especially when there is a cloud on the title.

Summons This is a document at the beginning of a lawsuit to tell the de- fendant what is being requested, and what must be done to respond to the complaint.

Tax Deed An instrument, similar to certificate of sale, given to a pur- chaser at a tax sale.

Tax Lien an encumbrance placed upon a property as a claim for payment of a tax liability. A tax lien may be imposed for failure to pay city, county, estate, income, payroll, property, sales, or school taxes. Tax liens and assessments take priority over most, if not all other liens.
Tax Sale The public sale of a property by the government for nonpayment of taxes.

Third-Party Pool Insurance Protects investors from any losses on the mortgage loans and is a form of credit enhancement. The bond insurer, paid an annual fee by the issuer, will absorb the losses. The CMBS issue is usually never rated higher than the credit rating of the third party insurer.

Time is of the Essence (TOE) A phrase in a contract that requires the performance of a certain act within a stated period of time.

Title Evidence that the owner of land is in lawful possession thereof, evidence of ownership.

Title Holding Trust Also known as a "land trust". Devised by Chicago Title Insurance Co. in 1891 as a legal, time-tested, fictitious entity that's primarily used to hold the title to real property to shield it from any clouds or liens that all individuals are susceptible to when they get sued, go through a divorce, die, etc. It's especially useful when several, non-related individuals jointly buy investment property.

Title Insurance Policy A "contract of indemnity" protecting the insured from loss due to unknown, hidden clouds, liens or defects affecting the title to the covered property. Since insurance benefits will be paid only to the "named insured" in the title policy, it's important that an owner purchase an "owner's title policy" (CLTA) that's separate from the "lender's policy" (ALTA).

Title Search A detailed check of the title records at the recorder's office to make certain that the buyer is purchasing a property from the legal owner and that there are no more liens against the property's title than those already disclosed by the seller.

Transfer Tax A tax collected from sellers upon the transfer of their title to real property (see closing costs)

Trust A legal arrangement where a person, called the grantor or testator, transfers assets to a person called a Trustee who will manage those assets for the benefit of the beneficiary.

Trust Deed An instrument used to create a mortgage lien by which the mortgagor conveys his or her title to a trustee, who holds it as security for the benefit of the note holder (the lender) also called a deed of trust.

Trustee Holds the mortgage collateral documents, issues the Certificates of Beneficial Ownership (securities) and passes all funds collected by the *master servicer* to the certificate holders. Distributes statements on distributions and status reports on the collateral. Acts as a supervisor to the master servicer and *special servicer*. Ensures that the servicers act in accordance with the terms of the Pooling and Servicing Agreement. If there is a violation of the agreement, the trustee has the right to assume the authority or to appoint a new *servicer*. The Trustee represents the Trust that holds the legal title to the collateral for the benefit of all class holders of the security. It must carry out its duties according to the indentures established within the Trust Indenture. Some Trustees actually collect the proceeds from the Master Servicer and distribute them to the certificate holders while some Trustees subcontract the distribution to " paying agents ". This sub contract does not release the Trustee from its legal obligations to protect the interests of the certificate holders.

Trustee's Deed The deed issued by a trustee to the highest bidder at a trustee's sale. The deed discloses on its face what the opening or minimum bid was at the sale and what the final winning bid actually amounted to.

Trustee's Responsibilities (land trust) In general the duties of a trustee are to honestly represent the best interests of the beneficiary. The trust agreement itself may set forth other more specific duties.

Trustee's Sale A non-judicial auction sale of real property, conducted by a trustee in the exercise of the power of sale clause, pursuant to the terms of the defaulted deed of trust.

Truth In Lending Act (TIL) Under this act a lender is required to provide you with a disclosure estimating the costs of the loan you have applied for, including your total finance charge and the Annual Percentage Rate *(APR) within three business days of your application for a loan.*

Unclean Hands is a legal doctrine that says you cannot win by claiming the other side is being unfair if you, yourself, were unfair to them.

Unrecorded Deed An unrecorded deed transfers ownership from one party to another without being officially recorded.

Unsecured Debt A debt that is not secured by any pledge of property. Examples: utility bills, student loans, credit cards, medical, hospital, or doctors' bills, etc.

Usury A rate of interest charged on a loan that is in excess of the statutory maximum.

VA **Veterans Administration** established under the Servicemen's Readjustment Act of 1944. It provides two very helpful housing benefits to servicemen and veterans by guaranteeing a lender's housing loan made to an eligible vet without any down payment requirement and by requiring that the subject property conform to VA's housing standards as determined by an on-site appraisal conducted by an approved VA appraiser.

Valid Contract A contract that complies with all the essentials of a contract and is binding and enforceable on all parties to it.

Variable Rate Loan A loan bearing an interest rate that fluctuates (vs. a fixed rate) according to some specified financial index of the current cost of money - wherein both the interest rate and the monthly payment are subject to adjustment at some pre-established interval.

Voidable Contract A contract that seems to be valid on the surface, but may be rejected or disaffirmed by one of the parties.

Void Contract A contract that has no legal force or effect because it does not meet the essential elements of a contract.

Voluntary Lien Any lien placed on property with the consent and cooperation of the owner (mortgage).

Warranty **Deed** A deed containing express and implied covenants as to good title and right to possession.

Workout A workout can be a variety of negotiated agreements you might arrange with creditors to address a debt that you are having trouble paying. Most commonly, a workout is devised between a mortgagee, and mortgagor to restructure or modify a loan to avoid foreclosure.

Workout Fee That portion of the Special Servicer's compensation payable with respect to each Corrected Mortgage Loan, as applicable per the Pooling and Servicing Agreement. This fee is payable out of and is calculated by applying a Workout Fee Rate to each collection of interest and principal (including scheduled payments, prepayments, balloon payments and payments at maturity) for a Mortgage Loan as long as it remains a Corrected Mortgage Loan. This fee ceases to be payable if the loan becomes a Specially Serviced Mortgage Loan again or becomes an REO property.

Wraparound Mortgage A loan arrangement whereby the existing loan is retained and a new loan is added to the property. Full payments on both mortgages are made to the wraparound mortgagee, who then forwards the payments on the first mortgage to the first mortgagee.

Printed in the United States
136906LV00003B/73/A